Czech
phrase book

Berlitz Publishing / APA Publications GmbH & Co.
Verlag KG, Singapore Branch, Singapore

Contacting the Editors
Every effort has been made to provide accurate information in this publication, but changes are inevitable. The publisher cannot be responsible for any resulting loss, inconvenience or injury. We would appreciate it if readers would call our attention to any errors or outdated information by contacting Berlitz Publishing, 95 Progress Street, Union, NJ 07083, USA. Fax: 1-908-206-1103
email: comments@berlitzbooks.com

Satisfaction guaranteed—If you are dissatisfied with this product for any reason, send the complete package, your dated sales receipt showing price and store name, and a brief note describing your dissatisfaction to: Berlitz Publishing, Langenscheidt Publishing Group, Dept. L, 46-35 54th Rd., Maspeth, NY 11378. You'll receive a full refund.

Cover photo: ©Royalty-Free/CORBIS

Printed in Singapore

Contents

Pronunciation

This section is designed to make you familiar with the sounds of Czech by using our simplified phonetic transcription. You'll find the pronunciation of the Czech letters and sounds explained below, together with their "imitated" equivalents. To use this system, found throughout the phrase book, simply read the pronunciation as if it were English, noting any special rules below.

The Czech language

Czech is a Slavic language, closely related to Russian, Polish, and Bulgarian. However, unlike Russian and Bulgarian, Czech (and Polish) use the Roman alphabet. In addition, it is related to the other modern Indo-European languages such as French, German, and English, as well as Latin and Greek. Many Czech and English words have a common origin in Latin, for example: **bratr** (brother) and **sestra** (sister).

Czech is a highly inflected language. This means that words are modified in their appearance to signal changes in such grammatical functions as gender, number, case, etc. ➤ 169.

Czech is a phonetic language, and its pronunciation is much more systematic than that of English. The spelling of words is simple and their pronunciation can be almost always predicted.

Pronunciation of Czech consonants

As in English, certain consonants are termed "voiced" because their pronunciation is accompanied by a resonance of the voice. In Czech, these "voiced" consonants are **b, g, d, ď** (*dy*), **h, z, ž** (*zh*), and **v**. Each of them has an "unvoiced" equivalent, that is a consonant which is pronounced in exactly the same way, but without any resonance of the voice, almost as though whispered. These are respectively **p, k, t, ť** (*ty*), **ch, s, š** (*sh*), and **f**.

Voiced consonants become unvoiced when they appear at the beginnings and ends of words, and before unvoiced consonants. For example: **oběd** is pronounced *obyet,* **ztratit** as *stratyit,* and **tužka** as *tooshka.*

Conversely, unvoiced consonants become voiced when they occur before a voiced consonant. This involves mainly **k** becoming **g**. For example: **kde** is pronounce as *gdeh* and **nikdo** as *nyig-do'.*

Soft consonants

The sign ˇ written over the letter "e" (ě) makes the
preceding consonant soft. A similar effect is produced by
pronouncing y as in yet. When d, n, and t precede ě, they are
pronounced as 'soft' ď (dy), ň (ny), and ť (ty). The same happens if
they precede the letters i/í. For example: děkuji is pronounced as _dye-koo-yih_, **nic** as _nyits_, and **ještě** as _yesh-tyeh_.

When b, f, m, p, and v precede ě and i/í, they are pronounced 'soft' _by, fy, my, py,_ and _vy._ For example: **pět** is pronounced as _pyet_, **věc** as _vyets_, and **město** as _myesto'_.

Consonants

Letter	Approximate pronunciation	Symbol	Example	Pron.
b, d, f, g, k, m, n, p t, v, z	approximately as in English			
c	like *ts* in ca*ts*	ts	cesta	tsesta
č	like *ch* in *ch*urch	ch	klíč	kleech
ď	like *d* in *d*uty	dy	láďa	lah-dya
g	like *g* in *g*ood	g	galerie	galeri-yeh
h	like *h* in *h*alf	h	hotel	hotel
ch	like *ch* in Scottish lo*ch*	kh	chyba	khiba
i	like *y* in *y*es	y	jídlo	yeedlo'
ň	like *ny* in ca*ny*on	ny	píseň	peeseny'
r	rolled, like a Scottish *r*	r	ruka	rooka
ř	a sound unique to Czech like **r** + **ž** (zh) pronounced in quick succession	rzh	řepa	rzhepa
s	like *s* in *s*eat	s	sobota	sobota
š	like *sh* in *sh*ort	sh	šest	shest
ť	like *t* in *t*une	ty'	chuť	khooty'
w	like *v* in *v*an; found only in foreign words	v	watt	vut
ž	like *s* in plea*s*ure	zh	žena	zhena

Vowels

Vowels in Czech can be either short (**a, e, i/y, o, u**) or long (**á, é, í/ý, ó, ú/ů**). The length of the vowel is an essential feature since it can differentiate the meaning of words which are otherwise written with the same spelling.

Letter	Approximate pronunciation	Symbol	Example	Pron.
a	between the *a* in c**a**t and the *u* in c**u**t	a/u	**tady/tam**	*tadih/tum*
á	like *a* in f**a**ther	ah	**máma**	*mah-ma*
e	like *e* in m**e**t; this *e* is always pronounced, even at the end of a word	e	**den**	*den*
é	like *a* in m**a**re	eh	**mléko**	*mleh-ko'*
i/y	like *i* in b**i**t	i	**pivo**	*pivo'*
í/ý	like *ee* in s**ee**	ee	**bílý**	*beelee*
o	like *o* in h**o**t	o	**slovo**	*slovo'*
ó	like *au* in g**au**l	au	**gól**	*gaul*
u	like *oo* in b**oo**k	oo	**ruka**	*rooka*
ú/ů	like *oo* in m**oo**n	uh	**úkol/vůz**	*uhkol/vuhs*

All vowels (long and short) should be pronounced the same way in all positions including at the end of a word.

Where an apostrophe is used in the phonetic transcription after a vowel, mainly after **o**, it indicates that the sound should be pronounced in full, but not rounded as in English words like *no, go, toe*. For example: in the word **pivo**, pronounce the **o** as the *o* in h**o**t, rather than as the *o* in h**e**ro.

In places where confusion may arise over pronunciation, hyphens have been inserted into the phonetic transcription to help differentiate the syllables, for example: **můžete** = *muh-zheteh* and **tohle** = *toh-leh*.

Diphthongs

Letter	Approximate pronunciation	Symbol	Example	Pron.
au	like *ow* in c**ow**	ow	**auto**	*ow-to'*
ou	like the exclamation *oh*	oh	**mouka**	*moh-ka*

Stress

Stress in Czech falls always on the first syllable of a word, though it is weaker than in English. Prepositions in Czech are generally pronounced together with their object as a single word, so the stress falls on the preposition.

Kolik to stojí <u>na</u> den?   *kolik to' sto-yee <u>na</u>den*

Note that stress and the length of vowels are two independent features: long vowels are not necessarily stressed vowels; conversely, stressed vowels are not automatically long vowels.

The Czech alphabet

A	*ah*	**Ň**	*eny'*
B	*beh*	**O**	*o*
C	*tseh*	**P**	*peh*
Č	*cheh*	**Q**	*kveh*
D	*deh*	**R**	*er*
Ď	*dyeh*	**Ř**	*erzh*
E	*eh*	**S**	*es*
F	*ef*	**Š**	*esh*
G	*geh*	**T**	*teh*
H	*hah*	**Ť**	*tyeh*
CH	*chah*	**U**	*uh*
I	*ee*	**V**	*veh*
J	*yeh*	**W**	*dvo-yiteh veh*
K	*kah*	**X**	*iks*
L	*el*	**Y**	*ipsilon*
M	*em*	**Z**	*zet*
N	*en*	**Ž**	*zhet*

Basic Expressions

ESSENTIAL

Yes.	**Ano.** *ano'*
No.	**Ne.** *neh*
Okay.	**Dobře.** *dob-rzheh*
Please.	**Prosím.** *proseem*
Thank you.	**Děkuji.** *dyekoo-yeih*
Thank you very much.	**Děkuji mnohokrát.** *dyekoo-yeih mno-ho-kraht*

Greetings/Apologies Pozdravy/Omluvy

Hello./Hi!	**Nazdar./Ahoj!** *nazdar/ahoy*
Good morning. *(early/late morning)*	**Dobré ráno./Dobrý den.** *dob-reh rah-no'/dob-ree den*
Good afternoon.	**Dobré odpoledne.** *dobreh otpoledneh*
Good evening.	**Dobrý večer.** *dobree vecher*
Good night.	**Dobrou noc.** *dobroh nots*
Good-bye.	**Na shledanou.** *nas-khledanoh*
Excuse me! *(getting attention)*	**Promiňte!** *prominye'-teh*
Excuse me. *(May I get past?)*	**Dovolte prosím!** *dovolteh proseem*
Sorry!	**Pardon!** *pardon*
Don't mention it.	**To je v pořádku.** *to' yeh fpo-rzhah-tkooh*
Never mind.	**Nic se nestalo.** *nits seh nestalo'*

Communication difficulties
Potíže s dorozumíváním

Do you speak English?	**Mluvíte anglicky?** *mlooveeteh anglitskih*
Does anyone here speak English?	**Mluví tady někdo anglicky?** *mloovee tadih nyegdo' anglitskih*
I don't speak much Czech.	**Neumím moc česky.** *ne-oomeem mots cheskih*
Could you speak more slowly?	**Můžete mluvit pomaleji?** *muh-zheteh mloovit pomale-yei*
Could you repeat that?	**Můžete to zopakovat?** *muh-zheteh to' zopakovat*
Excuse me? [Pardon?]	**Prosím?** *proseem*
What was that?	**Co jste říkal(a)?** *tso' yesteh rzheekal(a)*
Could you spell it?	**Můžete to hláskovat?** *muh-zheteh to' hlah-skovat*
Please write it down.	**Můžete mi to napsat?** *muh-zheteh mih to' napsat*
Can you translate this for me?	**Můžete mi tohle přeložit?** *muh-zheteh mih to-hleh purzhe-lo-zhit*
What does this/that mean?	**Co to/tamto znamená?** *tso' to'/tumto' znamenah*
Please point to the phrase in the book.	**Můžete mi tu větu ukázat v příručce?** *muh-zheteh mih tooh vyetooh ukah-zat fpurzhee-rooch-tseh*
I understand.	**Rozumím.** *rozoomeem*
I don't understand.	**Nerozumím.** *nerozoomeem*
Do you understand?	**Rozumíte?** *rozoomeeteh*

– Bude to sto šedesát sedm korun.
(That's 167 korun.)
– Nerozumím. (I don't understand.)
– Bude to sto šedesát sedm korun.
(That's 167 korun.)
– Můžete mi to napsat? ... Hmm, "167 korun".
Prosím.
(Please write it down. ... Ah, "167 korun".
Here you are.)

Questions Otázky

GRAMMAR

Simple questions can be formed in Czech:

1. by repeating the positive statement, without altering the word order, but adding interrogatory intonation.

| **Mluvíte dobře česky.** | You speak good Czech. |
| **Mluvíte dobře česky?** | Do you speak good Czech? |

2. by inverting the subject and the verb.

| **Hotel má garáž.** | The hotel has a garage. |
| **Má hotel garáž?** | Does the hotel have a garage? |

3. by using other question words *where* (**kde/kam**), *when* (**kdy**), etc.

| **Kde to je?** | Where is it? |
| **Kdy jedete?** | When are you going? |

Where? Kde?/Kam?*

Where is it?	**Kde to je?** *gdeh to' yeh*
Where are you going?	**Kam jdete?** *kum yede-teh*
across the road	**přes ulici** *purzhes oolitsih*
around the town	**po městě** *pomyes-tyeh*
far from here	**daleko odtud** *daleko' ot-tood*
from the U.S.	**ze Spojených států** *zeh spo-yeneekh stah-tuh*
here	**sem** *sem*
in the Czech Republic	**v České republice** *fcheskeh repoobli-tseh*
in the car	**v autě** *vow-tyeh*
inside	**uvnitř** *oov-nyiturzh'*
near the bank	**blízko u banky** *bleesko' oobankih*
next to the post office	**vedle pošty** *vedleh poshtih*
opposite the market	**naproti tržnici** *naprotyih tur-zhnyi-tsih*
on the left/right	**vlevo/vpravo** *vlevo'/fpravo'*
on the sidewalk [pavement]	**na chodníku** *na-khod-nyeekooh*
outside the café	**venku u kavárny** *ven-kooh ookavahr-ni*
there	**tam** *tum*
to the hotel	**k hotelu** *ghotelooh*
towards Prague	**směrem k Praze** *smyerem kprazeh*
up to the traffic light	**až k semaforům** *azh kse-ma-fo-ruhm*

* **Kde** is used to ask a question about where something is positioned. **Kam** is used to ask a question about where something/someone is going.

When? Kdy?

When does the museum open?	**Kdy v muzeu otvírají?** *gdih vmoozeh-ooh otfee-ra-yee*
When does the train arrive?	**Kdy vlak přijede?** *gdih vlak purzhi-yedeh*
10 minutes ago	**před deseti minutami** *purzhet desetyih minootamih*
after lunch	**po obědě** *po-obye-dyeh*
always	**vždy** *vuzhdih*
around midnight	**kolem půlnoci** *kolem puhl-no-tsih*
at 7 o'clock	**v sedm hodin** *fsedum ho-dyin*
before Friday	**do pátku** *do' paht-kooh*
by tomorrow	**do zítřka** *dozee-turzh-ka*
every week	**každý týden** *kazhdee teeden*
for 2 hours	**dvě hodiny** *dvyeh ho-dyi-nih*
from 9 a.m. to 6 p.m.	**od devíti ráno do šesti večer** *od-devee-tyih rah-no' do-shes-tyih vecher*
in 20 minutes	**za dvacet minut** *za-dva-tset minoot*
never	**nikdy** *nyig-dih*
not yet	**ještě ne** *yesh-tyeh neh*
now	**teď** *tetye'*
often	**často** *chus-to'*
on March 8	**osmého března** *osmeh-ho' burzhe-zna*
on weekdays	**v pracovní dny** *fpra-tsov-nyee dnih*
sometimes	**někdy** *nyeg-dih*
soon	**brzo** *bur-zo'*
then	**potom** *potom*
within 2 days	**do dvou dnů** *do-dvoh dnuh*

What sort of …? Jaký …?

I'd like something …	**Chtěl(a) bych něco …**	khutyel(a) bikh nye-tso'
It's …	**Je to …**	yeh to'
beautiful/ugly	**krásné/ošklivé**	krah-sneh/osh-kliveh
better/worse	**lepší/horší**	lep-shee/hor-shee
big/small	**velké/malé**	vel-keh/maleh
cheap/expensive	**levné/drahé**	lev-neh/dra-heh
clean/dirty	**čisté/špinavé**	chis-teh/shpinaveh
dark/light	**tmavé/světlé**	tma-veh/svyet-leh
delicious/revolting	**chutné/odporné**	khoot-neh/ot-por-neh
early/late	**brzo/pozdě**	bur-zo'/poz-dyeh
easy/difficult	**snadné/těžké**	snad-neh/tyezh-keh
empty/full	**prázdné/plné**	prahz-dneh/pul-neh
good/bad	**dobré/špatné**	dob-reh/shput-neh
heavy/light	**těžké/lehké**	tyezh-keh/lekh-keh
hot/warm/cold	**horké/teplé/studené**	hor-keh/tep-leh/stoo-deneh
narrow/wide	**úzké/široké**	uhz-keh/shirokeh
next/last	**další/poslední**	dul-shee/pos-led-nyee
old/new	**staré/nové**	stareh/noveh
open/shut	**otevřené/zavřené**	ote-vurzhe-neh/za-vurzhe-neh
pleasant/nice/unpleasant	**příjemné/hezké/nepříjemné**	purzhee-yem-neh/heskeh/ne-purzhee-yem-neh
quick/slow	**rychlé/pomalé**	rikh-leh/poma-leh
quiet/noisy	**tiché/hlučné**	tyi-kheh/hlooch-neh
right/wrong	**správné/chybné**	sprah-vneh/khib-neh
tall/short	**vysoké/nízké**	visokeh/nees-keh
thick/thin	**silné/slabé**	sil-neh/slabeh
vacant/occupied	**volné/obsazené**	volneh/op-sazeneh'
young/old	**mladé/staré**	mla-deh'/stareh'

GRAMMAR

Czech nouns are either masculine, feminine, or neuter.
They change their endings according to the case they are in
(that is, the "role" they play in the sentence), and according
to whether they are singular or plural ➤ 169.

Masculine nouns usually end in a consonant, e.g., **vlak** (train)

Feminine nouns usually end in **-a** or **-e**, e.g., **žena** (woman),
ulice (street), but some also end in a consonant

Neuter nouns usually end in **-o**, **-e**, or **-í**, e.g., **město** (town),
pole (field), **náměstí** (square)

How much/many? Kolik?

How much is that?	**Kolik to stojí?**	*kolik to' sto-yee*
How many are there?	**Kolik jich tam je?**	*kolik yeikh tum yeh*
1/2/3	**jeden/dva/tři**	*yeden/dva/trzhih*
4/5	**čtyři/pět**	*chti-rzhih/pyet*
none	**žádný**	*zhahd-nee*
about 100 korun	**asi sto korun**	*asih sto' koroon*
a little	**trochu**	*tro-khooh*
a lot of people	**hodně lidí**	*hod-nyeh li-dyee*
enough	**dost**	*dost*
few/a few of them	**málo/několik**	*mah-lo'/nyekolik*
more than that	**o něco více**	*onye-tso' vee-tseh*
less than that	**o něco méně**	*onye-tso' meh-nyeh*
much more	**mnohem více**	*mno-hem vee-tseh*
nothing else	**už nic**	*oozh nits*
too much	**příliš mnoho**	*purzhee-lish mno-ho'*

Why? Proč?

Why is that?	**Proč?**	*proch*
Why not?	**Proč ne?**	*proch neh*
It's because of the weather.	**Je to kvůli počasí.**	
	yeh to' kvuh-lih pochasee	
It's because I'm in a hurry.	**Protože pospíchám.**	
	protozheh pos-pee-khahm	
I don't know why.	**Nevím proč.**	*neveem proch*

Who?/Which? Kdo?/Který?

Who is it for? **Pro koho je to?** *prokoho' yeh to'*

(for) her/him **(pro) ni/něho** *(pro') nyih/nye-ho'*

(for) me **(pro) mne** *(pro') mneh*

(for) you **(pro) vás** *(pro') vahs*

(for) them **(pro) ně** *(pro') nyeh*

someone **někdo** *nyeg-do'*

no one **nikdo** *nyig-do'*

Which one do you want? **Který chete?** *kteree khutse-teh*

this one/that one **tenhle/tamten** *ten-hleh/tum-ten*

one like that **jako tento** *yuko' ten-to'*

not that one **ten ne** *ten neh*

something **něco** *nye-tso'*

nothing **nic** *nits*

Whose? Čí?

Whose is that? **Čí je to?** *chee yeh to'*

It's … **Je to …** *yeh to'*

mine/ours/yours **moje/naše/vaše**
mo-yeh/na-sheh/va-sheh

his/hers/theirs **jeho/její/jejich**
ye-ho'/ye-yee/ye-yeikh

This is … hotel. **To je … hotel.** *to' yeh … hotel*

my/our/your **můj/náš/váš**
muh-yeh/nah-sh/vah-sh

his/her/their **jeho/její/jejich**
yeh-ho'/yeh-yee/yeh-yeikh

GRAMMAR

Pronouns, like nouns, decline according to gender, plurality, and case.
Personal pronouns (I, you, he, she, etc.) can look very different from
their base forms according to what "role" they play in the sentence.
Possessive pronouns (my, your, his, her, etc.) behave like adjectives
and vary according to the gender, plurality, and case of the noun they
modify ➤ 169.

How? Jak?

How would you like to pay?	**Jak budete platit?** *yuk boodeteh pla-tyit*
by cash	**hotově** *hotovyeh*
by credit card	**kreditní kartou** *kredit-nyee kar-toh*
How are you getting here?	**Jak sem přijedete?** *yuk sem przhi-yedeteh*
by car/bus/train	**autem/autobusem/vlakem** *owtem/ow-toboosem/vlakem*
on foot	**pěšky** *pyesh-kih*
quickly	**rychle** *rikh-leh*
slowly	**pomalu** *pomalooh*
too fast	**příliš rychle** *purzhee-lish rikh-leh*
very	**velmi** *vel-mih*
with a friend	**s přítelem** *sprzhee-telem*
without a passport	**bez cestovního pasu** *bes tses-tov-nyee-ho' pa-sooh*

Is it …?/Are there …? Je to …?/Jsou tam …?

Is it free of charge?	**Je to zadarmo?** *yeh to' zadar-mo'*
It isn't ready.	**Není to hotové.** *ne-nyee to' hotoveh*
Is there a shower in the room?	**Je to pokoj se sprchou?** *yeh to' pokoye' se-spr-khoh*
Is there a bus into town?	**Jede do města autobus?** *yedeh domyes-ta ow-toboos*
Are there buses into town?	**Jezdí do města autobusy?** *yez-dyee domyes-ta ow-toboosi*
There aren't any towels in my room.	**V mém pokoji nejsou ručníky.** *vmehm poko-yei neye'-soh rooch-nyee-kih*
Here it is./Here they are.	**Tady je to./Tady jsou.** *tadih yeh to'/tadih yesoh*
There it is./There they are.	**Tam je to./Tam jsou.** *tum yeh to'/tum yesoh*

17

Can/May ...? Mohu ...?

Can I ...?	**Mohu ...?** *mohooh*
May we ...?	**Můžeme ...?** *muh-zhemeh*
Can you show me ...?	**Můžete mi ukázat ...?** *muh-zheteh mih ukah-zat*
Can you tell me ...?	**Můžete mi říci ...?** *muh-zheteh mih rzhee-tsih*
Can you help me?	**Můžete mi pomoci?** *muh-zheteh mih pomotsih*
May I help you?	**Mohu vám pomoci?** *mohooh vahm pomo-tsih*
Can you direct me to ...?	**Můžete mi říci, jak se dostanu k ...?** *muh-zheteh mi rzhee-tsih yuk seh dostanooh k*
I can't.	**Nemohu.** *nemohooh*

What do you want? Co si přejete?

I'd like ...	**Chtěl(a) bych ...** *khutyel(a) bikh*
Could I have ...?	**Můžete mi dát ...?** *muh-zheteh mih daht*
We'd like ...	**Chtěli bychom ...** *khutye-lih bi-khom*
Give me ...	**Dejte mi ...** *deye-teh mih*
I'm looking for ...	**Hledám ...** *hledahm*
I need to ...	**Potřebuji ...** *po-turzhe-boo-yih*
go ...	**jít ...** *yeet*
find ...	**najít ...** *na-yeet*
see ...	**vidět ...** *vidyet*
speak to ...	**mluvit s ...** *mloovit s*

– Promiňte, prosím. (Excuse me.)
– *Ano? Mohu vám pomoci? (Yes? May I help you?)*
– Mohu mluvit s panem Novákem?
(Can I speak to Mr. Novák?)
– *Okamžik, prosím. (Just a moment, please.)*

Other useful words
Další užitečné výrazy

fortunately	**naštěstí**	nush-tyes-tyee
hopefully	**snad**	snut
of course	**samozřejmě**	samoz-rzheye'-myeh
perhaps	**možná**	mozh-nah
unfortunately	**bohužel**	bohoo-zhel
also/but	**také/ale**	takeh/aleh
and/or	**a/nebo**	ah/nebo'

Exclamations Zvolání

At last!	**Konečně!**	konech-nyeh
Go on.	**Ale jděte.**	aleh yedye-teh
Nonsense!	**Nesmysl!**	nes-mi-sul
That's true.	**To je pravda.**	to yeh prav-da
No way!	**Rozhodně ne!**	roz-hod-nyeh neh
How are things?	**Jak se máte?**	yuk se mahteh
great/terrific	**moc dobře/báječně**	mots dob-rzheh/bah-yech-nyeh
very good	**skvěle**	skvye-leh
fine	**fajn**	fein
not bad	**jde to**	yedeh to'
okay	**dobře**	dob-rzheh
not good	**ne moc dobře**	neh mots dob-rzheh
fairly bad	**dost špatně**	dost shput-nyeh
terrible	**hrozně**	hroz-nyeh

GRAMMAR

Czech has no articles, i.e., no words for *a/an* or *the*. Thus *a telephone* and *the telephone* are simply conveyed as **telefon**.
However, remember that the noun will change according to number and case ➤ 169.

19

Accommodations

Local tourist information offices **Turistická cestovní kancelář, Informační kancelář**, and **Čedok**, the country's main tourist bureau, have information on various types of accommodations, from private rooms to five-star hotels. If you plan on visiting a popular tourist destination, particularly between Easter and September or around Christmas/New Year, make your reservations as far in advance as possible.

Hotel *hotel*

Hotels vary. Simple ones do not have private bathrooms, but there is usually a wash basin in the room. A Czech double bed consists of two single beds bolted together, with separate mattresses, sheets, and quilts. For deluxe accommodations, particularly in Prague, expect to pay Western prices. Some of the best hotels are located in former castles and palaces.

Penzión *pen-zi-on*

Pensions are often small, family run businesses offering simple accommodation facilities, with or without breakfast. Usually a lot cheaper than hotels.

Motel *motel*

Motels are found in the countryside and along the main highways; they are reasonably priced.

Rekreační chaty *rek-re-ach-nyee kha-tih*

Country chalets have varying facilities and you generally cook for yourself. Designed for a longer stay (a week or more), they have to be booked well in advance, particularly for the summer months (July and August).

Privát *pri-vaht*

Private rooms, equivalent to those at a bed and breakfast. Facilities vary. Dinner is usually available by private arrangement.

Turistická ubytovna *tooris-tits-kah oobi-tov-na*

Similar standard to a youth hostel, with a number of beds in a room and shared facilities. Meals usually not provided.

Reservations Rezervace

In advance Předem

Can you recommend a hotel in …?
Můžete mi doporučit hotel v …? *moo-zheteh mih doporoochit hotel v*

Is it near the center of town?
Je to blízko centra? *yeh to' blees-ko' tsen-tra*

How much is it per night?
Kolik stojí jedna noc? *kolik sto-yee yed-na nots*

Do you have a cheaper room?
Máte levnější pokoj? *mah-teh lev-nyeye'-shee pokoye'*

Could you reserve me a room there, please?
Mohli byste mi tam zamluvit pokoj? *mo-hlih bis-teh mih tum za-mloovit pokoye'*

How do I get there?
Jak se tam dostanu? *yuk se tum dos-tanooh*

At the hotel V hotelu

Do you have a room?
Máte volný pokoj? *mahteh volnee pokoye'*

I'm sorry, we're full.
Bohužel máme obsazeno. *bohoozhel mah-meh obsazeno'*

Is there another hotel nearby?
Je tu poblíž jiný hotel? *yeh tooh pobleezh yinee hotel*

I'd like a single/double room.
Chtěl(a) bych jednolůžkový/dvoulůžkový pokoj. *khutyel(a) bikh yedno-luh-shkovee/ dvoh-luh-shkovee pokoye'*

Can I see the room, please?
Mohu se na pokoj podívat? *mohooh se napokoye' po-dyee-vat*

I'd like a room with …
Chtěl(a) bych pokoj s … *khutyel(a) bikh pokoye' s*

twin beds
dvěma lůžky *dvye-ma luh-shkih*

a double bed
manželskou postelí *man-zhel-skoh postelee*

a bath/shower
vanou/sprchou *vanoh/spr-khoh*

– Máte volný pokoj? (Do you have a room?)
– *Bohužel máme obsazeno. (I'm sorry, we're full.)*
– Aa. Je tu poblíž jiný hotel?
(Oh. Is there another hotel nearby?)
– *Ano, paní/pane. Hotel Ambassador je hodně blízko.*
(*Yes, madam/sir. The Hotel Ambassador is very near.*)

Reception Recepce

I have a reservation. **Mám tu zamluvený pokoj.**
mahm tooh za-mloo-venee pokoye'

My name is … **Jmenuji se …** *yeme-noo-yih seh*

We've reserved a double and a single room. **Máme zamluvený dvoulůžkový a jednolůžkový pokoj.** *mah-meh za-mloo-venee dvoh-luh-shkovee ah yedno-luh-shkovee pokoye'*

I've reserved a room for two nights. **Mám rezervaci na dvě noci.** *mahm rezer-va-tsih nadvyeh no-tsih*

I confirmed my reservation by mail. **Potvrdil(a) jsem rezervaci poštou.** *potvur-dil(a) yesem rezer-va-tsih posh-toh*

Could we have adjoining rooms? **Mohli byste nám dát sousední pokoje?** *mo-hlih bis-teh nahm daht soh-sed-nyee poko-yeh'*

Amenities and facilities Příslušenství a vybavení

Is there (a) … in the room? **Je v pokoji … ?** *yeh fpoko-yih*

air conditioning **klimatizace** *klimatiza-tseh*

TV / telephone **televize/telefon** *televizeh/telefon*

Does the hotel have (a) …? **Je v hotelu … ?** *yeh vhotelooh*

fax **fax** *fux*

laundry service **prádelní služba** *prah-del-nyee sloozhba*

satellite TV **satelitní televize** *satelit-nyee elevizeh*

sauna **sauna** *sa-oona*

swimming pool **bazén** *ba-zehn*

Could you put … in the room? **Mohli byste dát do pokoje …?** *mo-hlih bis-teh daht dopoko-yeh'*

an extra bed **lůžko navíc** *luh-shko' na-veets*

a crib [child's cot] **kolébku** *kolehp-kooh*

Do you have facilities for children / the disabled? **Máte vybavení pro děti/tělesně postižené?** *mahteh vibave-nyee pro-dye-tyih/tye-les-nyeh pos-tyi-zheneh*

How long ...? Jak dlouho ...?

We'll be staying ...	**Zůstaneme tady ...** *zoos-tanemeh tadih*
overnight only	**pouze přes noc** *poh-zeh przhez-nots*
a few days	**několik dní** *nye-kolik dnyee*
a week (at least)	**(nejméně) týden** *(neye'-meh-nyeh) teeden*
I'd like to stay an extra night.	**Rád(a) bych tu zůstal(a) ještě jednu noc.** *raht(rahda) bikh tooh zuhs-tal(a) yesh-tyeh yed-nooh nots*

– Dobrý den, mám tu zamluvený pokoj.
Jmenuji se John Newton.
(Hello, I have a reservation. My name's John Newton.)
– *Dobrý den, pane Newton. (Hello, Mr. Newton.)*
– Mám rezervaci na dvě noci.
(I've reserved a room for two nights.)
– *Dobře. Vyplňte prosím tuto registrační kartu.*
(Very good. Please fill out this registration form.)

Ukažte mi pas, prosím.	May I see your passport, please?
Vyplňte prosím tento formulář/ tady se podepište.	Please fill out this form / sign here.
Jakou má vaše auto poznávací značku?	What is your license plate [registration] number?

NOCLEH ... KČ	room ... Kč (*korun*)
SE SNÍDANÍ	breakfast included
TEPLÁ KUCHYNĚ	meals available
PŘÍJMENÍ/JMÉNO	last name / first name
BYDLIŠTĚ/ULICE/ČÍSLO	home address / street / number
STÁTNÍ PŘÍSLUŠNOST/ POVOLÁNÍ	nationality / profession
DATUM/MÍSTO NAROZENÍ	date / place of birth
ČÍSLO PASU	passport number
POZNÁVACÍ ZNAČKA VOZIDLA	license plate [registration] number
MÍSTO/DATUM	place / date (*of signature*)
PODPIS	signature

Price Ceny

How much is it …?	**Kolik stojí …?** *kolik sto-yee*
per night/week	**jedna noc/týden** *yed-na nots/teeden*
for bed and breakfast	**nocleh se snídaní** *nots-leh' se-snyee-da-nyee*
excluding meals	**bez jídla** *bez yee-dla*
for full board (American Plan [A.P.])	**plná penze** *pulnah pen-zeh*
for half board (Modified American Plan [M.A.P.])	**polopenze** *polopen-zeh*
Does the price include …?	**Je v ceně …?** *ye ftse-nyeh*
breakfast	**snídaně** *snyee-danyeh*
sales tax [VAT]	**DPH** *deh-peh-hah*
Do I have to pay a deposit?	**Musím zaplatit zálohu?** *mooseem zaplatyit zah-lohooh*
Is there a reduction for children?	**Je na děti sleva?** *yeh nadye-tyih sleva*

Decisions Rozhodnutí

May I see the room?	**Mohu se na pokoj podívat?** *mohooh se napokoye' po-dyeevat*
That's fine. I'll take it.	**To je v pořádku. Vezmu si ho.** *to' yeh fpo-rzhat-kooh. vez-mooh sih ho'*
It's too …	**Je moc …** *yeh mots*
dark/small	**tmavý/malý** *tmavee/malee*
noisy	**hlučný** *hlooch-nee*
Do you have anything …?	**Máte něco …?** *mahteh nye-tso'*
bigger/cheaper	**většího/levnějšího** *vyet-sheeho'/lev-nyey'-shee-ho'*
quieter/warmer	**tiššího/teplejšího** *tish-shee-ho'/tepleye'-shee-ho'*
No, I won't take it.	**Ne, nevezmu si ho.** *neh nevez-mooh sih ho'*

Problems Problémy

The ... doesn't work.
... nefunguje.
... nefoon-goo-yeh

air conditioning / fan
klimatizace/větrák
klimatiza-tseh/vyet-rahk

heating / light
topení/světlo *tope-nyee/svyet-lo'*

I can't turn the heat [heating] on/off.
Nemohu zapnout/vypnout topení.
nemohooh zup-noht/vip-noht tope-nyee

There's no hot water.
Neteče horká voda. *netecheh hor-kah voda*

There's no toilet paper.
Není tam toaletní papír.
ne-nyee tum to-alet-nyee papeer

The faucet [tap] is dripping.
Kohoutek kape. *kohoh-tek kapeh*

The sink is blocked.
Umyvadlo je ucpané.
oomivad-lo' yeh oots-paneh

The toilet is blocked.
Záchod je ucpaný.
zah-khot yeh oots-panee

The door is jammed.
Dveře nejdou otevřít.
dve-rzheh neydoh ote-vurzheet

The window is jammed.
Okno nejde otevřít.
okno' neydeh ote-vurzheet

My room has not been made up.
Neuklidili mi pokoj.
ne-ookli-dyi-lih mih pokoye'

The blinds are broken.
Roleta je rozbitá. *roleta yeh roz-bitah*

The shutters are broken.
Okenice jsou rozbité.
okeni-tseh yesoh roz-biteh

The lamp is broken.
Lampa je rozbitá. *lum-pa yeh roz-bitah*

The lock is broken.
Zámek je rozbitý. *zah-mek yeh roz-bitee*

There are insects in our room.
V našem pokoji je hmyz.
vna-shem poko-yih' yeh hmis

Action Náprava

Could you have that taken care of?
Mohli byste to napravit?
mo-hlih bis-teh to' na-pravit

I'd like to move to another room.
Chtěl(a) bych se přestěhovat do jiného pokoje. *khutyel(a) bikh se purzhe-stye-hovat do-yineh-ho' pokoyeh*

I'd like to speak to the manager.
Chtěl(a) bych mluvit s vedoucím.
khutyel(a) bikh mloovit sve-doh-tseem

About the hotel O hotelu

If you bring your own personal appliances, such as a hair dryer or an electric razor, you will need a 220-volt A.C. adapter with you. Note: Hair dryers are only provided in deluxe or first-class hotels.

Where's the …?	**Kde je …?** *gdeh yeh*
bar	**bar** *bar*
bathroom [toilet]	**záchod** *zah-khot*
dining room	**jídelna** *yee-delna*
elevator [lift]	**výtah** *vee-tah'*
parking lot [car park]	**parkoviště** *par-kovish-tyeh*
shower room	**sprcha** *spr-kha*
swimming pool	**bazén** *ba-zehn*
tour operator's bulletin board	**nástěnka cestovní kanceláře** *nahs-tyen-ka tsestov-nyee kan-tselah-rzheh*
Does the hotel have a garage?	**Má hotel garáž?** *mah hotel garah-zh*
Can I use this adapter here?	**Mohu tady použít tento adaptér?** *mohooh tadih po-oo-zheet tento' adap-tehr*

POUZE NA HOLICÍ STROJKY	razors [shavers] only
NOUZOVÝ VÝCHOD	emergency exit/fire door
NERUŠIT	Do not disturb.
EXTERNÍ LINKA …	Dial … for an outside line.
RECEPCE …	Dial … for reception.
NEBERTE Z POKOJE RUČNÍKY	Do not remove towels from room.

Personal needs Osobní potřeby

The key to room …, please.	**Klíč od pokoje …, prosím.** *kleech ot-pokoyeh …* *proseem*
I've lost my key.	**Ztratil(a) jsem klíč od pokoje.** *stra-tyil(a) yesem kleech ot-pokoyeh*
I've locked myself out of my room.	**Zabouchl(a) jsem si dveře.** *za-boh-khul(khla) yesem si dve-rzeh*
Could you wake me at …?	**Vzbudili byste mě v …?** *vuzboo-dyi-lih bis-teh myeh v*
I'd like breakfast in my room.	**Mohu snídani na pokoj?** *mohooh sneeda-nyih napoko-ye'*
Can I leave this in the safe?	**Mohu tohle nechat v sejfu?** *mohooh to-hleh ne-khat fsey-fooh*
Could I have my things from the safe?	**Chtěl(a) bych si vyzvednout své věci ze sejfu.** *khutyel(a) bikh sih viz-ved-noh-t sveh vye-tsih zesey-fooh*
Where can I find (a) …?	**Kde najdu …?** *gdeh naye'-dooh*
maid	**pokojskou** *pokoye-skoh*
our tour guide (*masc./fem.*)	**našeho průvodce/naši průvodkyni** *na-sheho' proo-vot-tseh/na-shih* *proo-vot-ki-nyih*
May I have (an) extra …?	**Mohu dostat … navíc?** *mohooh dostat … naveets*
bath towel	**ručník** *rooch-nyeek*
blanket	**přikrývku** *przhi-kreef-kooh*
hangers	**ramínka** *ra-meen-ka*
pillow	**polštář** *polsh-tah-rzh*
soap	**mýdlo** *mee-dlo'*
Is there any mail for me?	**Je tu pro mě pošta?** *yeh tooh pro-myeh posh-ta*
Are there any messages for me?	**Jsou tu pro mě vzkazy?** *yesoh tooh pro-myeh vska-zih*
Could you mail this for me, please?	**Mohli byste mi tohle poslat?** *mo-hlih bis-teh mih to-hleh pos-lat*

BREAKFAST ➤ *43; CHANGING MONEY* ➤ *138*

Renting Pronájem

We've reserved an apartment/cottage ...	**Zamluvili jsme si byt/chatu ...** za-mloovilih yesmeh sih bit/kha-tooh
in the name of ...	**na jméno ...** na-yemeh-no'
Where do we pick up the keys?	**Kde si vyzvedneme klíče?** gdeh sih viz-ved-nemeh klee-cheh
Where's the electric meter?	**Kde jsou elektrické hodiny?** gdeh yesoh elek-trits-keh ho-dyi-nih
Where's the fuse box?	**Kde jsou pojistky?** gdeh yesoh po-yist-kih
Where's the valve [stopcock]?	**Kde je uzavírací kohout?** gdeh yeh ooza-vee-ra-tsee ko hoht
Where's the water heater?	**Kde je ohřívač vody?** gde yeh o-hurzhee-vach vodih
Are there any spare ...?	**Jsou tu náhradní ... ?** yesoh tooh nah-hrad-nyee
fuses	**pojistky** po-yist-kih
gas bottles	**plynové bomby** plinoveh bom-bih
Are there any spare sheets?	**Je tu náhradní povlečení?** yeh tooh nah-hrad-nyee po-vleche-nyee
Which day does the maid come?	**Kdy sem chodí pokojská?** gdih sem kho-dyee pokoye-skah
When do I put out the trash [rubbish]?	**Kdy se odvážejí odpadky?** gdih se odvah-zhe-yee ot-pat-kih

Problems Problémy

Where can I contact you?	**Kde se s vámi mohu spojit?** gdeh se svah-mih mohooh spo-yit
How does the stove [cooker]/ water heater work?	**Jak funguje vařič/ohřívač vody?** yuk foon-goo-yeh va-rzhich/o-hurzhee-vach vodih
The ... is dirty.	**... je špinavý.** ... yeh shpi-na-vee
The ... are dirty.	**... jsou špinavé.** ... yesoh shpi-na-veh
The ... has broken down.	**... je rozbitý.** ... yeh roz-bitee
We accidentally broke/lost ...	**Neúmyslně jsme rozbili/ztratili ...** ne-uh-mi-sul-nyeh yesmeh roz-bilih/ stra-tyi-lih
That was already damaged when we arrived.	**To bylo poškozené už před naším příjezdem.** to' bilo' posh-kozeneh oozh purzhet na-sheem purzhee-yez-dem

HOUSEHOLD ARTICLES ➤ 148

Useful terms Užitečné výrazy

boiler	**kotel** *kotel*
crockery	**nádobí** *nah-dobee*
cutlery	**příbory** *przhee-borih*
freezer	**mraznička** *mraz-nyich-ka*
frying pan	**pánev** *pah-nef*
kettle	**konvice** *kon-vi-tseh*
lamp	**lampa** *lum-pa*
refrigerator	**lednice** *led-nyi-tseh*
saucepan	**hrnec** *hur-nets*
stove [cooker]	**vařič** *va-rzhich*
washing machine	**pračka** *pruch-ka*

Rooms Pokoje

balcony	**balkón** *bal-kaun*
bathroom	**koupelna** *koh-pel-na*
bedroom	**ložnice** *lozh-nyi-tseh*
dining room	**jídelna** *yee-del-na*
kitchen	**kuchyň** *koo-khinye'*
living room	**obývací pokoj** *obee-va-tsee pokoye'*
toilet	**záchod** *zah-khot*

Youth hostel Mládežnická ubytovna

Do you have any places left for tonight?	**Máte na dnes ještě volná místa?** *mahteh nadnes yesh-tyeh vol-nah mees-ta*
Do you rent out bedding?	**Půjčujete přikrývky a povlečení?** *puh'ye-choo-yeteh przhi-kreef-kih ah po-vle-che-nyee*
What time are the doors locked?	**V kolik hodin se zamyká vchod?** *fkolik ho-dyin seh zamikah fukhot*
I have an International Student Card.	**Mám mezinárodní studentský průkaz.** *mahm mezinah-rod-nyee student-skee pruh-kaz*

REQUIREMENTS ➤ 26; CAMPING ➤ 30

Camping Kempink

Facilities at campsites vary, and not many are equipped for trailers [caravans]. Visit or contact a local tourist office for specific information.

Reservations Rezervace

Is there a campsite near here?	**Je tu poblíž kempink?** *yeh tooh po-bleezh kem-pink*
Do you have space for a tent/trailer [caravan]?	**Máte místo na stan/obytný přívěs?** *mah-teh mees-toh na-stun/obit-nee przhee-vyes*
What is the charge …?	**Jaký je poplatek za … ?** *Yukee yeh po-platek za*
per day/week	**den/týden** *den/teeden*
for a tent/car	**stan/auto** *stun/ow-to'*
for a trailer [caravan]	**obytný přívěs** *obit-nee przhee-vyes*

Facilities Vybavení

Are there cooking facilities on site?	**Je na kempinku kuchyňské vybavení?** *yeh nakem-pin-kooh koo-khiny'skeh viba-ve-nyee*
Are there any electrical outlets [power points]?	**Jsou tu elektrické zásuvky?** *yesoh tooh elek-trits-keh zah-soov-kih*
Where is the drinking water?	**Kde je pitná voda?** *gdeh yeh pit-nah voda*
Where are the trashcans [dustbins]?	**Kde jsou popelnice?** *gdeh yesoh popel-nyi-tseh*
Where are the laundry facilities?	**Kde je prádelna?** *gdeh yeh prah-del-na*
Where are the showers?	**Kde jsou sprchy?** *gdeh yesoh spr-khih*
Where can I get some butane gas?	**Kde si mohu opatřit plyn?** *gdeh sih mohuoh opat-rzhit plin*

ZÁKAZ KEMPOVÁNÍ	no camping
PITNÁ VODA	drinking water
ZÁKAZ ROZDĚLÁVÁNÍ OHNĚ/ POUŽITÍ GRILU	no fires/barbecues

Complaints Stížnosti

It's too sunny here.	**Tady je to moc na slunci.** *tadih yeh to' mots na-sloon-tsih*
It's too shady / crowded here.	**Tady je to moc ve stínu/ přeplněné.** *tadih yeh to' mots ve-styee-nooh/przhe-pul-nye-neh*
The ground's too hard / uneven.	**Zem je moc tvrdá/hrbolatá.** *zem yeh mots tvur-dah/hur-bolatah*
Do you have a more level spot?	**Máte rovnější místo?** *mah-teh rov-nyey'shee mees-to'*
You can't camp here.	**Tady nemůžete kempovat.** *tadih nemuh-zheteh kem-povat*

Camping equipment Kempovací vybavení

butane gas	**plyn** *plin*
campbed	**stanové lůžko** *sta-noveh luh-shko'*
charcoal	**dřevěné uhlí** *drzhe-vye-neh ooh-lee*
flashlight [torch]	**ruční svítilna** *rooch-nyee svee-tyil-na*
groundcloth [groundsheet]	**podlážka** *pod-lah-shka*
guy rope	**kotevní lano** *kotev-nyee lano'*
hammer	**kladivo** *kla-dyivo'*
kerosene [primus] stove	**primus** *pri-moos*
knapsack	**ruksak** *rook-suck*
mallet	**palice** *pali-tseh*
matches	**zápalky** *zah-pal-kih*
(air) mattress	**(nafukovací) matrace** *nafookova-tsee ma-tra-tseh*
paraffin	**parafín** *parafeen*
sleeping bag	**spací pytel** *spa-tsee pitel*
tent	**stan** *stun*
tent pegs	**stanové kolíčky** *sta-noveh koleech-kih*
tent pole	**stanová tyč** *sta-novah tich*

Checking out Odjezd

What time do we have to check out?
V kolik hodin musíme uvolnit pokoj?
fkolik ho-dyin moo-see-meh oo-vol-nyit pokoye'

Could we leave our baggage here until ... p.m.?
Můžeme si tu nechat zavazadla až do ... hodin odpoledne? *muh-zhemeh sih tooh ne-khat zavazad-la azh do' ... ho-dyin ot-poled-neh*

I'm leaving now.
Odjíždím.
od-yeezh-dyeem

Could you order me a taxi, please?
Můžete mi zavolat taxi?
muh-zheteh mih zavolat taksi

It's been a very enjoyable stay.
Moc se mi tu líbilo.
mots seh mih tooh lee-bi-lo'

Paying Placení

Smaller hotels do not always have bellhops [porters], although somebody is usually available to offer assistance if required. Porters in larger hotels will expect 10–20 korun (Kč) per item.

May I have my bill, please?
Účet, prosím.
uh-chet proseem

How much is my telephone bill?
Kolik zaplatím za telefon?
kolik zapla-tyeem zatelefon

I think there's a mistake in this bill.
Myslím, že v účtu je chyba.
mis-leem zhe v-uh-chtooh yeh khi-ba

I've made ... telephone calls.
Měl(a) jsem ... telefonických hovorů.
myel(a) yesem ... telefonits-keekh hovoruh

I've taken ... from the mini-bar.
Vzal(a) jsem si ... z minibaru.
vzal(a) yesem sih ... zminibarooh

Can I have an itemized bill?
Mohli byste mi účet rozepsat?
mo-hlih bis-teh mih uh-chet ro-zepsat

Could I have a receipt, please?
Mohli byste mi dát stvrzenku?
mo-hlih bis-teh mih daht stuvur-zen-kooh

Eating Out

Restaurants Restaurace

A three-course meal can cost anything from 200 Kč in a simple country restaurant to well over 1,000 Kč in some Prague restaurants and hotels.

Rychlé občerstvení *rikh-leh opchers-tve-nyee*

Snack bars serving a range of open-faced sandwiches; hot meals and snacks; tea and coffee; beer and wine. Generally standing places only.

Pivnice/Hospoda *piv-nyi-tseh/hospoda*

Pubs/bars serving draft [draught] beer and sometimes also simple hot and cold meals.

Vinárna *vinahr-na*

These are restaurants offering a wide selection of wine. The cuisine is usually Czech. Often open for dinner only.

Cukrárna *tsook-rahr-na*

A pastry shop, an essential component of every town's main square. Many of them are open on Sundays, as well as during the week, and offer a wide choice of pastries, cakes, and ice cream. Some have seating and serve coffee, iced coffee, tea, and cold drinks, too. Many will have tables outside in the summer.

Kavárna *kavahr-na*

A coffee-house. The true coffeehouse will offer a really
good selection of coffees, along with a limited selection
of cakes or ice cream. Traditionally they provide broadsheet
newspapers in long wooden frames.

Restaurace *res-ta-oora-tseh*

Traditional restaurant. They range from the simple to the stylish.
The cuisine is usually Czech, although recently Chinese, Vietnamese,
and Italian restaurants have appeared.

Pizzerie *pi-tse-ri-yeh*

Pizzeria. Some serve exclusively pizza, others pizza and pasta.
Some have the traditional ovens and their pizzas are true to the
Italian original.

Meal times Denní jídla

Breakfast (**snídaně** *snyee-da-nyeh*): served from 6:00 to 9:30 a.m.

Lunch (**oběd** *ob-yed*): served from 11:30 a.m. to 2:00 p.m. Mostly a two-
or three-course meal, often offered as a set menu. Generally still the main
meal for Czechs.

Dinner (**večeře** *veche-rzheh*): served from 6:00 to 10:00 p.m. The Czechs
eat their dinner early.

Czech cuisine Česká kuchyně

Czech cuisine is traditionally meat based, with pork and poultry being
the most popular meats. Dumplings made from flour, semolina, or
potatoes are a frequent accompaniment to meat often prepared in a rich
gravy or a cream sauce ➤ 45. Potatoes are also popular and are served in
a variety of ways. Many local soups can be a meal in themselves. You will
probably find the range of vegetarian dishes limited.

The Czech Republic is a landlocked country and most fish on offer will be
fresh-water fish like the carp and trout. Seafood is still a bit of a rarity.
When you do find it, it is usually frozen. If you find fresh seafood, it is
likely to be very expensive.

Czechs have a sweet tooth and are very fond of desserts and cakes. They
also enjoy excellent rich coffee, traditionally served in the Turkish style
(**turecká káva**), with the coffee grounds left in the bottom of the cup, or in
the Viennese style (**vídeňská káva**), with the coffee topped with whipped
cream.

A table for ..., please.	**Stůl pro ... , prosím.** *stuhl pro' ... proseem*
1/2/3/4	**jednoho/dva/tři/čtyři** *yed-no-ho'/dva/trzhih/chti-rzhih*
Thank you.	**Děkuji.** *dye-koo-yih*
The bill, please.	**Účet, prosím.** *uh-chet proseem*

Finding a place to eat Kde se najíst

Can you recommend a good restaurant?	**Můžete mi doporučit dobrou restauraci?** *muh-zheteh mih doporoochit dobroh res-ta-oora-tsih*
Is there a(n) ... restaurant near here?	**Je tu poblíž ... restaurace?** *yeh tooh pob-leezh ... res-ta-oora-tseh*
Chinese	**čínská** *cheens-kah*
fish	**rybí** *ribee*
inexpensive	**levná** *lev-nah*
Italian	**italská** *ital-skah*
traditional Czech	**tradiční česká** *tra-dich-nyee cheskah*
vegetarian	**vegetariánská** *vegetari-ahn-skah*
Where can I find a(n) ...? (*masc./fem.*)	**Kde bych našel/našla ...?** *gdeh bikh nashel (nashla)*
burger stand	**stánek s párky** *stahnek spahr-kih*
café/coffeehouse	**bufet/kavárnu** *boofet/kavahr-nooh*
restaurant	**restauraci** *res-ta-oora-tsih*
with a terrace/garden	**s terasou/se zahradou** *sterasoh/seza-hra-doh*
fast-food restaurant	**rychlé občerstvení** *rikh-leh op-chers-tve-nyee*
ice-cream parlor	**cukrárnu se zmrzlinou** *tsook-rahr-nooh se-zmur-zli-noh*
pizzeria	**pizzerii** *pi-tse-ri-yih*

DIRECTIONS ➤ 94

Reserving a table Rezervace

I'd like to reserve a table …	**Chtěl(a) bych si zamluvit stůl …** *khuteyl(a) bikh sih zamloovit stuhl*
for two	**pro dva** *pro dva*
for this evening/tomorrow at …	**na dnes večer/na zítra na …** *na-dnes vecher/na-zeet-ra na*
We'll come at 8:00.	**Přijdeme v osm hodin.** *purzhiye-demeh vo-sum ho-dyin*
A table for two, please.	**Stůl pro dva, prosím.** *stuhl pro-dva proseem*
We have a reservation.	**Máme to rezervaci.** *mah-meh to' rezerva-tsih*

Na kolik hodin?	For what time?
Na jaké jméno?	What's the name, please?
Je mi líto. Máme obsazeno.	I'm sorry. We're very busy/full up.
Budeme mít volný stůl asi za … minut.	We'll have a free table in … minutes.
Přijďte znovu za … minut.	Please come back in … minutes.

Where to sit Kde se posadit

Could we sit …?	**Mohli bychom si sednout …?** *moh-lih bi-khom sih sed-noht*
over there	**tamhle** *tum-hleh*
outside	**venku** *ven-kooh*
in a non-smoking area	**v části pro nekuřáky** *fchahs-tyih pro' ne-koo-rzhah-kih*
by the window	**u okna** *oo-okna*
Smoking or non-smoking?	**Pro kuřáky nebo nekuřáky?** *pro-koo-rzhah-kih nebo' ne-koo-rzhah-kih*

– Chtěl(a) bych si zamluvit stůl na dnes na večer.
(I'd like to reserve a table for this evening.)
– Pro kolik osob? (For how many people?)
– Pro čtyři. (For four.)
– Na kolik hodin? (For what time?)
– Přijdeme v osm. (We'll come at eight o'clock.)
– Na jaké jméno?
(And what's the name, please?)
– Smith. (Smith.)
– Dobře. Budeme se těšit.
(Thank you. See you then.)

Ordering Objednávání

Waiter! / Waitress!	**Pane vrchní! / Paní vrchní!** *paneh vur-khnyee / panyee vur-khnyee*
May I see the wine list, please?	**Mohl(a) bych vidět nápojový lístek?** *mohl(a) bikh vi-dyet nah-po-yo-vee lees-tek*
Do you have a set menu?	**Máte hotové menu?** *mah-teh hotoveh menooh*
Can you recommend some typical local dishes?	**Můžete mi doporučit nějaké typické místní jídlo?** *muh-zheteh mih doporuchit nye-ya-keh meest-nyee yeed-lo'*
Could you tell me what … is?	**Můžete mi říci, co je …?** *muh-zheteh mih rzhee-tsih tso yeh*
What's in it?	**Co v tom je?** *tso' ftom yeh*
What kind of … do you have?	**Jaké máte …?** *yakeh mah-the*
I'd like … / I'll have …	**Chtěl(a) bych … / Vezmu si …** *khutyel(a) bikh / vezmooh sih*
a bottle / glass / carafe of …	**láhev / sklenici / džbánek …** *lah-hef / skle-nyi-tsih / duzh-bah-nek*

Chcete si objednat?	Are you ready to order?
Co byste si přáli?	What would you like?
A co si přejete k pití?	What would you like to drink?
Doporučil(a) bych …	I recommend …
Nemáme …	We don't have …
Bude to trvat … minut.	That will take … minutes.
Nechte si chutnat.	Enjoy your meal.

– *Chcete si objednat?* (Are you ready to order?)
– *Můžete mi doporučit typické místní jídlo?*
  (Can you recommend a typical local dish?)
– *Ano. Doporučil bych vám uzené se zelím a knedlíkem.*
  (Yes. I recommend the smoked pork with
   sauerkraut and dumplings.)
– *Dobře, já si to vezmu.*
  (OK, I'll have that, please.)
– *Dobře. A co si přejete k pití?*
  (Certainly. And what would you like to drink?)
– *Džbánek červeného vína, prosím.*
  (A carafe of red wine, please.)
– *Samozřejmě.* (Certainly.)

DRINKS ➤ 49; MENU READER ➤ 52

Accompaniments Přílohy

Could I have … without the …?	**Mohu dostat … bez …?** _mohooh dostat … bes_
With a side order of …	**Jako přílohu …** _yako' przhee-lo-hooh_
Could I have salad instead of vegetables, please?	**Mohu dostat čerstvý salát místo zeleniny?** _mohooh dostat chers-tvee salaht meesto' zele-nyi-nih_
Does the meal come …?	**Je jídlo …?** _yeh yeed-lo'_
with vegetables / with potatoes	**se zeleninou / s bramborem** _sezele-nyi-noh / sbrum-bo-rem_
with rice / with pasta	**s rýží / s těstovinami** _sree-zhee / styes-to-vi-namih_
Do you have any …?	**Máte …?** _mah-teh_
ketchup / mayonnaise	**kečup / majonézu** _ke-choop / ma-yo-neh-zooh_
I'd like … with that.	**Chtěl(a) bych k tomu …** _khutyel(a) bikh kto-mooh_
vegetables / salad	**zeleninu / salát** _zele-nyi-nooh / sa-laht_
potatoes / French fries	**brambory / hranolky** _brum-bo-rih / hra-nol-kih_
sauce	**omáčku** _omahch-kooh_
ice	**led** _let_
May I have some …?	**Mohu dostat …?** _mohooh dostat_
bread	**chleba** _khle-ba_
butter	**máslo** _mah-slo'_
lemon	**citrón** _tsi-tron_
mustard	**hořčici** _horzh-chi-tsih_
pepper	**pepř** _peprzh_
salt	**sůl** _suhl_
oil and vinegar	**olej a ocet** _oleye ah o-tset_
sugar	**cukr** _tsoo-kur_
artificial sweetener	**umělé sladidlo** _oomye-leh sla-dyi-dlo'_
oil and vinegar [vinaigrette]	**francouzskou zálivku** _fran-tsohs-koh zah-lif-kooh_

General requests Obecné žádosti

Could I/we have (a/an) …, please?
Mohu/Můžeme dostat …?
mohooh/muh-zhemeh dostat

(clean) ashtray
(čistý) popelník
chis-tee popel-nyeek

(clean) cup/(clean) glass
(čistý) šálek/(čistou) sklenici
chis-tee shah-lek/chis-toh skle-nyi-tsih

(clean) fork/(clean) knife
(čistou) vidličku/(čistý) nůž
chis-toh vid-lich-kooh/chis-tee nuhzh

(clean) plate/(clean) spoon
(čistý) talíř/(čistou) lžíci
chis-tee ta-leerzh/chis-toh luzhee-tsih

(clean) napkin
(čistý) ubrousek *chis-tee oob-roh-sek*

I'd like some more …, please.
Chtěl(a) bych ještě …
khutyel(a) bikh yesh-tyeh

That's all, thanks.
To je všechno, děkuji.
to' yeh vushekh-no' dye-koo-yih

Where are the bathrooms [toilets]?
Kde jsou záchody?
gdeh yesoh zah-khodih

Special requirements Zvláštní přání

I can't eat food …
Nesmím jíst nic … *nes-meem yeest nits*

containing salt/sugar
se solí/s cukrem *se-solee/s-tsook-rem*

Do you have any dishes/drinks for diabetics?
Máte jídla/nápoje pro diabetiky?
mah-teh yeed-la/nah-po-yeh pro-di-abe-tikih

Do you have vegetarian dishes?
Máte vegetariánská jídla?
mah-teh vegeta-ri-ahn-ska yeed-la

For the children Pro děti

Do you have a children's menu?
Máte jídelníček pro děti?
mah-teh yee-del-nyee-chek pro-dye-tyih

Could you bring a child's seat, please?
Můžeme dostat dětskou sedačku?
moo-zhemeh dostat dyets-koh se-duch-kooh

Where can I change the baby?
Kde mohu přebalit dítě?
gdeh mo-hooh purzhe-balit dyee-tyeh

Where can I feed the baby?
Kde mohu nakojit dítě?
gdeh mo-hooh nako-yit dyee-tyeh

CHILDREN ➤ 113

Fast food / Café
Rychlé občerstvení / Bufet
Something to drink Něco k pití

I'd like (a) …	**Chtěl(a) bych …** *khutyel(a) bikh*
beer	**pivo** *pivo'*
tea	**čaj** *chuy*
Viennese coffee	**Vídeňskou kávu** *vee-denye-skoh kah-vooh*
… coffee	**… kávu** *… kah-vooh*
black / with milk [white]	**černou / bílou** *cher-noh / bee-loh*
I'd like a … of red / white wine.	**Chtěl(a) bych … červeného / bílého vína.** *khutyel(a) bikh … cher-ve-neh-ho' / bee-leh-ho' veena*
glass / carafe / bottle	**skleničku / džbánek / láhev** *skle-nyich-kooh / duzh-bah-nek / lah-hef*
I'd like a … beer.	**Chtěl(a) bych … pivo.** *khutye(a) bikh … pivo'*
bottled / draft [draught]	**láhvové / točené** *lah-voveh / to-cheneh*

And to eat A k jídlu

A piece / slice of …, please.	**Kousek / plátek …, prosím.** *koh-sek / plah-tek … proseem*
I'd like two of those.	**Chtěl(a) bych to dvakrát.** *khutyel(a) bikh to' dvuk-raht*
I'd like …	**Chtěl(a) bych …** *khutyel(a) bikh*
burger / fries	**karbanátek / hranolky** *kar-banah-tek / hra-nol-kih*
omelet / pizza	**omeletu / pizzu** *omeletooh / pi-tsooh*
sandwich / cake	**sendvič / zákusek** *send-vich / zah-koosek*
ice cream	**zmrzlinu** *zmur-zli-nooh*
chocolate / strawberry / vanilla	**čokoládovou / jahodovou / vanilkovou** *chokolah-dovoh / ya-ho-do-voh / va-nil-ko-voh*
A … portion, please.	**… porci, prosím.** *… por-tsih proseem*
small / large	**malou / velkou** *maloh / vel-koh*
regular [medium]	**obyčejnou** *obi-chey-noh*
It's to go [take away].	**Vezmu si to s sebou.** *vez-mooh sih to' seboh*
That's all, thanks.	**To je všechno, děkuji.** *to' yeh vushekh-no' dye-koo-yih*
To eat in or to go [take away]?	**Tady nebo s sebou?** *tadih nebo' seboh*

DRINKS ➤ 49–51

– Co byste si přáli? What would you like?
– Dvakrát kávi, prosím. (Two coffees, please.)
– Černou nebo bílou? (Black or with milk?)
– Bílou. (With milk, please.)
– Je to všechno? (Anything else?)
– To je všechno, děkuji.
(That's all, thanks.)

Complaints Stížnosti

I have no knife/fork/spoon.	**Nemám nůž/vidličku/lžíci.** *ne-mahm nuh-zh/vid-lich-kooh/luzhee-tsih*
There must be some mistake.	**To je asi nějaký omyl.** *to' yeh asih nye-yakee omil*
That's not what I ordered.	**To jsem si neobjednal(a).** *to' yesem sih ne-ob-yed-nal(a)*
I asked for …	**Objednal(a) jsem si …** *ob-yed-nal(a) yesem sih*
I can't eat this.	**Nemohu to jíst.** *ne-mo-hooh to' yeest*
The meat is …	**Maso je …** *maso' yeh*
overdone	**převařené** *przhe-va-rzhe-neh*
underdone	**nedovařené** *ne-do-va-rzhe-neh*
too tough	**moc tuhé** *mots too-heh*
This is too …	**Tohle je moc …** *to-hleh yeh mots*
bitter/sour	**hořké/kyselé** *horzh-keh/ki-seleh*
The food is cold.	**Jídlo je studené.** *yeed-lo' yeh stoo-deneh*
This isn't fresh.	**Není to čerstvé.** *ne-nyee to' chers-tveh*
How much longer will our food be?	**Jak dlouho budeme ještě na jídlo čekat?** *yak dloh-ho' boo-demeh yesh-tyeh na-yeed-lo' chekat*
We can't wait any longer. We're leaving.	**Už nemůžeme déle čekat. Odcházíme.** *oozh ne-moo-zhemeh deh-leh chekat. ot-khah-zee-meh*
This isn't clean.	**Tohle není čisté.** *to-hleh ne-nyee chis-teh*
I'd like to speak to the head waiter/to the manager.	**Chtěl(a) bych mluvit s vrchním/s vedoucím.** *khutyel(a) bikh mloo-vit svur-khnyeem/ sve-doh-tseem*

Paying Placení

Check before ordering if you plan to pay with a credit card, as not all restaurants will accept them. The usual amount for a tip is between 10 and 15 percent.

I'd like to pay.	**Zaplatím.** *zapla-tyeem*
The bill, please.	**Účet, prosím.** *uh-chet proseem*
We'd like to pay separately.	**Budeme platit každý samostatně.** *boodemeh pla-tyit kazh-dee samos-tut-nyeh*
It's all together.	**Všechno dohromady.** *vushekh-no' do-hro-ma-dih*
I think there's a mistake in this bill.	**Myslím, že v účtu je chyba.** *mis-leem zheh vuh-chtooh yeh khiba*
What's this amount for?	**Za co je tato částka?** *za-tso' yeh tato' chahs-tka*
I didn't have that. I had …	**To jsem neměl(a). Měl(a) jsem …** *to' yesem ne-myel(a). myel(a) yesem*
Is service included?	**Je v tom zahrnutá obsluha?** *yeh ftom za-hur-nootah op-sloo-ha*
Can I pay with this credit card?	**Mohu zaplatit touto kreditní kartou?** *mo-hooh zapla-tyit toh-to' kre-dit-nyee kar-toh*
I've forgotten my wallet.	**Zapomněl(a) jsem si peněženku.** *zapo-mnyel(a) yesem sih pe-nye-zhen-kooh*
I don't have enough cash.	**Nemám dost hotových peněz.** *ne-mahm dost ho-to-veekh pe-nyes*
Could I have a receipt, please?	**Mohu dostat stvrzenku, prosím?** *mo-hooh dostat st-vur-zen-kooh proseem*
That was a very good meal. *(for a man/woman)*	**Výborně jsem se najedl/najedla.** *vee-bor-nyeh yesem seh na-yedul/na-yed-la*

– Pane vrchní! Účet, prosím. (Waiter! The bill, please.)
– Jistě. Prosím, tady je. (Certainly. Here you are.)
– Je v tom zahrnutá obsluha?
(Is service included?)
– Ano, je. (Yes, it is.)
– Mohu zaplatit touto kreditní kartou?
(Can I pay with this credit card?)
– Ano, samozřejmě. (Yes, of course.)
– Děkuji. Výborně jsem se najedl(a).
(Thank you. That was a very good meal.)

Course by course Jednotlivé chody

Breakfast Snídaně

Czechs tend to eat breakfast – tea or coffee and bread with
butter and jam – on the run. Large, Western, tourist-oriented
hotels offer a buffet with a choice of cold meats, cheeses, pastries,
eggs, ham, bacon, cereal, fruit, etc.

I'd like …	**Chtěl(a) bych …** *khutyel(a) bikh*
bread	**chleba** *khle-ba*
butter	**máslo** *mah-slo'*
eggs	**vejce** *veye-tseh*
boiled/fried/scrambled	**vařená/smažená/míchaná** *va-rzhe-nah/sma-zhe-nah/mee-kha-nah*
fruit juice	**ovocný džus** *ovots-nee dzhoos*
grapefruit/orange	**grepový/pomerančový** *gre-po-vee/po-me-run-chovee*
honey	**med** *met*
jam	**džem** *dzhem*
marmalade	**pomerančovou marmeládu** *po-me-run-chovoh mar-me-lah-dooh*
milk	**mléko** *mleh-ko'*
rolls	**rohlíky** *ro-hlee-kih*
toast	**topinky** *topin-kih*

Appetizers/Starters Předkrmy

ham with gherkins	**šunka s okurkou** *shoon-ka so-koor-koh*
salami with gherkins	**salám s okurkou** *sa-lahm so-koor-koh*
egg mayonnaise	**ruské vejce** *roos-keh veye-tseh*
cod livers with onion	**tresčí játra s cibulkou** *tres-chee yah-tra s-tsi-bool-koh*
rolled pork with onion	**tlačenka s cibulí** *tla-chen-ka s-tsi-boo-lee*
smoked tongue	**uzený jazyk** *oozenee ya-zik*
ham and horseradish roll	**křenová rolka** *kurzhe-novah rol-ka*
ham in aspic	**šunka v aspiku** *shoon-ka vas-pi-kooh*
pickled herring [rollmops]	**zavináče** *za-vi-nah-cheh*

Soups Polévky

bramborová polévka	*brum-borovah po-lehf-ka*	potato soup
česneková polévka	*ches-nekovah po-lehf-ka*	garlic soup
čočková polévka	*choch-kovah po-lehf-ka*	lentil soup
fazolová polévka	*fazolovah po-lehf-ka*	bean soup
hovězí vývar (s nudlemi)	*ho-vye-zee vee-var (snood-lemih)*	consommé (with vermicelli)
hrachová polévka s uzeným	*hra-kho-vah po-lehf-ka sooze-neem*	pea soup with smoked meat
kapustová polévka	*ka-poos-tovah po-lehf-ka*	cabbage soup
kuřecí vývar (se zeleninou)	*koo-rzhe-tsee vee-var (se-ze-le-nyi-noh)*	chicken soup (with vegetables)
rajská polévka	*rai-skah po-lehf-ka*	tomato soup
rybí polévka	*ribee po-lehf-ka*	fish soup
zeleninová polévka	*zele-nyi-novah po-lehf-ka*	vegetable soup

Bramboračka *brum-bo-ruch-ka*
A thick soup with cubed potatoes, vegetables, mushrooms, and a touch of garlic.

Zelňačka *zel-nyach-ka*
A thick soup with cubed potatoes, chopped sauerkraut, and cream.

Hovězí vyvar s játrovými knedlíčky
ho-vye-zee vee-var syah-tro-vee-mih kuned-leech-kih
Beef broth (sometimes with shredded vegetables) and little round dumplings of finely chopped liver seasoned with nutmeg.

Egg dishes Vaječná jídla

omeleta	*omeleta*	omelet
omeleta se šunkou/ se sýrem	*omeleta se-shoon-koh/ se-see-rem*	omelet with ham/cheese
míchaná vejce na slanině	*mee-kha-nah veye-tseh na-sla-nyi-nyeh*	scrambled eggs with bacon
míchaná vejce na cibulce	*mee-kha-nah veye-tseh na-tsi-bool-tseh*	scrambled eggs with onion

Fish/seafood Ryby

The Czech Republic is a landlocked country and fresh salt-water fish is rare, as is seafood. Common varieties of fresh-water fish are carp and trout.

candát	tsan-daht	pike perch
garnát	gar-naht	shrimp [prawns]
humr	hoo-mur	lobster
chobotnice	kho-bot-nyi-tseh	octopus
kapr	ka-pur	carp
kaviár	ka-vi-ahr	caviar
krab	krub	crab
losos	losos	salmon
platýz	pla-tees	plaice
pstruh	pus-trooh	trout
rybí filé	ribee fi-leh	fish fillet
slaneček	sla-ne-chek	herring [whitebait]
štika	shtyi-ka	pike
treska	tres-ka	cod
tuňák	too-nyahk	tuna
ústřice	uhs-turzhi-tseh	oysters

Smažený kapr sma-zhe-nee kapur
Pieces of carp fried in bread crumbs.

Kapr na černo kapur na-cher-no
Pieces of carp portions baked in a thick sauce made with vegetables, black beer, and prunes.

Kapr na česneku kapur na-ches-nekooh
Pieces of carp grilled with butter and garlic.

Pstruh na másle pus-trooh na-mah-sleh
Grilled trout with butter, garnished with lemon.

Dumplings Knedlíky

Dumplings, a traditional part of Czech cuisine, are usually served as a savory accompaniment to meat dishes. They are cooked in long rolls and then sliced and served with sauce. Sweet dumplings are usually filled with fruit, traditionally fresh plums, and sprinkled with sieved curd cheese and sugar, and covered with melted butter.

houskové knedlíky	hoh-skoveh kned-leekih	bread dumplings
bramborové knedlíky	brumboroveh kned-leekih	potato dumpling
švestkové knedlíky	shvest-koveh kned-leekih	plum dumplings

Meat and poultry Maso a drůbež

bažant	*ba-zhunt*	pheasant
biftek	*bif-tek*	steak
hovězí	*ho-vye-zee*	beef
husa	*hoosa*	goose
jehněčí	*yeh-nye-chee*	lamb
kachna	*kakh-na*	duck
klobásy	*klo-bah-sih*	sausages
králík	*krah-leek*	rabbit
krůta	*kruh-ta*	turkey
kuře	*ku-rzheh*	chicken
párky	*pahr-kih*	chunky sausages
slanina	*sla-nyi-na*	bacon
šunka	*shoon-ka*	ham
telecí	*tele-tsee*	veal
vepřové	*vep-rzho-veh*	pork
zajíc	*za-yeets*	hare
zvěřina	*zvye-rzhi-na*	venison

Smažený vepřový řízek *sma-zhe-nee vep-rzho-vee rzhee-zek*
Wiener schnitzel with potatoes (**s bramborem**) or potato salad
(**bramborovým salátem**).

Uzené se zelím a knedlíky *oozeneh sezeleem a kned-leekih*
Smoked pork with sauerkraut and dumplings.

Svíčková na smetaně *sveech-kovah na-sme-ta-nyeh*
Roast tenderloin slices in a creamy root vegetable sauce, garnished with
cranberries and served with dumplings (**s knedlíkem**).

Pečená kachna *pechenah kakh-na*
Roast duck, served with cabbage or sauerkraut, usually accompanied by
dumplings.

Meat cuts Části masa

biftek	*bif-tek*	fillet/sirloin/rump/T-bone steak
játra	*yah-tra*	liver
hřbet	*hurz-bet*	saddle
ledvinky	*led-vin-kih*	kidneys
kotlety	*kot-letih*	chops
kýta	*kee-ta*	leg
plec	*plets*	shoulder
řízek	*rzhee-zek*	cutlet

Vegetables Zelenina

brambory	*brum-borih*	potatoes
celer	*tse-ler*	celery root [celeriac]
cibule	*tsi-booleh*	onions
cukety	*tsoo-ketih*	zucchini [courgettes]
červená řepa	*cher-venah rzhe-pa*	beets [beetroot]
česnek	*ches-nek*	garlic
fazolové lusky	*fazoloveh loos-kih*	green beans
houby	*hoh-bih*	mushrooms
hrášek	*hrah-shek*	peas
jarní cibulka	*yar-nyee tsi-bool-ka*	spring onions
květák	*kvye-tahk*	cauliflower
lilek	*lilek*	eggplant [aubergine]
mrkev	*mur-kef*	carrots
okurka	*okoor-ka*	cucumber
paprika	*pap-rika*	peppers
pórek	*paw-rek*	leeks
rajčata	*rai-cha-ta*	tomatoes
rýže	*ree-zheh*	rice
salát	*sa-laht*	lettuce
šalotka	*sha-lot-ka*	shallots
zelí	*zelee*	cabbage
žampiony	*zhum-pi-onih*	mushrooms

Smažený květák s bramborem
sma-zhe-nee kvye-tahk s-brum-borem
Cauliflower rosettes fried in bread crumbs, served with boiled potatoes and tartar sauce. A favorite vegetarian dish.

Salad Saláty

bramborový salát	*brum-borovee sa-laht*	potato salad
míchaný salát	*mee-kha-nee sa-laht*	mixed salad
okurkový salát	*okoor-kovee sa-laht*	cucumber salad
rajčatový salát s cibulkou	*rai-cha-tovee sa-laht s-tsi-bool-koh*	tomato and onion salad
zelený salát	*zelenee sa-laht*	green salad
zelný salát	*zel-nee sa-laht*	cabbage salad

Cheese Sýry

jemný sýr	*yem-nee seer*	mild cheese
kozí sýr	*kozee seer*	goat cheese
měkký tvaroh	*mye-kee tva-rokh*	cottage cheese
ostrý sýr	*os-tree seer*	sharp / tangy cheese
ovčí sýr	*of-chee seer*	ewe's milk cheese
plísňový sýr	*plees-nyo-vee seer*	blue cheese
smetanový sýr	*sme-tanovee seer*	cream cheese
tvrdý sýr	*tuvur-dee seer*	hard cheese

Niva® *nyi-va*
This is the most common brand of blue cheese available. It often appears on menus as **… s Nivou** (… with blue cheese), the assumption being that everyone will know what **Niva** is.

Smažený sýr *sma-zhe-nee seer*
Slices of Edam or Gouda fried in bread crumbs; served with a garnish as a hot appetizer or with potatoes as a main dish.

Syrečky *si-rech-kih*
A cheese with a strong smell and sharp taste made with beer. It comes in small disk-like shapes.

Dessert Moučníky/Zákusky

jablečný závin	apple strudel
koblihy	donuts [doughnuts]
makový koláč	poppy seed cake
ovocný koláč	fruit cake
ovocný koláč s drobenkou	fruit crumble pie
palačinky	pancakes
sachr dort	Sacher torte [Black Forest gateau]
trubičky se šlehačkou	brandy snaps with cream
tvarohové taštičky	cottage cheese pastries
zmrzlinový pohár	ice-cream sundae

Lívance *lee-vun-tseh*
Small pancakes, spread with plum cheese and a layer of cottage cheese, and topped with yogurt or thick sour cream.

Švestkové knedlíky *shvest-koveh kned-leekih*
Plum dumplings sprinkled with sieved curd cheese and sugar, and covered with melted butter.

Fruit Ovoce

banány	*banah-nih*	bananas
borůvky	*bo-roof-kih*	blueberries
broskve	*brosk-veh*	peaches
cukrový meloun	*tsook-rovee me-lown*	melon
grepy	*grepih*	grapefruit
hroznové víno	*hroz-noveh veeno'*	grapes
jablka	*ya-bul-ka*	apples
jahody	*yahodih*	strawberries
maliny	*malinih*	raspberries
meloun	*me-lown*	watermelon
meruňky	*me-roony'-kih*	apricots
pomeranče	*pome-run-cheh*	oranges
švestky	*shvest-kih*	plums
třešně	*trzhesh-nyeh*	cherries
višně	*vish-nyeh*	morello cherries

Drinks Nápoje

Aperitifs Aperitivy

meruňkovice	apricot brandy
slivovice	plum brandy / slivovitz (sometimes served with small snacks)

Karlovarská Becherovka® is a famous herb brandy from Karlsbad. Generally served chilled as an aperitif or as a liqueur with strong coffee. Believed to aid digestion.

Beer Pivo

All beers in the Czech Republic are lagers, not ales. They are generally quite strong and bitter and always served chilled. There are many brands, each region having its own brewery.

plzeňské	pilsen
Budvar	Budweiser
černé	black (slightly sweet)

Do you have … beer?	**Máte … pivo?**	*mah-teh … pivo'*
bottled / draft [draught]	**láhvové/točené**	*lah-voveh/to-cheneh*

Wine Víno

Bohemia and, in particular, the warmer region of Moravia have a number of local wines, which are increasingly available in restaurants and liquor stores. Many **vinárna** – a type of restaurant with a wide selection of wines – serve local wines; they are open late and also offer typical regional snacks and/or meals. Look for the mature "archive" wine (**archívní víno**). Compared to imported wine, all Czech wines are relatively inexpensive.

Popular Czech wines to look for:

White:	**Vlašský ryzlink, Rulandské bílé, Müller-Thurgau, Veltlínské zelené**
Red:	**Frankovka, Vavřinec**

Can you recommend a ... wine?	**Můžete mi doporučit ... víno?** moo-zheteh mih doporuchit ... vee-no'
red/white/blush [rosé]	**červené/bílé/růžové** cher-veneh/bee-leh/ruh-zhoveh
dry/sweet/sparkling	**suché/sladké/šumivé** soo-kheh/slut-keh/shoo-miveh

Spirits and liqueurs Destiláty a likéry

Apart from **slivovitz** and apricot brandy, another popular Czech drink worth trying is **borovička**, which is made with juniper berries and is similar to gin. Most other hard liquors, e.g., cognac, whisky, rum, gin, and vodka, are imported and usually priced rather high.

straight [neat]	**čistý** chis-tee
on the rocks [with ice]	**s ledem** sledem
with water/with tonic water/ with lemon	**s vodou/s tonikem/s citrónem** zvo-doh/sto-ni-kem/s-tsi-tro-nem
I'd like a single/double gin.	**Chtěl(a) bych malý/dvojitý gin.** khutyel(a) bikh malee/dvo-yee-tee dzhin
I'd like a single/double ...	**Chtěl(a) bych malou/dvojitou ...** khutyel(a) bikh maloh/dvo-yei-toh
brandy/whisky/vodka	**brandy/whisky/vodku** bren-dih/vis-kih/vot-kooh

Non-alcoholic drinks
Nealkoholické nápoje

Mineral water (**minerálka**) is inexpensive and comes in many
different varieties; all are genuine local mineral waters,
sometimes with natural gas. The brand "Good Water" is sold in
large bottles in most supermarkets. Look for "Mattoni," the well-known
and highly regarded mineral water from Karlsbad. It comes in glass
bottles, and its fresh flavor is well worth the extra weight. Imported
mineral water is also available, but it tends to be much more expensive.
Various well-known soft drink brands and sodas are generally available,
as are fruit juices.

Tea and coffee Čaj a káva

Tea is seldom drunk with milk. It is more usual to have it with lemon
(**s citrónem**). Also popular are rose hip tea (**šípkový čaj**) and camomile tea
(**heřmánkový čaj**).

Czechs like their coffee richly brewed, and you will find Turkish-style coffee
(**turecká káva**), with coffee grounds left in the bottom of the cup, and
Viennese-style coffee (**videňská káva**), with the coffee topped with whipped
cream, widely available. Cappuccino and espresso are popular, too.

I'd like (a) …	**Chtěl(a) bych …** *khutye(a) bikh*
tea with milk/with lemon	**čaj s mlékem/s citrónem** *chuy sumleh-kem/sutsit-ronem*
black coffee	**černou kávu** *cher-noh kah-vooh*
coffee with milk	**bílou kávu** *bee-loh kah-vooh*
hot chocolate/cocoa	**horkou čokoládu/kakao** *hor-koh choko-lah-dooh/kakao*
cola/lemonade	**kolu/limonádu** *ko-looh/limo-nah-dooh*
fruit juice	**ovocnou šťávu** *ovots-noh shtyah-vooh*
orange/pineapple/tomato	**pomerančovou/ananasovou/rajskou** *pome-run-cho-voh/ana-na-sovoh/rai-skoh*
milk shake	**mléčný koktejl** *mleh-chnee kok-teyel*
mineral water	**minerálku** *mine-rahl-kooh*
carbonated/non-carbonated [still]	**s bublinkami/bez bublinek** *zboob-lin-kamih/bez-boob-linek*

Menu Reader

This Menu Reader is an alphabetical glossary of terms that you may find on a menu. Certain traditional dishes are cross-referenced to the relevant page in the *Course by course* section, where they are described in more detail.

dobře upečené	*dob-rzheh oopecheneh*	well-done
dušené	*doo-she-neh*	braised/stewed
dušené v páře	*doo-sheneh fpah-rzheh*	steamed
grilované	*grilovaneh*	grilled
hodně krvavé	*hod-nyeh kur-vaveh*	very rare
kořeněné	*ko-rzhe-nye-neh*	spicy
krvavé	*kur-vaveh*	rare
marinované	*marinovaneh*	marinated
mírně propečené	*meer-nyeh propecheneh*	medium
nakrájené na kostičky	*na-krah-yeneh na-kos-tyich-kih*	diced
na másle	*na-mah-sleh*	sautéed
pečené	*pe-che-neh*	baked/roasted
plněné	*pul-nye-neh*	stuffed
smažené	*sma-zhe-neh*	fried
uzené	*oozeneh*	smoked
vařené	*va-rzhe-neh*	boiled
ve smetaně	*ve-sme-ta-nyeh*	creamed
ve strouhance	*ve-stroh-hun-tseh*	breaded

A **alkoholické nápoje** alcoholic drinks
ananas pineapple
angrešt gooseberry
anýz aniseed
anýzovka aniseed liqueur
aperitiv aperitif
arašídy peanuts
artyčok artichoke
aspik jelly
avokádo avocado

B **banán** banana
banán v čokoládě chocolate-covered banana
bazalka basil
bažant pheasant
bez kofeinu decaffeinated
biftek steak
bílá with milk/white (*coffee*)
bílé hrozny white grapes
bílé zelí white cabbage
bílek egg white
bílý chléb white bread
bobkový list bay leaf
boby broad beans
bonbony candy [sweets]
borůvkové knedlíky blueberry dumplings
borůvkový koláč blueberry pie/tart
borůvky blueberries

borovička brandy
bramboračka thick soup with potatoes and vegetables ➤ 44
bramborák potato pancake
bramborová kaše mashed potato
bramborová polévka potato soup
bramborové hranolky French fries
bramborové knedlíky potato dumplings
bramborové krokety potato croquettes
bramborové taštičky s masitou nádivkou potato ravioli with meat filling
brambory potatoes
brokolice broccoli
broskev peach
brusinky cranberries
brzlík sweetbreads
buchta bun
bůček pork belly
burské oříšky peanuts
bylinková směs mixed herbs
bylinky herbs

C **candát** pike perch
celer celery root [celeriac]
celozrnná mouka whole-wheat flour
cemr loin (*pork, etc.*)
cibule onions
citrón lemon

citrónová šťáva lemon juice

citrónový lemon (adj.)

cukety zucchini [courgettes]

cukr sugar

cukrová kukuřice corn [sweet corn]

cukroví small sweet pastries

cukrový meloun melon

Č

čaj tea (beverage)

čekanka chicory

černá black (coffee)

černý rybíz blackcurrants

čerstvé datle fresh dates

čerstvé fíky fresh figs

čerstvé ovoce fresh fruit

čerstvý fresh

čerstvý tvaroh fresh curd cheese

červená řepa beets [beetroot]

červené hrozny black grapes

červené zelí red cabbage

červený red (wine)

červený rybíz redcurrants

česnek garlic

česneková majonéza garlic mayonnaise

česneková omáčka garlic sauce

česneková polévka garlic soup

čevapčiči meatballs

čínské zelí Chinese cabbage

čistý straight [neat]

čočka lentils

čočková polévka lentil soup

čočkový salát lentil salad

čokoláda chocolate

D

datle dates

dezert dessert

dezertní víno dessert wine

divočák/divoký kanec wild boar

domácí home-made

dort cake

drůbež poultry

drůbky giblets

dršťková polévka tripe soup

dršťky tripe

dýně pumpkin/marrow

dušená ryba steamed fish

dušená rýže steamed rice

dušené pot roasted

dušené hovězí pot roast

dušené ovoce stewed fruit

dušené telecí maso na víně veal braised in wine

dušený stewed

dvojitý double (a double shot)

džem jam

džin gin

džin fiz gin fizz

džin s tonikem gin and tonic

džus fruit juice

E estragon tarragon

F fíky figs
fazole beans (*pulses*)
fazolové klíčky bean sprouts
fenykl fennel
francouzská zálivka vinaigrette
[French dressing]
fazolová polévka bean soup

G garnáti shrimp [prawns]
granátová jablka
pomegranates
gratinovaný gratin / au gratin
grep grapefruit
gril grill
grilované kuře grilled chicken
grilovaný grilled
grilovaný na dřevěném uhlí
charcoal-grilled
guláš goulash, stew
gulášová polévka Hungarian
goulash soup

H heřmánkový čaj camomile
tea ➤ 51
hladká mouka flour
hlavní jídla entrées
hlíva ústřičná oyster mushrooms
hodně kořeněný highly seasoned

holoubě pigeon
horká čokoláda hot
chocolate
horká voda hot water
horký hot (*temperature*)
hořčice mustard
houby mushrooms
houska roll (*bread*)
houskový knedlík
bread dumpling
hovězí beef
hovězí pečeně roast beef
hovězí tokáň beef in wine and
tomato purée
hovězí vývar beef broth
hovězí vývar s játrovými knedlíčky
beef broth with liver dumplings
➤ 44
hrachor sugar snap peas
[mangetout]
hrachová polévka s uzeným
masem pea soup with smoked
meat
hranolky French fries
hrášek peas
hrozinky raisins
hrozny/hroznové víno grapes
hruška pear
hřbet saddle (*lamb, etc.*)
hřebíček cloves
hřiby ceps (*mushrooms*)
humr lobster
husa goose

CH chlazené nápoje cold drinks

chlazený chilled (*wine, etc.*)/iced (*drink*)

chléb bread

chlebíček open sandwich

chlupaté knedlíky dumplings with diced smoked meat and sauerkraut

chobotnice octopus

chřest asparagus

chuťovky savories

J jablečná šťáva apple juice

jablečný mošt cider (*non-alcoholic*)

jablečný závin apple strudel

jablko apple

jablkový koláč apple pie/tart

jahody strawberries

jarní cibulka spring onions

játra liver

játrová paštika liver pâté

játrové knedlíčky liver balls (*served in broth*)

jazyk tongue

jehněčí lamb

jehněčí guláš lamb stew

jehněčí kýta leg of lamb

jelínek brandy

jelení venison

jelito black pudding

jemný mild (*flavor*)

jídelní lístek menu

jídlo dish (*meal*)

jitrnice white sausage

jogurt yogurt

K kachna duck

kakao cocoa

kandované ovoce candied fruit

kapary capers

kapoun capon

kapr carp

kapr na černo baked carp in a beer, prune, and vegetable sauce ➤ 45

kapr na česneku carp grilled with butter and garlic ➤ 45

kapr na kmíně carp baked with caraway seeds

kapustová polévka cabbage soup

karafa carafe

karamel caramel

karbanátek fried burger

Karlovarská Becherovka® herb brandy ➤ 49

kaštany chestnuts

káva coffee

kaviár caviar

kečup ketchup

kedlubna kohlrabi

kiwi kiwi fruit

klobásky sausages (*made with coarsely ground pork*)

kmín caraway
knedlík dumpling
knedlíky s vejci dumpling with scrambled egg
kobliha donut [doughnut]
kohout cockerel
kokos coconut
koktejl milk shake
koláč pie/tart (*sweet/savory*)
koláček tartlette (*sweet/savory*)
kompot stewed fruit
konsomé consommé
kopr dill
koroptev partridge
kořeněná klobása spicy sausage
koření seasoning/spices
kořeněný hot/spicy/seasoned
kost bone
kotleta T-bone
kotlety chops
koza goat
kozí sýr goat cheese
krab crab
krájený sliced
králík rabbit
králík na smetaně roast rabbit in rich cream sauce
krekry crackers
krémovitá polévka cream soup
kroketa croquette
kroupy barley
krůta turkey
křen horseradish
křepelka quail

kukuřice corn
kuře chicken
kuře na paprice pan-roasted chicken with creamy paprika sauce
kuřecí játra chicken liver
kuřecí prso breast of chicken
kuřecí vývar chicken broth/soup
kuře pečené s nádivkou roast chicken with stuffing
květák cauliflower
kyselé okurky sour pickles
kýta leg (*cut of meat*)
kyselé zelí sauerkraut

L langoš fried dough coated in garlic
led ice
ledvinky kidneys
lehký light (*sauce, etc.*)
ležák lager
lihoviny spirits
likér liqueur
lilek eggplant [aubergine]
limetta lime
limettová šťáva lime juice
limonáda lemonade
lískové ořechy hazelnuts
lístkové těsto puff pastry
lišky chanterelle mushrooms
lívance small pancakes with plum and cottage cheese, topped with yogurt or sour cream ➤ 48

lívanečky fritters
losos salmon
luštěniny pulses

M **mák** poppy seeds
máslo butter
máta mint
majonéza mayonnaise
majoránka marjoram
makový koláč poppy seed cake
makrela mackerel
malé občerstvení snacks
maliny raspberries
mandarínka tangerine
mandle almond
marcipán marzipan
marinovaný (v octě) marinated (in vinegar)
marmeláda jam
maso meat (*general*)
masová směs na roštu mixed grill
masový a zeleninový vývar meat and vegetable broth
mečoun swordfish
med honey
melasa molasses [treacle]
meloun watermelon
meruňkové knedlíky apricot dumplings
meruňkovice apricot brandy
meruňky apricots
míchaná zelenina mixed vegetables

míchaný salát mixed salad
minerálka/minerální voda mineral water
místní speciality local specialties
mléko milk
mleté maso minced meat [mince]
mletý minced
moravský vrabec stewed slice of pork stuffed with ham, egg, and gherkin
moruše mulberry
mořský jazyk sole
moučník dessert
mouka flour
mozeček brains
mrkev carrots
muškátový oříšek nutmeg

N **na česneku** in garlic
nadívané olivy stuffed olives
nádivka stuffing
na grilu cooked on a grill
nakládané houby pickled mushrooms
nakládané okurky gherkins
nakládaný marinated
na kosti on the bone
nakrájený na plátky sliced
nakyselo sour (*taste*)
na másle sautéed
naměkko soft-boiled (*eggs*)
na oleji in oil

nápojový lístek wine list
na roštu barbecued
na rožni spit-roasted
na špízu skewered
natvrdo hard-boiled (*egg*)
naťový celer celery
nealkoholické nápoje non-alcoholic/soft drinks
nektarinka nectarine
Niva® blue cheese (*the most common brand*) ➤ 48
nudle noodles
nudle s mákem wide noodles with poppy seeds, butter, and sugar
nugát nougat

O **obalovaný (ve strouhance)** breaded (*cutlet, etc.*)
oběd lunch
obloha garnish, trimming
obložený chlebíček open sandwich
okoun perch
okurka cucumber
olivy olives
omáčka gravy/sauce
omeleta omelet
oplatky wafers
ořechy nuts
ostrá pepřová omáčka hot pepper sauce

ostružinová marmeláda blackberry jam
ostružinový koláč blackberry pie
ostružiny blackberries
ostrý hot (*spicy*)
ovesná kaše porridge
ovesné vločky porridge oats
ovoce fruit
ovoce z konzervy canned fruit
ovocná šťáva fruit juice
ovocný koláč fruitcake
ovocný kompot fruit compote
ovocný nápoj fruit drink

P **palačinky** pancakes
palačinky s čokoládou pancakes with chocolate sauce
palačinky s ovocem a se zmrzlinou pancakes with fruit and ice cream
pálenka brandy
párek v rohlíku hot dog
párky sausages (*made with finely ground pork*)
paštika pâté
pažitka chives
pečená kachna roast duck, served with cabbage or sauerkraut ➤ 46
pečená ryba baked fish
pečeně roasted
pečené brambory roast potatoes

pečené kuře roast chicken

pečeně se slaninou roasted with bacon

pečený baked / roasted

pečivo pastries

perlička guinea fowl

perlivý carbonated

perník gingerbread

petržela parsley

pfeferonka chili pepper

piškot sponge cake

pivo beer

plátek slice

platýs halibut

plecko shoulder (*cut of meat*)

plísňový sýr blue cheese

plněné papriky v rajčatové omáčce stuffed peppers in tomato sauce

plněný stuffed

podmáslí buttermilk

poleva icing

polévka soup

pomazánka z Nivy blue cheese spread

pomeranč orange

pomerančová marmeláda marmalade

pomerančová šťáva/pomerančový džus orange juice

pomfrity French fries

porce portion

pórek leek

pórková polévka leek soup

porstké víno port

pražené arašídy roasted peanuts

pražené mandle roasted almonds

prso/prsíčko breast

předrkmy appetizers

přírodní řízek unbreaded cutlet

pstruh trout

pstruh na másle trout grilled with butter ➤ 45

pudink custard

pudinkový krém cream

punč punch

R rajčata tomatoes

rajčatová omáčka tomato sauce

rajská polévka tomato soup

rak crayfish

ramstejk rumpsteak

rebarbora rhubarb

rizoto risotto

rohlíky rolls (*bread*)

rosol jelly

roštěnka sirloin steak

roštěnky na pivě carbonade, a stew of beef and onion cooked in beer

rozinky raisins

rozmarýna rosemary

ruláda fillet steak

ruské vejce mayonnaise

růžičková kapusta Brussel sprouts

růžový blush [rosé] (*wine*)
ryba fish
rybí filé fish fillet
rybí polévka fish soup
rýže rice

Ř **ředkvička** radish
řeřicha cress/watercress
řízek cutlet (*esp. veal*)

S **s citrónem** with lemon
s cukrem with sugar
s ledem on the rocks
s mlékem with milk
salám salami
salát green salad/lettuce
salát ze syrového zelí coleslaw
sardelky anchovies
sardelová pasta anchovy paste
sardinky sardines
sekaná minced beef
selátko suckling pig
sendvič sandwich
sirup syrup
sklenice/sklenička glass
skopové mutton
skopový guláš mutton stew
skořice cinnamon
skotská whisky Scotch whisky
sladký sweet
sladkokyselá omáčka
  sweet-and-sour sauce

slané mandle salted
  almonds
slaneček salted
  herring
slanina bacon
slaný savory/salty
slávky mussels
sleď herring
slepičí vývar s nudlemi chicken
  broth with vermicelli
slivovice plum brandy
slunečnicová semínka sunflower
  seeds
smažená ryba fried fish
smažená vejce scrambled eggs
smažené kuře fried chicken
smaženka croquette
smažený fried
smažený kapr carp fried in
  breadcrumbs ➤ 45
smažený květák cauliflower
  rosettes fried in breadcrumbs
  ➤ 47
smažený sýr slices of Edam or
  Gouda fried in breadcrumbs
  ➤ 48
smažený v těstíčku fried in batter
smažený vepřový řízek Wiener
  schnitzel ➤ 46
smetana cream
smetanová omáčka white sauce
smetanový creamy
sněhová pusinka meringue
snídaně breakfast

sodová voda soda water
sója soya
solené arašídy salted peanuts
solený salted
specialita dne dish of the day
speciality šéfa kuchyně specialties of the house
srdce heart
srnčí venison
srnčí hřbet dušený na víně saddle of venison braised in wine
stehno leg (*cut of meat*)
stolní víno table wine
strouhanka breadcrumbs
strouhaný grated
studená jídla cold dishes
studená polévka cold soup
studená voda iced water
studený hot
suchý dry
sůl salt
sultánky sultanas/raisins
sušené datle dried dates
sušené fíky dried figs
sušené švestky prunes
sušenky cookies [biscuits]
svíčková tenderloin (*cut of meat*)
svíčková na smetaně tenderloin of beef in creamy root vegetable sauce ➤ 46
sýr cheese
syrový raw

Š **šafrán** saffron
šalotka shallots
šalvěj sage
šery sherry
šípkový čaj rosehip tea ➤ 51
škubánky s mákem bread dumplings with poppy seeds and sugar
šlehačka whipped cream
šopský salát tomato and cucumber salad with feta-type cheese
špagety spaghetti
špek spek (*bacon*)
špekáčky wieners (*smoked sausage/frankfurter*)
špekové knedlíky se zelim dumplings stuffed with bacon, served with sauerkraut
špenát spinach
šproty sprats (*small herrings*)
šťáva gravy (*meat*)/juice (*fruit*)
štika pike
štrůdl apple strudel
šumivé víno sparkling wine
šumivý fizzy/sparkling (*drinks*)
šunka ham
šunka od kosti ham on the bone
šunka s vejci ham and eggs
švestkové knedlíky plum dumplings, sieved curd cheese and sugar ➤ 48
švestky plums

T tatarský biftek steak tartare

tavený sýr soft cheese

telecí veal

telecí játra veal liver

teplý warm

těsto pastry

těstoviny pasta

těžký full-bodied (*wine*)

tmavý chléb black bread

tonik tonic water

topinka toast

tresčí játra cod liver

treska cod

třešně cherries

tučný fatty

tuňák tuna

turecká káva Turkish-style coffee ➤ 51

tykev squash [marrow]

tymián thyme

U uherský salám Hungarian salami

úhoř eel

umělé sladidlo sweetener

ústřice oysters

utopenci sausage marinated in vinegar

uzená makrela smoked mackerel

uzená šunka smoked ham

uzenáč smoked herring

uzené maso smoked pork

uzené se zelím a knedlíky smoked pork with sauerkraut and dumplings ➤ 46

uzený cured/smoked (*ham, etc.*)

uzený bůček smoked pork belly

uzený jazyk smoked tongue

uzený losos smoked salmon

uzený sýr smoked cheese

uzený úhoř smoked eel

V v těstíčku in batter

vafle waffles

vajíčka eggs

vaječná jídla egg dishes

vanilka vanilla

vanilková zmrzlina vanilla ice cream

vařené brambory boiled potatoes

vařený v páře steamed

vařící boiling (*water*)

večeře dinner

vejce eggs

velmi suchý very dry (*wine, etc.*)

vepřové pork

vepřové klobásy pork sausages

vepřové žebírko stewed rib of pork

vermut vermouth

vídeňská káva Viennese-style coffee with the coffee topped with whipped cream ➤ 51

víno wine
višně morello cherries
vlašské ořechy walnuts
voda water
vuřt sausage
vývar consommé

Z **zajíc** hare
zajíc na divoko hare cooked bacon, with onions and vegetables in red wine
zajíc na smetaně roast hare in rich cream sauce
zákusek cake/dessert
zapékaný gratin/au gratin
zavináče pickled herrings [rollmops]
zázvor ginger
zázvorky ginger cookies
zelí cabbage
zelená paprika green peppers
zelené fazole green beans
zelené fazolky French beans
zelenina vegetables (*general*)
zeleninová jídla vegetable dishes
zeleninová polévka vegetable soup

zelňačka thick soup with potatoes, sauerkraut, and cream ➤ 44
zelná polévka s klobásou cabbage soup with smoked sausage
zmrzlina ice cream
zmrzlinový pohár (s ovocem) ice-cream sundae (with fruit)
znojemská pečeně slices of roast beef in a gherkin sauce
zralý ripe
zvěřina game

Ž **žampiony** mushrooms
žebírka ribs
želé jelly
žemle bun
žitný chléb rye bread
žloutek egg yolk

Travel

ESSENTIAL

A train/bus ticket to …	**Jednu jízdenku* do …** *yed-nooh yeez-denkooh do'*
2/3 train/bus tickets to …	**Dvě/Tři jízdenky* do …** *dvyeh/trzhih yeez-denkih do'*
To Brno, please.	**Do Brna, prosím.** *doburna proseem*
one-way [single]	**jedním směrem** *yed-nyeem smyerem*
round-trip [return]	**zpáteční** *spahtech-nyee*
How much …?	**Kolik stojí …?** *kolik sto-yee*

* **jízdenka** is a "train/bus ticket," for "plane ticket" the word is **letenka**.

Safety Bezpečnost

Would you accompany me to the bus stop?	**Doprovodil(a) byste mne na autobusovou zastávku?** *doprovodyil(a) bis-teh mneh na-ow-toboo-so-voh zas-tahf-kooh*
I don't want to … on my own.	**Nechci … sám (sama).** *nekh-tsih … sahm (sama)*
stay here	**zde zůstat** *zdeh zuh-stat*
walk home	**jít domů** *yeet domuh*
I don't feel safe here.	**Necítím se zde bezpečně.** *ne-tsee-tyeem seh zdeh bes-pech-nyeh*

POLICE ➤ 159; EMERGENCY ➤ 224

Arrival Příjezd

Citizens of the U.K., the U.S., Ireland, Canada, and New Zealand need only a valid passport for visits of 90 days or less to the Czech Republic; citizens of Australia and South Africa need to obtain a visa. However, visa regulations change from time to time, so do check with your travel agent before you leave. There are no restrictions on the amount of foreign currency you can take into or out of the Czech Republic, but it is illegal for visitors to take more than 100 Czech korun out of the country without the authorization of the Czech National Bank.

Duty free into:	Cigarettes	Cigars	Tobacco	Spirits	Wine
Canada	200 and	50 and	400 g.	1l. or	1l.
Czech Rep.	250 and	50 and	250 g.	1l. or	2l.
the U.K.	200 or	50 or	250 g.	1l. and	2l.
the U.S.	200 and	100 and	discretionary	1l. or	1l.

Passport control Pasová kontrola

> **Mohu vidět váš pas?**
> **Jaký je účel vaší cesty?**
> **S kým jste přijel?**

May I see your passport, please?
What's the purpose of your visit?
Who are you here with?

We have a joint passport.
Máme společný pas.
mah-meh spolech-nee pas

The children are on this passport.
Děti jsou v tomto pasu.
dye-tyih yesoh ftom-to' pasooh

I'm here on vacation [holiday]/ business.
Jsem zde na dovolené/služebně.
yesem zdeh nadovoleneh/sloo-zheb-nyeh

I'm just passing through.
Pouze projíždím.
poh-zeh pro-yeezh-dyeem

I'm going to …
Jedu do … *yedooh do'*

I'm on my own.
Jsem sám (sama). *yesem sahm (sama)*

I'm with my family.
Jsem s rodinou. *yesem sro-dyi-noh*

I'm with a group.
Jsem se skupinou. *yesem se-skoo-pi-noh*

WHO ARE YOU WITH? ➤ 120

Customs Celní prohlídka

I have only the normal allowances.
Mám pouze běžně povolené zboží. *mahm poh-zeh byezh-nyeh povoleneh zbo-zhee*

It's a gift.
Je to dárek. *yeh to' dah-rek*

It's for my personal use.
Je to pro mou osobní potřebu. *yeh to' pro' moh osob-nyee po-trzhe-booh*

Máte něco k proclení?	Do you have anything to declare?
Za tohle musíte platit clo.	You must pay duty on this.
Kde jste to koupil(a)?	Where did you buy this?
Otevřte laskavě tuhle tašku.	Please open this bag.
Máte další zavazadla?	Do you have any more luggage?

I would like to declare …
Rád(a) bych přihlásil(a) k proclení … *raht(rahda) bikh przhi-hlah-sil(a) kpro-tsle-nyee*

I don't understand.
Nerozumím. *nerozoomeem*

Does anyone here speak English?
Mluví zde někdo anglicky? *mloo-vee zdeh nyeg-do' anglitskih*

PASOVÁ KONTROLA	passport control
HRANIČNÍ PŘECHOD	border crossing
CELNÍ PROHLÍDKA	customs
NIC K PROCLENÍ	nothing to declare
ZBOŽÍ K PROCLENÍ	goods to declare

Duty-free shopping Nákup zboží bez cla

What currency is this in?
V jaké je to měně? *vyakeh yeh to' mye-nyeh*

Can I pay in …
Mohu zaplatit v … *mohooh zapla-tyit v*

dollars
dolarech *dolarekh*

korun
korunách *koroonah-kh*

pounds
librách *librah-kh*

Plane Letadlo

There are few internal flights in the Czech Republic; the country is small and a car/bus/train is often cheaper and faster.
Frequent flights between Prague and Ostrava are used mainly by business travelers.

Tickets and reservations Letenky a rezervace

When is the … flight to New York?	**Kdy letí … letadlo do New Yorku?** *gdih le-tyee … letadlo' do' nyoo-yorkooh*
first/next/last	**první/další/poslední** *pr-vnyee/dul-shee/posled-nyee*
I'd like two tickets to New York.	**Chtěl(a) bych dvě letenky do New Yorku.** *khutel(a) bikh dvyeh letenkih do' nyoo-yorkooh*
I'd like two round-trip [return] tickets to …	**Chtěl(a) bych dvě zpáteční letenky do …** *khutel(a) bikh dvyeh spah-tech-nyee letenkih do'*
I'd like two … tickets.	**Chtěl(a) bych dvě letenky.** *khutel(a) bikh dvyeh letenkih*
first/business/economy class	**do první/obchodní/ekonomické třídy** *do pr-vnyee/op-khod-nyee/ekonomits-keh trzhee-dih*
How much is a flight to …?	**Kolik stojí letenka do …?** *kolik sto-yee letenka do'*
Are there any supplements/reductions?	**Platí nějaké přirážky/slevy?** *pla-tyee nye-yukeh purzhi-rah-zhkih/slevih*
I'd like to … my reservation for flight number …	**Chtěl(a) bych … svou rezervaci na linku číslo …** *khutyel(a) bikh … svoh rezerva-tsih nalin-kooh chees-lo'*
cancel/change/confirm	**zrušit/změnit/potvrdit** *zroo-shit/zmye-nyit/pot-fr-dyit*

Inquiries about the flight Dotazy o letu

How long is the flight?	**Jak dlouho let trvá?** *yuk dloh-ho' let tr-vah*
What time does the plane leave?	**V kolik hodin letadlo odlétá?** *fkolik ho-dyin letadlo' odleh-tah*
What time will we arrive?	**V kolik hodin přistaneme?** *fkolik hodyin przhis-tanemeh*
What time do I have to check in?	**V kolik hodin se musím dostavit k odbavení?** *fkolik ho-dyin seh mooseem dostavit kod-bave-nyee*

Checking in Odbavení

Where is the check-in desk for flight ...?

U které přepážky se odbavuje let ...? *ookte-reh przhe-pah-zhkih seh odba-voo-yeh let*

I have ...

Mám ... *mahm*

three cases to check in

tři zavazadla k odbavení *trzhih zavazadla kod-bave-nyee*

two pieces of hand luggage

dvě příruční zavazadla *dvyeh przhee-rooch-nyee zavazadla*

How much hand luggage is allowed free?

Kolik příručních zavazadel je povoleno zadarmo? *kolik przhee-rooch-nyeekh zavazadel yeh povoleno' zadarmo'*

Ukažte mi letenku/pas, prosím.	Your ticket / passport, please.
Chcete sedadlo u okna nebo do chodbičky?	Would you like a window or an aisle seat?
Pro kuřáky nebo nekuřáky?	Smoking or non-smoking?
Postupte laskavě do odletové haly.	Please go through to the departure lounge.
Kolik máte zavazadel?	How many pieces of baggage do you have?
Máte nadváhu.	You have excess baggage.
Musíte zaplatit přirážku čtyři sta korun.	You'll have to pay a supplement of four hundred korun.
Tohle je na příruční zavazadlo příliš těžké/velké.	That's too heavy/large for hand baggage.
Balil(a) jste tato zavazadla sám (sama)?	Did you pack these bags yourself?
Jsou v nich nějaké ostré nebo elektronické předměty?	Do they contain any sharp or electronic items?

PŘÍLETY	arrivals
ODLETY	departures
BEZPEČNOSTNÍ KONTROLA	security check
NENECHÁVEJTE ZAVAZADLA BEZ DOZORU	Do not leave bags unattended.

BAGGAGE ➤ 71

Information Informace

Is there any delay on flight …?	**Má let … zpoždění?** *mah let … spozh-dye-nyee*
How late will it be?	**Jaké bude mít zpoždění?** *yakeh boodeh meet spozh-dye-nyee*
Has the flight from … landed?	**Přistálo letadlo z …?** *purzhis-tah-lo' letadlo' z*
Which gate does flight … leave from?	**Od kterého východu linka … odlétá?** *ot-kte-reh-ho' vee-kho-dooh linka odleh-tah*

Boarding/In-flight Nástup/Na palubě letadla

Your boarding pass [card], please.	**Předložte palubní vstupenku, prosím.** *przhed-lozhteh paloob-nyee vstoo-penkooh proseem*
Could I have a drink/ something to eat, please?	**Mohu dostat něco k pití/k jídlu?** *mohooh dostat nye-tso' kpi-tyee/kyee-dlooh*
Please wake me for the meal.	**Vzbuďte mne laskavě na jídlo.** *vuzboodye'-teh mneh laskavyeh na-yeed-lo'*
What time will we arrive?	**V kolik hodin budeme přistávat?** *fkolik ho-dyin boodemeh przhi-stah-vat*
An airsickness bag, please.	**Sáček na zvracení, prosím.** *sah-chek na-zuvra-tse-nyee proseem*

Arrival Přílet

Where is/are (the) …?	**Kde je/jsou …?** *gdeh yeh/yesoh*
buses	**autobusy** *ow-to-boosih*
car rental	**půjčovna aut** *puhye-chov-na owt*
currency exchange	**směnárna** *smye-nahr-na*
exit	**východ** *vee-khot*
taxis	**taxi** *taksih*
Is there a bus into town?	**Jede do města autobus?** *yedeh do' myesta ow-to-boos*
How do I get to the … hotel?	**Jak se dostanu do hotelu …?** *yuk seh dostanooh dohotelooh*

BAGGAGE ➤ 71; CUSTOMS ➤ 67

Baggage Zavazadla

Luggage carts are available at Prague airport. If you need a porter, you will find them waiting near the baggage reclaim section.

Porter! Excuse me!	**Nosič! Promiňte, prosím!** *nosich! pro-miny'-teh proseem*
Could you take my luggage to …?	**Vzal byste mi laskavě zavazadla do …?** *vzal bis-teh mih laskavyeh zavazadla do'*
a taxi/bus	**taxi/autobusu** *taksih/ow-toboosooh*
Where is/are (the) …?	**Kde je/jsou …?** *gdeh yeh/yesoh*
luggage carts [trolleys]	**vozíky** *vozeekih*
baggage check [left-luggage office]	**úschovna zavazadel** *uhs-khov-na zavazadel*
baggage reclaim	**výdej zavazadel** *vee-deye' zavazadel*
Where is the luggage from flight …?	**Kde jsou zavazadla z letu …?** *gdeh yesoh zavazadla zle-tooh*

Loss, damage, and theft Ztráta, poškození a krádež

I've lost my baggage.	**Ztratila se mi zavazadla.** *stra-tyi-la seh mih zavazadla*
My baggage has been stolen.	**Někdo mi ukradl zavazadla.** *nyeg-do' mih ook-radul zavazadla*
My suitcase was damaged.	**Můj kufr je poškozený.** *mooye' koofr yeh po-shko-zenee*
Our baggage has not arrived.	**Naše zavazadla nepřišla.** *nasheh zavazadla ne-przhi-shla*

Jak vaše zavazadlo vypadá?	What does your baggage look like?
Máte zavazadlový lístek?	Do you have the claim check [reclaim tag]?
Vaše zavazadlo …	Your luggage …
asi poslali do …	may have been sent to …
přijde asi později	may arrive later today
Přijďte laskavě zítra.	Please come back tomorrow.
Zavolejte si na tohle číslo a zeptejte se, zda vaše zavazadlo přišlo.	Call this number to check if your baggage has arrived.

POLICE ➤ 159; COLOR ➤ 143

Train Vlak

The Czech rail network is extensive and train fares are cheap. Express trains (**rychlík**) and international trains should be reserved in advance. Discounts are available for children, students, and senior citizens. European residents under 26 and holders of International Student Identity Cards can buy the *Eurotrain* Czech Explorer Pass, which gives a week's unlimited train travel. They must be bought before you arrive in the Czech Republic. *Inter-Rail* and *Inter-Rail 26+ Passes* are also valid on the Czech rail network.

Intercity (IC) *intersity*

Intercity express with very few stops. First- and second-class seats are available. Seat reservation is recommended, for which a special supplement is charged. Standard of service is much higher than in other Czech trains. The Intercity service covers only major Czech cities and international destinations.

Rychlík *rikh-leek*

Long-distance fast train stopping at major cities only. First- and second-class seats are available. The standard of service is much lower than on Intercity trains; first class travel is recommended. This is not a huge expense, since the prices of Czech train tickets are still very cheap for foreigners due to the favorable exchange rate – expect to pay around 250Kč (approximately $8) for a 250-kilometer trip.

Osobní vlak *osob–nyee vlak*

Local train stopping at many smaller locations. Often covers quite long distances. There is a good train service between Prague and some of the places of interest in its vicinity, such as the castle of Karlštejn and the town of Kutná Hora.

Jídelní vůz *yee-del-nyee vuhs*

Dining car; attached to most Intercity and fast trains. Serves snacks, drinks, and full meals.

Lůžkový vůz *luh-shkovee vuhs*

Sleeping car; up to three berths (**lůžka** *luh-shka*) per compartment. Cheaper couchettes (**lehátka** *le-haht-ka*) are also available. There are six couchettes per compartment. Basic washing facilities are available.

To the station Jedeme nádraží

How do I get to the train station?

Jak se dostanu na nádraží?
yuk se dostanooh nanah-dra-zhee

Do trains to Brno leave from ... station?

Jedou do Brna vlaky ze stanice ...? *yedoh doburna vla-kih zesta-nyi-tseh*

How far is it?

Jak je to daleko?
yak yeh to' daleko'

Can I leave my car there?

Mohu tam nechat auto?
mohooh tum ne-khat ow-to'

At the station Na nádraží

Where is/are the ...?

Kde je/jsou ...? *gdeh yeh/yesoh*

baggage check [left-luggage office]

úschovna zavazadel
uhs-khov-na zavazadel

currency exchange

směnárna *smye-nahr-na*

information desk

informace *informa-tseh*

Where's the lost-and-found [lost property] office?

Kde je ztráty a nálezy?
gdeh yesoh strah-tih ah nah-lezih

platforms

nástupiště
nah-stoo-pish-tyeh

snack bar

občerstvení
op-chers-tve-nyee

ticket office

pokladna *po-klad-na*

waiting room

čekárna *che-kahr-na*

VCHOD	entrance
VÝCHOD	exit
K NÁSTUPIŠTÍM	to the platforms
INFORMACE	information
REZERVACE	reservations
PŘÍJEZDY	arrivals
ODJEZDY	departures

DIRECTIONS ➤ 94

Tickets Jízdenky

Tickets for major routes and express trains should be reserved at the main train station in Prague (**Hlavní nádraží**). However, for local trips you can purchase your ticket at the local train station.

I'd like a ticket to Brno.	**Chtěl(a) bych jízdenku do Brna.** *khutyel(a) bikh yeez-denkooh dobur-na*
One-way [single] ticket.	**Jízdenku jedním směrem.** *yeez-denkooh yed-nyeem smye-rem*
I'd like a round-trip [return] ticket to Brno.	**Chtěl(a) bych zpáteční jízdenku do Brna.** *khutyel(a) bikh spah-tech-nyee yeez-denkooh dobur-na*
I'd like a … ticket to Brno.	**Chtěl(a) bych jízdenku … do Brna.** *khutyel(a) bikh yeez-denkooh … dobur-na*
first/second class	**do první/druhé třídy** *do-pur-vnyee/drooheh trzhee-dih*
concessionary	**se slevou** *se-slevoh*
I'd like to reserve a(n) … seat.	**Chtěl(a) bych si zarezervovat sedadlo …** *khutyel(a) bikh sih zarezervovat sedadlo'*
aisle seat	**do uličky** *do-oolich-kih*
window seat	**u okna** *ooh-okna*
Is there a sleeping car [sleeper]?	**Je tam lůžkový vůz?** *yeh tum luh-shko-vee vuhs*
I'd like a(n) … berth.	**Chtěl(a) bych lůžko …** *khutyel(a) bikh luh-shko'*
upper/lower	**nahoře/dole** *na-ho-rzheh/doleh*

Price Cena

How much is that?	**Kolik to stojí?** *kolik to' stoyee*
Is there a reduction for …?	**Je sleva pro …?** *yeh sleva pro'*
children/families	**děti/rodinu** *dye-tyih/rodyi-nooh*
senior citizens	**starší občany** *star-shee op-cha-nih*
students	**studenty** *stoo-den-tih*

Queries Dotazy

Do I have to change trains?	**Musím přestupovat?** *moo-seem przhe-stoo-povat*
Is it a direct train?	**Je to přímé spojení?** *yeh to' przee-meh spo-ye-nyee*
You have to change at …	**Musíte přestoupit v …** *moo-see-teh przhe-stoh-pit v*
How long is this ticket valid for?	**Jak dlouho tato jízdenka platí?** *yuk dloh-ho' tato' yeez-denka pla-tyee*
Can I take my bicycle on the train?	**Mohu si vzít do vlaku jízdní kolo?** *mohooh sih vzeet dovlakooh yeezd-nyee kolo'*
Can I return on the same ticket?	**Mohu se na stejnou jízdenku vrátit?** *mohooh seh na steye'-noh yeez-denkooh vrah-tyit*
In which car [coach] is my seat?	**V kterém vagónu je moje sedadlo?** *fkte-rehm vagau-nooh yeh mo-yeh sedadlo'*
Is there a dining car on the train?	**Je ve vlaku jídelní vůz?** *yeh vevlakooh yee-del-nyee vuhs*

– Chtěl(a) bych jízdenku do Olomouce, prosím.
 (I'd like a ticket to Olomouce, please.)
 – Jedním směrem nebo zpáteční?
 (One-way or round-trip?)
– Zpáteční, prosím. (Round-trip, please.)
 – Bude to pět set padesát šest korun.
 (That's 556 korun.)
– Musím přestupovat?
 (Do I have to change trains?)
 – Ano, musíte přestoupit v Hradci Králové.
 (Yes, you have to change at Hradec Králové.)
– Děkuji. Nashledanou. (Thank you. Good-bye.)

Train times Jízdní řád

Could I have a timetable, please?	**Máte jízdní řád, prosím?** *mah-teh yeez-dnyee rzaht proseem*
When is the … train to the airport?	**V kolik hodin jede … vlak na letiště?** *fkolik hodyin yedeh … vlak na le-tyish-tyeh*
first/next/last	**první/další/poslední** *purv-nyee/dul-shee/pos-led-nyee*

How frequent are the trains to …?	**Jak často jezdí vlaky do …?** *yak chus-to' yez-dyee vlakih do'*
once/twice a day	**jednou/dvakrát denně** *yed-noh/dva-kraht de-nyeh*
five times a day	**pětkrát denně** *pyet-kraht de-nyeh*
every hour	**každou hodinu** *kuzh-doh hodyi-nooh*
What time do they leave?	**V kolik hodin odjíždějí?** *fkolik hodyin od-yeezh-dye-yee*
on the hour	**každou celou** *kuzh-doh tseh-loh*
20 minutes past the hour	**za deset minut půl** *za deset minoot puhl*
What time does the train stop at …?	**V kolik hodin staví vlak v …?** *fkolik hodyin sta-vee vlak v*
What time does the train arrive in …?	**V kolik hodin přijede vlak do …?** *fkolik hodyin purzhi-yedeh vlak do'*
How long is the trip [journey]?	**Jak dlouho cesta trvá?** *yak dloh-ho' tses-ta tr-vah*
Is the train on time?	**Jede vlak na čas?** *yedeh vlak na-chus*

Departures Odjezd

Which platform does the train to … leave from?	**Ze kterého nástupiště odjíždí vlak do …?** *zeh ktereh-ho' nahs-too-pish-tyeh od-yeezh-dyee vlak do'*
Where is platform 4?	**Kde je čtvrté nástupiště?** *gdeh yeh chut-vur-teh nahs-too-pish-tyeh*
over there	**tamhle** *tum-hleh*
on the left/right	**vlevo/vpravo** *vlevo'/fpravo'*
Where do I change for …?	**Kde musím přestoupit na …?** *gdeh moo-seem przhe-stoh-pit nah*
How long will I have to wait for a connection?	**Jak dlouho budu čekat na spojení?** *yak dloh-ho' boodooh chekat naspo-yeh-nyee*

TIME ➤ 220; DIRECTIONS ➤ 94

Boarding Nástup

Is this the right platform for ...?	**Jede vlak do ... z tohoto nástupiště?** *yedeh vlak do' ... sto-ho-to' nahs-too-pish-tyeh*
Is this the train to ...?	**Je tohle vlak na ...?** *yeh to-hleh vlak na*
Is this seat taken?	**Je tohle místo obsazené?** *yeh to-hleh mees-to' opsazeneh*
I think that's my seat.	**Já myslím, že to je moje místo.** *yah misleem zheh to' yeh mo-yeh mees-to'*
Here's my reservation.	**Zde je moje místenka.** *zdeh yeh mo-yeh mees-tenka*
Are there any seats/berths available?	**Jsou zde volná sedadla/lůžka?** *yesoh zdeh vol-nah sedadla/luh-shka*
Do you mind if ...?	**Vadilo by vám, kdybych ...?** *va-dyi-lo' bih vahm gdi-bikh*
I sit here	**si tu sedl/sedla** *sih tooh sedul/sed-la*
I open the window	**otevřel(a) okno** *otevurzhel(a) ok-no'*

On the journey Během cesty

How long are we stopping here for?	**Na jak dlouho tu stavíme?** *nah yak dloh-ho' tooh sta-veemeh*
When do we get to ...?	**Kdy přijedeme do ...?** *gdih przhi-yedemeh do'*
Have we passed ...?	**Už jsme projeli ...?** *oozh yesmeh pro-ye-lih*
Where is the dining/sleeping car?	**Kde je jídelní/lůžkovývůz?** *gdeh yeh yee-del-nyee/luh-shko-vee vuhs*
Where is my berth?	**Kde je moje lůžko?** *gdeh yeh moyeh luh-shko'*
I've lost my ticket.	**Ztratil(a) jsem jízdenku.** *stra-tyil(a) yesem yeez-denkooh*

ZÁCHRANNÁ BRZDA	emergency brake
ALARM	alarm
AUTOMATICKÉ DVEŘE	automatic doors

Long-distance bus [Coach]
Dálkový autobus

Major routes radiate from the main bus terminal in Prague (**Autobusové nádraží Florenc**). Seats should be reserved in advance (the ticket office is at the terminus) as buses are popular, relatively fast and cheap, and get busy, particularly on weekends. Many local buses connect villages with the nearest town.

Where's the bus [coach] station?	**Kde je autobusové nádraží?** *gdeh yeh ow-to-boosoveh nah-dra-zhee*
When's the next bus [coach] to …?	**Kdy jede další autobus do …?** *gdih yedeh dul-shee ow-toboos do'*
Where does it leave from?	**Odkud odjíždí?** *ot-koot od-yeezh-dyee*
Does the bus [coach] stop at …?	**Staví autobus v …?** *stuvee ow-toboos v*
How long does the trip [journey] take?	**Jak dlouho cesta trvá?** *yak dloh-ho' tses-tah tr-vah*
Are there … on board?	**Je v autobuse …?** *yesoh vow-toboseh*
refreshments/toilets	**občerstvení/záchod** *op-chers-tve-nyee/zah-khot*

Bus/Streetcar [Tram] Autobus/Tramvaj

On Prague city transportation (bus, streetcar, and subway) you have a choice of buying a ticket or a pass (the latter come in 1-, 3-, 7- or 15-day increments). Don't forget to fill in your name on the back of the pass. Children under six ride free, children six to twelve pay a reduced price. Individual tickets – available at newsstands (**novinový stánek**) and tobacconists (**tabák**) – must be stamped on boarding the vehicle. Ticket inspectors check frequently; anyone without a valid ticket or pass (stamped or signed) is fined on the spot.

Where is the terminus?	**Kde je konečná?** *gdeh yeh konech-nah*
Where can I get a bus/streetcar [tram] to …?	**Kde staví autobus/tramvaj do …?** *gdeh stuvee ow-toboos/trum-vaye' do'*
What time is the … bus to Troja?	**V kolik hodin odjíždí … autobus do Troji?** *fkolik ho-dyin od-yeezh-dyee … ow-toboos do' tro-yih*

Musíte si přejít na tamhletu zastávku.	You need that stop over there.
Musíte jet autobusem číslo …	You need bus number …
Musíte přesednout v …	You must change buses at …

ZÁKAZ KOUŘENÍ	no smoking
VÝCHOD/NOUZOVÝ VÝCHOD	exit/emergency exit

Buying tickets Koupě jízdenek

Tickets are valid for all three types of transport (bus, streetcar, and subway) and also for the cable car to Petřín. A 12 Kč ticket allows unlimited travel for 60 minutes. A cheaper 8 Kč ticket allows up to 15 minutes bus or streetcar travel, or three stops on the subway.

Where can I buy tickets?	**Kde si mohu koupit jízdenku?** *gdeh sih mohooh koh-pit yeez-den-koo*
A(n) 8/12 korun ticket, please.	**Jízdenku za osm/dvanáct korun, prosím.** *yeez-den-koo za-osum/dva-nah-tsut ko-roon proseem*
A 1-/3-/5-day ticket, please.	**Jednodenní/třídenní/pětidenní jízdenku prosím.** *yedno-de-nyee/trzhee-de-nyee/pye-tyi-de-nyee yeez-den-koo proseem*
How much is the fare to ...?	**Kolik stojí jízdenka do ...?** *kolik sto-yee yeez-denka do'*

Traveling Na cestě

Is this the right bus/streetcar [tram] to ...?	**Je tohle autobus/tramvaj do/na ...?** *yeh to-hleh ow-toboos/trum-vaye' do'/na*
Could you tell me when to get off?	**Řekl(a) byste mi, kde mám vystoupit?** *rzhekul(rzhekla) bis-teh mih gdeh mahm vis-toh-pit*
Do I have to change buses?	**Musím přestupovat?** *mooseem przhes-toopovat*
How many stops are there to ...?	**Kolik je to stanic do ...?** *kolik yeh to' sta-nyits do'*
Next stop, please!	**Další stanici, prosím!** *dul-shee sta-nyi-tsih proseem*

POKLADNA	ticket office
PRODEJNÍ AUTOMAT	ticket vending machine

– Promiňte, prosím. Jede tenhle autobus
k městské radnici?
(Excuse me. Is this the right bus to the town hall?)
– Ano, číslo osm. (Yes, number 8.)
– Řekl(a) byste mi, kde mám vystoupit?
(Could you tell me when to get off?)
– Odtud jsou to čtyři stanice.
(It's four stops from here.)

NUMBERS ➤ *216;* *DIRECTIONS* ➤ *94*

Subway [Metro] Metro

The Prague subway [metro] has only three lines (A, B, and C), but it is clean, fast, safe, frequent, and runs from just before 5 a.m. until after midnight. Stations are clearly marked with an "M." Buy a ticket from a machine in the entrance hall, and don't forget to stamp it. The lines are marked on the city plan, available at hotels, tobacconists, newsstands, or tourist information offices.

General inquiries Informace

Where's the nearest subway [metro] station?	**Kde je nejbližší stanice metra?** *gdeh yeh neye'-bli-shee sta-nyi-tseh metra*
Where can I buy a ticket?	**Kde si mohu koupit jízdenku?** *gdeh sih mohooh koh-pit yeez-denkooh*
Could I have a map of the subway [metro], please?	**Mohu dostat plán metra.** *mohooh dostat plahn metrah*

Traveling Na cestě

Which line should I take for ...?	**Kterou trasou se dostanu do ...?** *kteroh tra-soh seh dostanooh do'*
Is this the right train for ...?	**Jede to do ...?** *yedeh to' do'*
Which stop is it for ...?	**Která stanice je na ...?** *kterah sta-nyi-tseh yeh nah*
How many stops is it to ...?	**Kolik stanic je to do ...?** *kolik sta-nyits yeh to' do'*
Is the next stop ...?	**Je příští stanice ...?** *yeh przhee-shtyee sta-nyi-tseh*
Where are we?	**Kde jsme?** *gdeh yesmeh*
Where do I change for ...?	**Kde musím přestoupit na ...?** *gdeh mooseem przhe-stoh-pit na*
What time is the last train to ...?	**V kolik hodin jede poslední metro do ...?** *fkolik ho-dyin yedeh pos-led-nyee metro' do'*

⊘ **PŘESTUP NA TRASU ...** transfer to line ... ⊖

NUMBERS ➤ 216; BUYING TICKETS ➤ 74, 79

Boats Lodě

When is the ... boat to Slapy?	**Kdy jede ... loď na Slapy?**
	gdih yedeh ... lotyeh'
	naslapih
first/next/last	**první/další/poslední**
	pr-vnyee/dul-shee/posled-nyee
hovercraft	**vznášedlo**
	vuz-nah-shedlo'
A round-trip [return]	**Zpáteční jízdenku pro ...**
ticket for ...	*spah-tech-nyee yee-zden-kooh pro'*
two adults and three children	**dva dospělé a tři děti**
	dvah dos-pye-leh ah turzhih dye-tyih
I want to reserve a ... seat.	**Chtěl(a) bych si zarezervovat ...**
	kuhtyel(a) bikh sih zarezervovat
single/double	**jedno místo/dvě místa**
	yed-no' meesto'/dvyeh meesta

⊘	**ZÁCHRANNÝ PÁS**	life preserver [life belt]	⊘
	ZÁCHRANNÝ ČLUN	lifeboat
	LODĚNICE	muster station
⊘	**PŘÍSTUP ZAKÁZÁN**	no access	⊘

Boat trips Projížďky lodí

Is there a ...?	**Je tu ...?**
	yeh tooh
boat trip/river cruise	**projížďka lodí/projížďka po řece**
	pro-yeezh-tye'-kah lo-dyee/
	pro-yeezh-tye'-kah po-rzhe-tseh
What time does it leave?	**V kolik hodin odjíždí?**
	fkolik ho-dyin od-yeezh-dyee
What time does it return?	**V kolik hodin se vrací?**
	fkolik ho-dyin seh vra-tsee
Where can we buy tickets?	**Kde si můžeme koupit lístky?**
	gdeh sih moozhemeh koh-pit leest-kih

TIME ➤ 220; BUYING TICKETS ➤ 74, 79

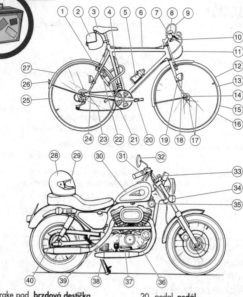

1 brake pad **brzdová destička**
2 bicycle bag **taška na kolo**
3 saddle **sedlo**
4 pump **pumpička**
5 water bottle **láhev na vodu**
6 frame **rám**
7 handlebars **řidítka**
8 bell **zvonek**
9 brake cable **brzdový kabel**
10 gear shift [lever]
 ovládání přehazovačky
11 gear control cable
 kabel přehazovačky
12 inner tube **duše**
13 front/back wheel **přední/zadní kolo**
14 axle **osa**
15 tire [tyre] **pneumatika**
16 wheel **kolo**
17 spokes **výplet**
18 bulb **žárovka**
19 headlamp **přední světlo**

20 pedal **pedál**
21 lock **zámek**
22 generator [dynamo] **dynamo**
23 chain **řetěz**
24 rear light **zadní světlo**
25 rim **ráfek**
26 reflectors **reflektory**
27 fender [mudguard] **blatník**
28 helmet **helma**
29 visor **štítko**
30 fuel tank **palivová nádrž**
31 clutch lever **spojka**
32 mirror **zrcátko**
33 ignition signal **spínač zapalování**
34 turn switch [indicator] **směrové světlo**
35 horn **houkačka**
36 engine **motor**
37 gear shift [lever] **řadicí páka**
38 kick stand [main stand] **nožní stojánek**
39 exhaust pipe **výfuk**
40 chain guard **kryt řetězu**

82

Bicycle / Motorbike
Jízdní kolo/Motocykl

I'd like to rent a …   **Chtěl(a) bych si půjčit …**
khutyel(a) bikh sih pooye'-chit

3-/10-speed bicycle   **jízdní kolo s třemi/deseti převody**
yeez-dnyee kolo' strzhemih/dese-tyih przhe-vo-dih

moped   **mopeda** *mopeda*

motorbike   **motocykl** *moto-tsikul*

How much does it cost per day / week?   **Kolik to stojí na den/na týden?**
kolik to' stoyee naden/nateeden

Do you require a deposit?   **Potřebujete zálohu?**
po-trzhe-boo-yeteh zah-lo-hooh

The brakes don't work.   **Brzdy nefungují.** *br-zdih nefoon-goo-yee*

There are no lights.   **Nejsou tu světla.** *neye-soh tooh svyet-lah*

The front / rear tire [tyre] has a flat [puncture].   **Přední/Zadní pneumatika je píchlá.**
przhed-nyee/zud-nyee pne-ooma-tika yeh pee-khlah

Hitchhiking Stopování

Hitchhiking is not recommended for safety reasons. Public transportation is cheap and efficient and a much better choice.

Where are you heading?   **Kam se chcete dostat?**
kum seh khutse-teh dostat

I'm heading for …   **Chci do …** *khutsih do'*

Is that on the way to …?   **Je to směrem na …?**
yeh to' smye-rem na

Could you drop me off …?   **Můžete mne vysadit …?**
moozheteh mneh vi-sadyit

here/at …   **tady/v …** *tadih/v*

at the … exit   **na sjezdu …** *na-syez-dooh*

downtown   **v centru města** *f-tsen-trooh myes-ta*

Thanks for giving me a lift.   **Děkuji za svezení.**
dye-koo-yih za-sve-ze-nyee

DIRECTIONS ➤ 94; NUMBERS ➤ 216

Taxi/Cab Taxi

All taxis have meters; their rates are displayed in the vehicle, and the driver will print a receipt at the end of your trip. The standard rate is 17 Kč/km; taxis at Prague airport and some hotel taxis have higher rates. However, you do not have to take a taxi from the airport – look for buses and minibuses provided by Czech Airlines and other operators. They charge around 300 Kč per person for a trip downtown.

Where can I get a taxi?	**Kde najdu taxi?** *gdeh naye'-dooh taksih*
Do you have the number for a taxi?	**Máte číslo na taxi?** *mah-teh chees-lo' nataksih*
I'd like a taxi …	**Chtěl(a) bych taxi …** *khutyel(a) bikh taksih*
now	**nyní** *ni-nyee*
in an hour	**za hodinu** *zahodyi-nooh*
for tomorrow at 9:00	**zítra v devět ráno** *zeet-rah vde-vyet rah-no'*
The address is …	**Adresa je …** *adresa yeh*
I'm going to …	**Chci jet do …** *khutsis yet do'*
Please take me to (the) …	**Dovezte mě laskavě na …** *doves-teh myeh laskavyeh na*
airport	**letiště** *le-tyish-tyeh*
train station	**nádraží** *nah-drazhee*
this address	**tuhle adresu** *too-hleh adresooh*
How much will it cost?	**Kolik to bude stát?** *kolik to' boodeh staht*
How much is that?	**Kolik je to?** *kolik yeh to'*
Keep the change.	**Nechte si drobné.** *nekh-teh sih drob-neh*

– Dovezte mě laskavě na nádraží.
(Take me to the train station, please.)
– Jistě. (Certainly.)
– Kolik to bude stát? (How much will it cost?)
– Šest set padesát korun. … Prosím.
(650 korun. … Here we are.)
– Děkuji. Nechte si drobné.
(Thank you. Keep the change.)

Car/Automobile Automobil

When driving in towns, watch out for streetcars [trams] which always have the right of way. They can be passed on the right, but not when there are passengers getting on or off. Avoid driving in Prague if you can; the city has an intricate system of one-way and no-entry streets, and parking is very limited.

When driving, you must carry a valid full driver's license, vehicle registration documents, Green Card insurance, and a red warning triangle. Seat belts must be warn at all times, and children under 12 are not allowed in the front seat.

The alcohol limit is 50 mg./100 ml. – and on-the-spot fines can be fierce.

Conversion Chart

km	1	10	20	30	40	50	60	70	80	90	100	110	120	130
miles	0.62	6	12	19	25	31	37	44	50	56	62	68	74	81

Road network

Speed limits kmph (mph)	Cars/motorbikes	Trailers [caravans]
Residential/Built-up area	50 (31)	50 (31)
Main roads	90 (56)	80 (50)
Highway [motorway]	130 (81)	80 (50)

Fuel

gasoline [petrol]	**benzín**	ben-zeen
leaded regular/premium [super]	**special/super**	spe-tsi-ahl/super
unleaded regular/premium [super]	**natural 91/95**	na-too-ral devade-saht yedna/ devade-saht pyet
diesel	**nafta**	nafta

Car rental Půjčovna aut

To rent a car you must be over 21 and have a valid driver's license. All the major international car rental companies have branches in Prague, the major cities, and tourist resorts. Car rental is expensive, but local firms charge less than the international chains. Rates vary greatly, so do check out prices first.

Where can I rent a car?	**Kde si mohu půjčit auto?** *gdeh sih mohooh puh-ye'-chit ow-to'*
I'd like to rent a(n) …	**Chtěl(a) bych si půjčit …** *khuteyl(a) bikh sih puh-ye'chit*
2--door car	**dvoudveřové auto** *dvohdve-rzho-veh ow-to'*
4-door car	**čtyřdveřové auto** *chutirzh-dve-rzho-veh ow-to'*
automatic	**auto s automatickou převodovkou** *ow-to' sow-toma-tits-koh przhe-vodof-koh*
car with 4-wheel drive	**auto se čtyřkolovým pohonem** *ow-to' seh chutirzh-koloveem po-honem*
car with air conditioning	**auto s klimatizací** *ow-to' skli-matiza-tsee*
I'd like it for a day / week.	**Chci je na den/na týden.** *khutsih yeh naden/nateeden*
How much does it cost per day/week?	**Kolik to stojí na den/týden?** *kolik to' sto-yee naden/nateeden*
Is insurance included?	**Je v tom zahrnuté pojištění?** *yeh ftom za-hur-noo-teh po-yeish-tye-nyee*
Are there special weekend rates?	**Máte speciální víkendové sazby?** *mah-teh spe-tsi-ahl-nyee vee-kendoveh saz-bih*
Can I return the car at …?	**Mohu auto vrátit v …?** *mohooh ow-to' vrah-tyit v*
What sort of fuel does it take?	**Na jaké palivo to jezdí?** *na-yakeh palivo' to' yez-dyee*
Where is the high [full]/low [dipped] beam?	**Kde se zapínají dálková/potkávací světla?** *gdeh seh za-pee-na-yee dahl-ko-vah/pot-kah-va-tsee svyet-la*
Could I have full insurance?	**Mohu dostat maximální možné pojištění?** *mohooh dostat ma-ksi-mahl-nyee mozh-neh po-yeish-tye-nyee*

Gas [Petrol] station Benzínová pumpa

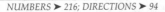

Where's the next gas [petrol] station, please?	**Kde je nejbližší benzínová pumpa, prosím?** *gdeh yeh neye'-bli-shee ben-zee-novah poompa proseem*
Is it self-service?	**Je to samoobsluha?** *yeh to' samo-ops-looha*
Fill it up, please.	**Plnou nádrž, prosím.** *pul-noh nah-dr-zh proseem*
… liters, please.	**… litrů, prosím.** *… litruh proseem*
premium [super]/regular	**super/obyčejný** *sooper/obi-cheye-nee*
lead-free/diesel	**bezolovnatý/naftu** *bezolovna-tee/nuf-tooh*
I'm at pump number …	**Jsem u pumpy číslo …** *yesem oopoom-pih chees-lo'*
Where's the air pump/water?	**Kde je vzduch/voda?** *gdeh yeh vus-dookh/voda*

CENA ZA LITR   price per liter

Parking Parkování

Major cities have extremely limited parking areas, and a permit is usually required. A car parked in a restricted zone without a permit (**parkovací lístek**) can be booted [clamped] or towed away. Some areas have underground parking (**parkoviště**), guarded parking areas (**hlídané parkoviště**), or parking meters.

Is there a parking lot [car park] nearby?	**Je tu poblíž parkoviště?** *yeh tooh po-bleesh parkovish-tyeh*
What's the charge per hour/day?	**Kolik se platí na hodinu/den?** *kolik seh pla-tyee naho-dyinooh/naden*
Do you have some change for the parking meter?	**Máte drobné na parkovací hodiny?** *mah-teh drob-neh naparkova-tsee ho-dyinih*
My car has been booted [clamped]. Who do I call?	**Dostal(a) jsem botičku. Kam mám zavolat?** *dost-tal(a) yesem bo-tyich-kooh. kum mahm zavolat*

NUMBERS ➤ 216; DIRECTIONS ➤ 94

Breakdown Porucha

Autotourist Road Service can help you if your car breaks down. Look for emergency telephones on the highway or ☎ 158 for the police.

Where's the nearest garage?	**Kde je nejbližší servis?** *gdeh yeh neye'-bli-shee servis*
My car broke down.	**Mám na autě poruchu.** *mahm na-ow-tyeh poroo-khooh*
Can you send a mechanic/tow [breakdown] truck?	**Můžete mi poslat mechanika/havarijní službu?** *moozheteh mih poslat me-khanika/havariye'-nyee sloozh-booh*
I'm a member of …	**Jsem členem …** *yesem chlenem*
My license plate [registration] number is …	**Mám poznávací značku …** *mahm poznah-va-tsee znuch-kooh*
The car is …	**Auto je …** *ow-to' yeh*
on the highway [motorway]	**na dálnici** *na-dahl-nyi-tsih*
2 km from …	**dva kilometry od …** *dva kilometrih ot*
How long will you be?	**Za jak dlouho přijedete?** *zah yuk dloh-ho' przhi-yedeteh*

What's wrong? Co se stalo?

My car won't start.	**Auto nechce nastartovat.** *ow-to' nekh-tseh nastartovat*
The battery is dead.	**Je vybitá baterie.** *yeh vibitah bateri-yeh*
I've run out of gas [petrol].	**Došel mi benzín.** *do-shel mih ben-zeen*
I have a flat [puncture].	**Mám píchlou pneumatiku.** *mahm peekh-loh pne-oomatikooh*
There is something wrong with …	**Něco se stalo s …** *nye-tso' seh stalo' s*
I've locked the keys in the car.	**Zamkl(a) jsem si klíče v autě.** *zum-kul(zum-kla) yesem sih klee-cheh vow-tyeh*

88

TELEPHONING ➤ 127; *CAR PARTS* ➤ 90–91

Repairs Opravy

Do you do repairs?

Provádíte opravy?
provah-dyee-teh opravih

Can you repair it?

Můžete to opravit?
moozheteh to' opravit

Please make only essential repairs.

Udělejte jenom nezbytné opravy.
oodye-leye-teh yenom nez-bit-neh opravih

Can I wait for it?

Mohu si na to počkat?
mohooh sih na to' poch-kat

Can you repair it today?

Můžete to opravit dnes?
moozheteh to' opravit dnes

When will it be ready?

Kdy to bude hotové?
gdih to' boodeh ho-to-veh

How much will it cost?

Kolik to bude stát?
kolik to' boodeh staht

That's outrageous!

To je nestydaté! *to' yeh nes-ti-dateh*

Can I have a receipt for my insurance?

Mohu dostat paragon pro pojišťovnu?
mo-hooh dostat paragon pro' po-yeish-tyov-nooh

... nefunguje.	The ... isn't working.
Nemám potřebné náhradní díly.	I don't have the necessary parts.
Budu muset objednat náhradní díly.	I will have to order the parts.
Mohu provést pouze dočasnou opravu.	I can only repair it temporarily.
Vaše auto nejde opravit.	Your car is beyond repair.
Nejde to opravit.	It can't be repaired.
Bude to hotové ...	It will be ready ...
ještě dnes	later today
zítra	tomorrow
do ... dnů	in ... days

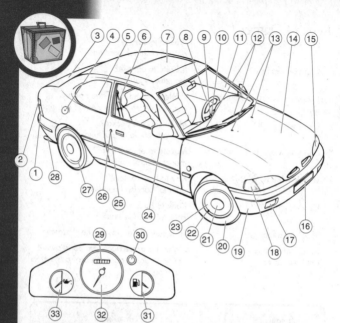

1	taillights [back lights] **koncová světla**
2	brakelights **brzdová světla**
3	trunk [boot] **zavazadlový prostor**
4	gas cap [petrol cap] **víko palivové nádrže**
5	window **okno**
6	seat belt **bezpečnostní pás**
7	sunroof **posuvná střecha**
8	steering wheel **volant**
9	ignition **zapalování**
10	ignition key **klíč zapalování**
11	windshield [windscreen] **čelní sklo**
12	windshield [windscreen] wipers **stěrače čelního skla**
13	windshield [windscreen] washer **ostřikovač čelního skla**
14	hood [bonnet] **kapota**
15	headlights **světlomety**
16	license [number] plate **státní poznávací značka**
17	fog lamp **světlo do mlhy**
18	turn signals [indicators] **směrová světla**
19	bumper **nárazník**
20	tires [tyres] **pneumatiky**
21	wheel cover [hubcap] **kryt kola**
22	valve **ventil**
23	wheels **kola**
24	outside [wing] mirror **vnější zrcátko**
25	automatic locks [central locking] **centrální zamykání**
26	lock **zámek**
27	wheel rim **ráfek kola**
28	exhaust pipe **výfuková roura**
29	odometer [milometer] **počítač ujetých kilometrů**
30	warning light **výstražné světlo**

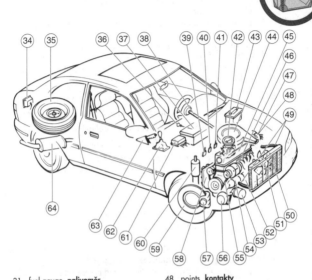

31 fuel gauge **palivoměr**	48 points **kontakty**
32 speedometer **rychloměr**	49 radiator hose (top/bottom)
33 oil gauge **měrka oleje**	**hadice chladiče (horní/spodní)**
34 backup [reversing] lights	50 radiator **chladič**
zpětná světla	51 fan **větrák**
35 spare wheel **náhradní kolo**	52 engine **motor**
36 choke **sytič**	53 oil filter **čistič oleje**
37 heater **topení**	54 starter motor **motor spouštěče**
38 steering column **sloupek volantu**	55 fan belt **řemen větráku**
39 accelerator **plyn**	56 horn **houkačka**
40 pedal **pedál**	57 brake pads **brzdové destičky**
41 clutch **spojka**	58 transmission [gearbox] **převodovka**
42 carburetor **karburátor**	59 brakes **brzdy**
43 battery **baterie**	60 shock absorbers **tlumiče pérování**
44 air filter **vzduchový filtr**	61 fuses **pojistky**
45 camshaft **vačkový hřídel**	62 gear shift [lever] **řadicí páka**
46 alternator **alternátor**	63 handbrake **ruční brzda**
47 distributor **rozdělovač**	64 muffler [silencer] **tlumič výfuku**

CAR REPAIRS ➤ 89

Accidents Nehody

In the event of an accident:

1. put your red warning triangle (**trojúhelník**) about 100 meters behind your car;

2. report the accident to the police (☎ 158), and do not leave before they arrive;

3. you will be asked for your driver's license, vehicle documents, your name and address, and will have to give a statement – ask for a copy;

4. get the other party's name, address, driver's license number, and the names and addresses of any independent witnesses.

There has been an accident.	**Stala se nehoda.** *stala seh ne-hoda*
It's …	**Je to …** *yeh to'*
on the highway [motorway]	**na dálnici** *nadahl-nyi-tsih*
near …	**poblíž …** *po-bleesh*
Where's the nearest telephone?	**Kde je nejbližší telefon?** *gdeh yeh neye'-bli-shee telefon*
Call …	**Zavolejte …** *zavoleye'-teh*
an ambulance	**sanitku** *sa-nit-kooh*
a doctor	**doktora** *dok-tora*
the fire department [brigade]	**hasiče** *ha-si-cheh*
the police	**policii** *poli-tsi-yei*
Can you help me, please?	**Můžete mi pomoci?** *muh-zhe-teh mih pomo-tsih*

Injuries Úrazy

There are people injured.	**Jsou tu zranění lidé.** *yesoh tooh zra-nye-nyee lideh*
No one is hurt.	**Nikomu se nic nestalo.** *nyi-komooh seh nits ne-sta-lo'*
He's seriously injured.	**Je vážně zraněný.** *yeh vah-zhnyeh zra-nye-nee*
She's unconscious.	**Je v bezvědomí.** *yeh vbez-vye-domee*
He can't breathe.	**Nemůže dýchat.** *ne-moozheh dee-khat*
He can't move.	**Nemůže se pohnout.** *ne-moozheh seh po-hnoht*
Don't move him.	**Nehýbejte s ním.** *ne-hee-beye-teh snyeem*

92

Legal matters Právní záležitosti

What's your insurance company?
Jak se jmenuje vaše pojišťovna? *yuk seh yeme-noo-yeh vasheh po-yeish-tyov-na*

What's your name and address?
Vaše jméno a adresa? *vasheh yeme-no' ah adresa*

The car ran into me.
Auto mě porazilo. *ow-to' myeh porazilo'*

The car was going too fast.
Auto jelo příliš rychle. *ow-to' ye-lo' przhee-lish rikh-leh*

The car was driving too close.
Auto jelo příliš blízko. *ow-to' ye-lo' przhee-lish blees-ko'*

I had the right of way.
Měl(a) jsem přednost. *meyl(a) yesem przhed-nost*

I was (only) driving … kmph.
Jel(a) jsem (jen) rychlostí … kilometrů za hodinu. *yel(a) yesem (yen) rikh-los-tyee … kilometrooh zaho-dyi-nooh*

I'd like an interpreter.
Chtěl(a) bych tlumočníka. *khutyel(a) bikh tloo-moch-nyee-ka*

I didn't see the sign.
Neviděl(a) jsem tu značku. *nevi-dyel(a) yesem tooh znach-kooh*

This man/woman saw it happen.
Ten pán (ta paní) viděl(a), co se stalo. *ten pahn (tapa-nyee) vidyel(a) tso' seh stalo'*

The license plate [registration] number was …
Poznávací značka byla … *poz-nah-va-tsee znuch-ka bila*

Ukažte mi …, prosím.	Can I see your …, please?
řidičský průkaz	driver's license
pojistku	insurance card
dokumenty na auto	vehicle registration documents
V kolik hodin se to stalo?	What time did it happen?
Kde se to stalo?	Where did it happen?
Týká se to ještě někoho jiného?	Was anyone else involved?
Byli u toho svědkové?	Are there any witnesses?
Jel(a) jste příliš rychle.	You were speeding.
Nefungují vám světla.	Your lights aren't working.
Musíte (na místě) zaplatit pokutu.	You'll have to pay a fine (on the spot).
Musíte na policejní stanici udělat prohlášení.	You have to make a statement at the station.

TIME ➤ 220

Asking directions
Ptáme se na cestu

Excuse me, please.	**Promiňte, prosím.** *pro-minye'-teh proseem*
How do I get to …?	**Jak se dostanu do …?** *yuk seh dostanooh do'*
Where is …?	**Kde je …?** *gdeh yeh*
Can you show me on the map where I am?	**Můžete mi na mapě ukázat, kde jsem?** *muh-zhe-teh mih nama-pyeh ukah-zat gdeh yesem*
I've lost my way.	**Ztratil(a) jsem se.** *stra-tyil(a) yesem seh*
Can you repeat that, please?	**Můžete to zopakovat, prosím?** *muh-zhe-teh to' zopakovat proseem*
More slowly, please.	**Pomaleji, prosím.** *pomale-yih proseem*
Thanks for your help.	**Děkuji vám za pomoc.** *dye-koo-yih vahm zapomots*

Traveling by car Cestování autem

Is this the right road for …?	**Jedu správně na …?** *yedooh sprah-vnyeh na*
Is it far?	**Je to daleko?** *yeh to' daleko'*
How far is it to … from here?	**Jak daleko je to odtud do …?** *yuk daleko' yeh to' ot-tood do'*
Where does this road lead?	**Kam tahle silnice vede?** *kum ta-hleh sil-nyi-tseh vedeh*
How do I get onto the highway [motorway]?	**Jak se dostanu na dálnici?** *yuk seh dostanooh na dahl-nyi-tsih*
What's the next town called?	**Jak se jmenuje nejbližší město?** *yuk seh yeme-noo-yeh neye'-bli-shee myes-to'*
How long does it take by car?	**Jak dlouho to trvá autem?** *yuk dloh-ho' to' tr-vah ow-tem*

> – Promiňte, prosím. Jak se dostanu na nádraží?
> (Excuse me, please. How do I get to
> the train station?)
> – Zahněte do třetí ulice vpravo a bude přímo před vámi.
> (Take the third right and it's straight ahead.)
> – Třetí ulice vpravo. Je to daleko?
> (Third right. Is it far?)
> – Pěšky je to deset minut. (It's ten minutes on foot.)
> – Děkuji za pomoc. (Thanks for your help.)
> – Není zač. (You're welcome.)

Location Umístění

Je to ...	It's ...
přímo před vámi	straight ahead
vlevo	on the left
vpravo	on the right
na konci ulice	at the end of the street
na rohu	on the corner
za rohem	around the corner
směrem na ...	in the direction of ...
naproti .../za ...	opposite .../behind ...
vedle .../za ...	next to .../after ...
Jděte ...	Go down the ...
postranní ulicí/hlavní ulicí	side street/main street
Přejděte přes ...	Cross the ...
náměstí/most	square/bridge
Zahněte do třetí ulice vpravo.	Take the third right.
Odbočte doleva ...	Turn left ...
po prvních semaforech	after the first traffic light
na druhé křižovatce	at the second intersection [crossroad]

By car Autem

Je to ... odtud.	It's ... of here.
na sever/na jih	north/south
na východ/na západ	east/west
Jeďte silnicí na ...	Take the road for ...
Jedete špatně.	You're on the wrong road.
Musíte se vrátit k ...	You'll have to go back to ...
Jeďte podle směrovek na ...	Follow the signs for ...

How far? Jak daleko?

Je to ...	It's ...
blízko/daleko	close/a long way
5 minut pěšky	5 minutes on foot
10 minut autem	10 minutes by car
asi 100 metrů odtud	about 100 meters down the road
asi 10 kilometrů odtud	about 10 kilometers away

TIME ➤ 220; NUMBERS ➤ 216

Road signs Dopravní značky

OBJÍŽĎKA	detour [diversion]
JEDNOSMĚRNÝ PROVOZ	one-way street
CESTA UZAVŘENA	road closed
POZOR ŠKOLA	school zone [path]
STOP	stop
ZÁKAZ PŘEDJÍŽDĚNÍ	no passing [overtaking]
JEĎTE POMALU	drive slowly
ZAPNĚTE SVĚTLA	use headlights

Town plans Plán města

autobusová/tramvajová trasa	bus/streetcar [tram] route
autobusová/tramvajová zastávka	bus/streetcar [tram] stop
banka	bank
divadlo	theater
hlavní ulice	main [high] street
hřiště	playing field [sports ground]
informační kancelář	information office
Jste zde.	You are here.
kino	movie theater [cinema]
kostel	church
letiště	airport
nádraží	train station
nemocnice	hospital
obchodní dům	department store
park	park
parkoviště	parking lot [car park]
pěší zóna	pedestrian zone [precinct]
policejní stanice	police station
pošta	post office
přechod pro chodce	pedestrian crossing
stadion	stadium
stanice metra	subway [metro] station
stanoviště taxi	taxi stand [rank]
škola	school

Sightseeing

Tourist information office
Turistická informační kancelář

Tourist information offices – called **turistická kancelář**, **cestovní kancelář**, or simply **informace** – are located in all major towns but are not always open. Local tobacconists (**tabák**) can be a useful source of information and usually have maps and good knowledge of local events.

Where's the tourist office?	**Kde je turistická kancelář?** *gdeh yeh tooris-tits-kah kan-tse-lahrzh*
What are the main points of interest?	**Kde jsou hlavní zajímavosti?** *gdeh yesoh hlav-nyee za-yee-mavos-tyih*
We're here for …	**Jsme tady na …** *yesmeh tadih na*
a few hours	**pár hodin** *pahr ho-dyin*
a day	**den** *den*
a week	**týden** *tee-den*
Can you recommend …?	**Můžete mi doporučit …?** *muh-zheteh mih doporoochit*
a sightseeing tour	**prohlídku** *pro-hleet-kooh*
an excursion	**výlet** *veelet*
a boat trip	**výlet lodí** *veelet lo-dyee*
Do you have any information on …?	**Máte nějaké informace o …?** *mah-teh nye-yakeh in-for-ma-tseh o*
Are there any trips to …?	**Pořádají se nějaké zájezdy na …?** *po-rzhah-da-yee seh ney-ya-keh zah-yez-dih na*

Excursions Výlety

How much does the tour cost?	**Kolik zájezd stojí?** *kolik zah-yezd sto-yee*
Is lunch included?	**Je do ceny zahrnutý oběd?** *yeh do-tse-nih za-hur-nootee ob-yet*
Where do we leave from?	**Odkud budeme odjíždět?** *ot-koot boo-demeh od-yeezh-dyet*
What time does the tour start?	**V kolik hodin zájezd začíná?** *fkolik ho-dyin zah-yezt za-chee-nah*
What time do we get back?	**V kolik hodin se vrátíme?** *fkolik ho-dyin seh vrah-tyee-meh*
Do we have free time in …?	**Budeme mít v … volný čas?** *boo-demeh meet v … volnee chas*
Is there an English-speaking guide?	**Bude s námi anglicky mluvící průvodce?** *boo-deh snah-mih an-glits-kih mloo-vee-tsee pruh-vot-tseh*

On tour Na výletě

Are we going to see …?	**Uvidíme …?** *oo-vi-dyee-meh*
We'd like to have a look at the …	**Rádi bychom viděli …** *rah-dyih bi-khom vi-dye-lih*
Can we stop here …?	**Mohli bychom tady zastavit na …?** *mo-hlih bi-khom tadih zas-tavit na*
to take photographs	**pár fotografií** *pahr foto-gra-fi-yee*
to buy souvenirs	**nákup suvenýrů** *nah-koop soove-nee-ruh*
to use the bathrooms [toilets]	**záchod** *zah-khot*
Would you take a photo of us, please?	**Můžete nás vyfotografovat?** *muh-zhe-teh nahs vi-foto-gra-fovat*
How long do we have here/in …?	**Jak dlouho tady/v … budeme?** *yuk dloh-ho' tadih/v … boo-demeh*
Wait! … isn't back yet.	**Počkejte! … se ještě nevrátil(a).** *poch-keye'-teh! … seh yesh-tyeh ne-vrah-tyil(a)*

Sights Památky

Town maps are usually displayed in town centers. They can also be purchased at tourist information offices, newsstands, tobacconists, and souvenir stores.

Where is the …?	**Kde je …?** *gdeh yeh*
art gallery	**galerie** *gale-ri-yeh*
battle site	**bitevní pole** *bitev-nyee poleh*
botanical garden	**botanická zahrada** *bota-nits-kah za-hra-da*
castle	**hrad** *hrat*
cathedral	**chrám** *khurahm*
cemetery	**hřbitov** *hurzhubi-tof*
church	**kostel** *kos-tel*
downtown area	**centrum** *tsen-troom*
fountain	**kašna** *kash-na*
historic site	**památková oblast** *pamaht-kovah ob-last*
market	**tržnice** *tur-zhnyi-tseh*
(war) memorial	**pomník (obětem války)** *pom-nyeek (ob-yetem vahl-kih)*
monastery	**klášter** *klah-shter*
museum	**muzeum** *moo-ze-oom*
old town	**staré město** *stareh myes-to'*
opera house	**operní divadlo** *oper-nyee dyi-vad-lo'*
palace	**palác** *palah-ts*
park	**park** *park*
parliament building	**budova parlamentu** *boo-dova par-la-men-tooh*
ruins	**zříceniny** *zurzhee-tse-nyi-nih*
shopping area	**oblast s obchody** *ob-last sop-kho-dih*
statue	**socha** *so-kha*
theater	**divadlo** *dyi-vad-lo'*
tower	**věž** *vyezh*
town hall	**radnice** *rad-nyi-tseh*
viewpoint	**vyhlídka** *vi-hleet-ka*
Can you show me on the map?	**Můžete mi to ukázat na mapě?** *muh-zheteh mih to' ookah-zat na-ma-pyeh*

DIRECTIONS ➤ 94

Admission Vstupné

Admission varies according to the venue. Most museums and galleries are closed on Mondays.

Is the … open to the public?	**Je … přístupný pro veřejnost?** *yeh … purzhee-stoop-nee pro-ve-rzheye'-nost*
Can we look around?	**Můžeme si to tady prohlédnout?** *muh-zhemeh sih to' tadih pro-hlehd-noht*
When is it open?	**Kdy je otevřeno?** *gdih yeh otev-rzhe-no'*
When does it close?	**Kdy se zavírá?** *gdih seh zavee-rah*
Is … open on Sundays?	**Má … otevřeno v neděli?** *mah … otev-rzhe-no' vne-dye-lih*
When's the next guided tour?	**V kolik hodin je další prohlídka s průvodcem?** *fkolik ho-dyin yeh dul-shee pro-hleet-ka supruh-vot-stem*
Do you have a guidebook (in English)?	**Máte průvodce (v angličtině)?** *mah-teh pruh-vot-tseh (van-glich-tyi-nyeh)*
Can I take photos?	**Mohu tady fotografovat?** *mohooh tadih foto-gra-fovat*
Is there access for the disabled?	**Je tam přístup pro invalidy?** *yeh tum purzhee-stoop pro-in-validih*
Is there an audioguide in English?	**Je tam audio průvodce v angličtině?** *yeh tum ow-di-o' pruh-vot-tseh van-glich-tyi-nyeh*

Paying/Tickets Placení/Vstupenky

… tickets, please.	**… vstupenky, prosím.** *… vustoo-pen-kih proseem*
How much is the entrance fee?	**Kolik je vstupné?** *kolik yeh vustoop-neh*
Are there any reductions for …?	**Je sleva pro …?** *yeh sleva pro'*
children	**děti** *dye-tyih*
groups	**skupiny** *skoo-pinih*
senior citizens	**starší občany** *star-shee op-chanih*
students	**studenty** *stoo-dentih*
the disabled	**invalidy** *in-validih*
One adult and two children, please.	**Jeden dospělý a dvě děti, prosím.** *yeden dos-pye-lee a dvyeh dye-tyih proseem*
I lost my ticket.	**Ztratila(a) jsem vstupenku.** *stra-tyil(a) yesem vustoo-pen-kooh*

– Pět vstupenek, prosím. Platí nějaké slevy?
(Five tickets, please. Are there any reductions?)

– Ano. Děti a důchodci platí čtyřicet korun.
(Yes. Children and senior citizens are 40 Kč.)

– Dva dospělí a tři děti, prosím.
(Two adults and three children, please.)

– Dvě stě osmdesát korun. (That's 280 Kč, please.)

⊘ **VSTUP ZDARMA**	free admission
ZAVŘENO	closed
DÁRKY	gift shop
POSLEDNÍ PROHLÍDKA V 17.00 HODIN	latest entry at 5 p.m.
DALŠÍ PROHLÍDKA V ...	next tour at ...
VSTUP ZAKÁZÁN	no entry
ZÁKAZ FOTOGRAFOVÁNÍ S BLESKEM	no flash photography
ZÁKAZ FOTOGRAFOVÁNÍ	no photography
OTEVŘENO	open
⊘ **NÁVŠTĚVNÍ HODINY**	[opening] hours

Impressions Dojmy

It's ...	**To je ...** *to' yeh*
amazing	**obdivuhodné** *ob-dyi-voo-hod-neh*
beautiful	**krásné** *krah-sneh*
bizarre	**prapodivné** *prapo-dyiv-neh*
incredible	**neuvěřitelné** *ne-oovye-rzhi-tel-neh*
interesting/boring	**zajímavé/nudné** *za-yee-maveh/nood-neh*
lots of fun	**zábavné** *zah-bavneh*
magnificent	**velkolepé** *vel-kolepeh*
romantic	**romantické** *roman-tits-keh*
strange	**divné** *dyiv-neh*
superb	**skvělé** *sukvye-leh*
terrible/ugly	**hrozné/ošklivé** *hroz-neh/osh-kli-veh*
It's a good value.	**Je to dobrá cena.** *yeh to' dob-rah tsena*
It's a rip-off.	**Je to předražené.** *yeh to' przhe-dra-zheneh*
I like/don't like it.	**Líbí/Nelíbí se mi to.** *leebee/ne-leebee seh mih to'*

Tourist glossary
Slovníček pro turisty

akvarel watercolor
apartmá (královské) apartments (royal)
apsida apse
brána gate
budova building
cihla brick
cimbuří battlement
císařovna empress
daroval(a) ... donated by ...
detail detail
dočasně vystavený předmět temporary exhibit
dokončeno v ... completed in ...
drahokam gemstone
dřevo wood
dveře door
dveřní prostor doorway
email enamel
fontána fountain
formální zahrada formal garden
freska fresco
fronton pediment
hodiny clock
hrob grave
hrobka tomb
hrobní kámen headstone
chór choir (stall)
chrlič gargoyle
jíl clay
kámen stone
kašna fountain
kazatelna pulpit
klenoty jewelry

knihovna library
koruna crown
kostelní hřbitov churchyard
koupele baths
kování ironwork
krajina landscape
krajinomalba landscape (*painting*)
král king
královna queen
kresba drawing
krypta crypt/vault
křídlo wing (*of building*)
lept etching
listy foliage
malba painting
malíř painter
měřítko jedna ku stu scale 1:100
mince coin
mistr master
mistrovské dílo masterpiece
model model
mořská krajina seascape
mramor marble
nábytek furniture
nádvoří courtyard
náhrobek tombstone
namaloval ... painted by ...
napůl dřevěné half-timbered
narozen v ... born in ...
nástěnná malba mural
návrh design
navrhl ... designed by ...

na žádost ... commissioned by ...
objeveno v ... discovered in ...
obnoveno v ... restored in ...
obraz picture
okno window
okno z barevného skla
  stained-glass window
olejomalby oils
oltář altar, altarpiece
opěrná zeď buttress
padací most drawbridge
panel panel
panelové obložení paneling
plátno canvas
pódium stage
postaveno v ...
  built/erected in ...
pozlacený gilded
práce works
práce z vosku waxwork
přednáška lecture
přestavěno v ... rebuilt in ...
převislý overhanging
reprezentační místnost stateroom
rohový kámen cornerstone
rybinová vazba herringbone
rytina engraving
řemesla crafts
řezba carving
scéna tableau
schodiště staircase
schody stairs
skica sketch
sloup pillar
socha sculpture
stín shadow
století century
strop ceiling
střecha roof

střední loď nave
střelecká věž turret
stříbro silver/
  silverware
styl design
škola ... school of ...
štít gable
tapisérie tapestry
terakota terracotta
trám beam
uhel charcoal
varhany organ
ve stylu ... in the style of ...
věž spire/tower
vitrína display cabinet
vláda reign
vlys frieze
vodní příkop moat
vstupní hala foyer
výklenek alcove
výlisek molding
výstava exhibition
vystavit exhibit
výška height
výtvarné umění fine arts
zahájeno v ...
  started in ...
založeno v ...
  founded in ...
zapůjčeno on loan
zátiší still life
zbraň weapon
zbrojnice armory
zeď wall
zemřel v ... died in ...
zlatý gold(en)
zničeno ...
  destroyed by ...
žil lived

Who?/What?/When?
Kdo?/Co?/Kdy?

What's that building? **Co je to za budovu?**
tso' yeh to' za-boo-dovooh

When was it built? **Kdy byla postavena?** *gdih bila pos-tavena*

Who was the architect? **Kdo byl architekt?** *gdo' bil ar-khi-tekt*

What period is that? **Z jakého je to období?**
zya-keh-ho' yeh to' ob-dobee

What style is that? **V jakém je to stylu?**
vya-kehm yeh to' sti-looh

Románský styl (c. 9–12)

The Romanesque style is characterized by massive masonry wall construction, the rounded arch, the groin vault, and a restrained use of moldings. A fine example of this style is the St. George Basilica in Prague.

Gotika/Renesance (c. 12–16)

The Gothic style is characterized by the lancet arch, the ribbed vault, and the flying buttress. Fine examples of this style include St. Vitus Cathedral and Charles Bridge in Prague, and the Karlštejn Castle, near Prague. The influence of Renaissance style, a strong artistic movement based on classical Greek and Roman architecture, can be seen in the Wallenstein Palace in Prague and in the town of Telč in Moravia.

Baroko (c. late 16–early 18)

The Baroque style, characterized by extensive ornamentation, has left its mark on numerous buildings and churches all over the country. Some outstanding examples are St. Nicholas Church in Prague, the cathedral of the town of Kutná Hora near Prague, and the unique, newly restored baroque theater in Česky Krumlov in southern Bohemia.

Secese (c. late 18–19)

At the turn of the nineteenth century, the style that had the greatest impact on Prague's architecture was Art Nouveau, a movement characterized by stylized natural forms, such as flowers and leaves. The Municipal House and Grand Hotel Europa in Prague testify to its exquisite beauty. The most famous Czech exponent of the style was Alfons Mucha.

Kubismus (c. early 20)

In the early twentieth century, *cubism*, inspired by Picasso, found followers among Czech artists and architects. One of the best examples of this style is the *House of the Black Madonna* in the center of Prague.

History Historie

Great Moravian Empire   (mid-800s)
Byzantine priests Cyril and Methodius bring Slavonic script
to the Czech lands. Christianity adopted.

Václav I   (921–929)
Reign of King Václav I, "Good King Wenceslas."

Charles IV   (1346–78)
Charles IV crowned Holy Roman Emperor in 1353. Charles University in
Prague established (1348); Charles Bridge and New Town in Prague built.

Hussite revolution   (1419–36)
Religious reform movement undermines power of Roman Catholic Church.

Ferdinand I   (1526–64)
First Hapsburg king. Beginning of centralization and absolutism.

17th century
Counter-Reformation, the forced re-catholicizing of Czech lands.

Empress Maria Theresa/Joseph II   (1740–80)/(1741–90)
Period of reform: serfdom abolished, feudal power of nobles curtailed,
religious tolerance granted to non-Catholics.

1918
Break up of the Austro-Hungarian Empire after World War I. State of
Czechoslovakia founded; T.G. Masaryk first president.

1938–39
The Sudetenland, part of Czechoslovakia, ceded to Germany;
Czechoslovakia occupied by Nazi Germany. Start of World War II.

1948
Communist Party takes power; Czechoslovak Socialist Republic proclaimed.
In the "Prague Spring" of 1968, Dubček's democratic experiment is crushed
by Soviet invasion.

1989
"Velvet Revolution" and collapse of communist rule; Václav Havel elected
president. In 1993, the "Peaceful Divorce" sees the creation of separate
Czech and Slovak Republics.

Places of worship Místa bohoslužeb

About 40 percent of the population is Roman Catholic. There are also
Protestant and Jewish minorities.

Catholic/Protestant church	**katolický/krotestantský kostel** *katolits-kee/pro-tes-tun-tsukee kostel*
mosque/synagogue/temple	**mešita/synagoga/chrám** *meshita/sinagoga/khurahm*
What time is …?	**V kolik hodin je …?** *fkolik ho-dyin yeh*
mass/the service	**mše/bohoslužba** *musheh/bo-ho-sloozh-ba*

In the countryside Na venkově

I'd like a map of ...	**Chtěl(a) bych mapu ...** *khutyel(a) bikh mapooh*
this region	**této oblasti** *teh-to' ob-las-tyih*
walking routes	**turistických cest** *tooris-tits-keekh tsest*
cycle routes	**cyklistických stezek** *cik-lis-tits-keekh ste-zek*
How far is it to ...?	**Jak je to daleko do ...?** *yuk yeh to' daleko' do'*
Is there a right of way?	**Je cesta přístupná?** *yeh tses-ta przhee-stoop-nah*
Is there a trail/scenic route to ...?	**Je do ... pěší/vyhlídková cesta?** *yeh do' ... pye-shee/vi-hleet-kovah tses-ta*
Can you show me on the map?	**Můžete mi to ukázat na mapě?** *muh-zheteh mih to' ookah-zat na-ma-pyeh*
I'm lost.	**Ztratil(a) jsem se.** *stratyil(a) yesem seh*

Organized walks Organizované vycházky

When does the guided walk start?	**Kdy začíná vycházka s průvodcem?** *gdih za-chee-nah vi-khah-ska supruh-vot-tsem*
When will we return?	**Kdy se vrátíme?** *gdih seh vrah-tyee-meh*
Is it a hard course?	**Je cesta obtížná?** *yeh tses-ta op-tyeezh-nah*
gentle/medium/tough	**mírná/střední/obtížná** *meer-nah/sutrzhed-nyee/op-tyeezh-nah*
I'm exhausted.	**Jsem vyčerpaný(á).** *yesem vi-cher-panee(ah)*
How long are we resting here?	**Jak dlouho tady budeme odpočívat?** *yuk dloh-ho' tadih boo-demeh ot-po-cheevat*
What kind of ... is that?	**Co je to za ...?** *tso' yeh to' za*
animal/bird	**zvíře/ptáka** *zvee-rzheh/ptah-ka*
flower/tree	**květinu/strom** *kvye-tyi-nooh/strom*

Geographic features
Zeměpisné pojmy

beach	**pláž** *plah-zh*
bridge	**most** *most*
canal	**kanál** *kanahl*
cave	**jeskyně** *yes-ki-nyeh*
cliff	**útes** *uh-tes*
farm	**statek** *statek*
field	**pole** *poleh*
footpath	**pěšina** *pye-shina*
forest	**les** *les*
hill	**kopec** *kopets*
lake	**jezero** *yezero'*
mountain	**hora** *hora*
mountain pass	**horský průsmyk** *hor-skee pruh-smik*
mountain range	**horské pásmo** *hor-skeh pah-smo'*
nature preserve [reserve]	**přírodní rezervace** *przhee-rod-nyee rezer-vatseh*
nature trail	**přírodní stezka** *przhee-rod-nyee stes-kah*
panorama	**panoráma** *panorah-ma*
park	**park** *park*
peak	**vrchol** *vr-khol*
picnic area	**místo na piknik** *mees-to' na-pik-nik*
pond	**rybník** *rib-nyeek*
rapids	**peřeje** *pe-rzhe-yeh*
river	**řeka** *rzheka*
sea	**moře** *mo-rzheh*
stream	**potok** *potok*
valley	**údolí** *uh-dolee*
viewpoint	**vyhlídka** *vi-hleet-ka*
village	**vesnice** *ves-nyi-tseh*
vineyard	**vinice** *vi-nyi-tseh*
waterfall	**vodopád** *vodopahd*
wood	**les** *les*

Leisure

Tourist information offices and ticket agencies provide information in English. In Prague, a monthly English-language guide, *Culture in Prague*, is published, listing theater performances, concerts, movies, and cultural events. The English-language newspaper, *Prague Post*, is also a good source of information.

Events Kulturní akce

Do you have a program of events?	**Máte kulturní program?** *mah-teh kool-toor-nyee program*
Can you recommend a …?	**Můžete mi doporučit …?** *muh-zheteh mih dopo-roo-chit*
ballet/concert	**balet/koncert** *balet/kon-tsert*
movie [film]	**film** *film*
opera/play	**operu/představení** *operooh/przhet-sta-venyee*

Availability Čas a lístky

When does it start/end?	**Kdy to začíná/končí?** *gdih to' zacheenah/kon-chee*
Are there any seats for tonight?	**Máte lístky na dnes na večer?** *mah-teh leest-kih na-dnes na-vecher*
Where can I get tickets?	**Kde dostanu lístky?** *gdeh dos-tanooh leest-kih*
There are two/three/ four of us.	**Jsme dva/tři/čtyři.** *yesmeh dva/trzhih/chuti-rzhih*
I'd like to reserve …	**Chtěl(a) bych si zamluvit …** *khutyel(a) bikh sih zamloo-vit*
three tickets for Sunday evening	**tři lístky na neděli večer** *trzhih leest-kih na-ne-dye-lih vecher*
one ticket for the Friday matinée	**jeden lístek na pátek odpoledne** *yeden lees-tek na-pah-tek ot-poled-neh*

Tickets Lístky

How much are the seats?

Kolik stojí lístek na místa k sezení? *kolik sto-yee lees-tek na-mees-ta kse-ze-nyee*

Do you have anything cheaper?

Máte něco levnějšího? *mah-teh nye-tso' lev-nyeye'-shee-ho'*

Can I pay by credit card?

Mohu zaplatit kreditní kartou? *mohooh zapla-tyit kredit-nyee kar-toh*

I'll pay by …

Zaplatím … *zapla-tyeem*

Jaké má vaše kreditní karta číslo?	What's your credit card number?
Jaký je to typ kreditní karty?	What's your credit card type?
Kdy vaše kreditní karta přestane platit?	What's the expiration [expiry] date?
Zde se podepište, prosím.	Can you sign here, please.
Vstupenky si vyzvedněte …	Please pick up the tickets …
do … odpoledne	by … p.m.
u pokladny s rezervacemi	at the reservation desk

May I have a program, please?

Mohu dostat program? *mohooh dos-tat program*

Where's the coatcheck [cloakroom]?

Kde je šatna? *gdeh yeh shut-na*

– *Co si přejete? (Can I help you?)*
– Chtěl(a) bych dva lístky na dnešní koncert, prosím.
(I'd like two tickets for tonight's concert, please.)
– *Prosím. (Certainly.)*
– Mohu zaplatit kreditní kartou?
(Can I pay by credit card?)
– *Ano. (Yes.)*
– V tom případě zaplatím Visa kartou.
(In that case, I'll pay by Visa.)
– *Děkuji. Zde se laskavě podepište.*
(Thank you. Sign here, please.)

VYPRODÁNO	sold out
VSTUPENKY NA DNEŠEK	tickets for today
REZERVACE	advance reservations

NUMBERS ➤ 216

Movies [Cinema] Kino

Foreign films are sometimes dubbed into Czech, so it is best to check before you go.

Is there a movie theater [cinema] near here?
Je tu blízko kino?
yeh tooh blees-ko' kino'

What's playing at the movies [on at the cinema] tonight?
Co dnes večer hrají v kině?
tso' dnes vecher hra-yee fki-nyeh

Is the film dubbed?
Je film dabovaný?
yeh film dabovanee

Is the film subtitled?
Je film s titulky?
yeh film sti-tool-kih

Is the film in the original English?
Je film v angličtině?
yeh film van-glich-tyi-nyeh

A ..., please.
..., prosím. *... proseem*

box [carton] of popcorn
praženou kukuřici
pra-zhe-noh kookoo-rzhi-tsih

chocolate ice cream [choc-ice]
čokoládovou zmrzlinu
chokolah-dovoh zumur-zli-nooh

hot dog
párek v rohlíku
pah-rek vro-hlee-kooh

Theater Divadlo

Major theaters, concert halls, and some restaurants frown on jeans, T-shirts, shorts, and sneakers [trainers]. You may not be admitted if you are wearing such items. Use coatcheck [cloakroom] facilities if they are provided. A tip of 2 Kč is customary for the coatcheck attendant.

What's playing at the National Theater?
Co hrají v Národním divadle?
tso' hra-yee vnah-rod-nyeem dyi-vadleh

Who's the playwright?
Kdo to napsal? *gdo' to' napsal*

Do you think I'd enjoy it?
Myslíte, že by se mi to líbilo?
mis-lee-teh zheh bih seh mih to' lee-bilo'

I don't know much Czech.
Nerozumím moc česky.
nerozoomeem mots ches-kih

Opera/Ballet/Dance
Opera/Balet/Tanec

Major towns have their own theater/opera companies.
Musical tradition is very strong in Bohemia and Moravia.
Prague, in particular, has many theaters and concert halls. The
annual Prague Spring Music Festival attracts famous performers from
around the world – and thousands of visitors.

Where's the theater?	**Kde je divadlo?** *gdeh yeh dyi-vadlo'*
Who's the composer?	**Od jakého je to skladatele?** *od-ya-keh-ho' yeh to' skladateleh*
Who's the soloist?	**Který sólista hraje?** *kteree so-lis-sta hra-yeh*
Is formal dress required?	**Je nutné formální oblečení?** *yeh noot-neh formahl-nyee obleche-nyee*
Who's dancing?	**Kdo tančí?** *gdo' tun-chee*
I'm interested in contemporary dance.	**Zajímá mě moderní tanec.** *za-yee-mah myeh moder-nyee tanets*

Music/Concerts Hudba/Koncerty

Where's the concert hall?	**Kde je koncertní síň?** *dgeh yeh kon-tsert-nyee seenye'*
Which orchestra/band is playing?	**Který orchestr/Která skupina hraje?** *kteree or-khe-stur/kterah skoopina hra-yeh*
What are they playing?	**Co hrají?** *tso' hra-yee*
Who's the conductor/soloist?	**Kdo diriguje?** *gdo' diri-goo-yeh*
Who's the conductor/soloist?	**Který sólista hraje?** *kteree so-lis-ta hra-yeh*
I really like …	**Mám moc rád(a) …** *mahm mots raht(rah-dah)*
folk music/country music	**lidovou hudbu/country** *lidovoh hood-booh/kant-rih*
jazz/pop/rock music	**džez/pop/rock** *dzhez/pop/rok*
music of the sixties	**hudbu ze šedesátých let** *hood-booh ze-she-de-sah-teekh let*
soul music	**hudbu amerických černochů** *hood-booh amerits-keekh cher-no-khuh*
Have you ever heard of her/him/them?	**Znáte ho/ji/je?** *znah-teh ho'/yih/yeh*
Are they popular?	**Jsou populární?** *yesoh popoo-lahr-nyee*

Nightlife Noční život

What is there to do in the evenings?	**Co se tady dá dělat večer?** *tso' seh tadih dah dye-lat vecher*
Can you recommend a …?	**Můžete mi doporučit …?** *muh-zheteh mih dopo-roo-chit*
Is there a …?	**Je tady …?** *yeh tadih*
bar / restaurant	**bar/restaurace** *bar/res-ta-oora-tseh*
cabaret / casino	**kabaret/kasino** *kabaret/kasino'*
discotheque	**diskotéka** *dis-ko-teh-ka*
gay club	**klub pro homosexuály** *kloop pro' homo-sek-soo-ah-lih*
nightclub	**noční klub** *noch-nyee kloop*
What type of music do they play?	**Jaký druh hudby se tam hraje?** *yukee drooh hood-bih seh tum hra-yeh*
How do I get there?	**Jak se tam dostanu?** *yuk seh tum dos-tanooh*
Is there an admission charge?	**Platí se tam vstupné?** *pla-tyee seh tum vstoop-neh*

Admission Vstup

What time does the show start?	**V kolik hodin začíná představení?** *fkolik ho-dyin za-chee-nah przhet-stave-nyee*
Is there a cover charge?	**Platí se kuvert?** *pla-tyee seh koo-vert*
Is a reservation necessary?	**Je nutná rezervace?** *yeh noot-nah rezer-va-tseh*
Do we need to be members?	**Musíme být členy?** *moo-see-meh beet chle-nih*
Can you have dinner there?	**Můžeme se tam navečeřet?** *muh-zhemeh seh tum naveche-rzhet*
How long will we have to stand in line [queue]?	**Jak dlouho budeme muset stát ve frontě?** *yuk dloh-ho' boo-demeh mooset staht ve-fron-tyeh*
I'd like a good table.	**Chtěl(a) bych pěkný stůl.** *khutyel(a) bikh peyk-nee stuhl*

Children Děti

Can you recommend
something for the children?

**Můžete mi doporučit něco
pro děti?** *muh-zhete mih
dopo-roo-chit nye-tso' pro-
dye-tyi*

Are there changing facilities
here for babies?

Je tady prostor na přebalování? *yeh
tadih pros-tor na-przhe-balovah-nyee*

Where are the bathrooms
[toilets]?

Kde jsou záchody?
dgeh yesoh zah-kho-dih

amusement arcade

prostor s hracími automaty
pros-tor suhra-tsee-mih ow-tomatih

fairground

lunapark *loonapark*

kiddie [paddling] pool

dětský bazén *dyets-kee bazehn*

playground

dětské hřiště *dyets-keh hrzhish-tyeh*

play group

školka *shkolka*

zoo

zoo *zo'*

Baby-sitting Hlídání dětí

Can you recommend a reliable
baby-sitter?

**Můžete mi doporučit spolehlivou paní
k dětem?** *muh-zheteh mih dopo-roo-chit
spo-le-hli-voh panyee gdyetem*

Is there constant supervision?

Je tam nepřetržitý dozor?
yeh tum ne-przhe-tr-zhitee dozor

Is the staff properly trained?

Je personál řádně vyškolený?
yeh personahl rzhah-dnyeh vi-shko-lenee

When can I drop them off?

Kdy je mohu přivést?
gdih yeh mo-hooh przhi-veh-st

I'll pick them up at …

Vyzvednu je v …
viz-ved-nooh yeh v

We'll be back by …

Vrátíme se do …
vrah-tyee-me seh do'

She's 3, and he's 18 months.

Jí jsou tři a jemu osmnáct měsíců.
*yee yesoh trzhih a ye-mooh
osum-nah-tsut mye-see-tsuh*

Sports Sporty

Soccer [football] in summer and ice hockey in winter are the most popular spectator sports. Swimming, tennis, volleyball, and basketball are also popular. And if you enjoy walking and hiking, you will find numerous well-marked paths and walking/hiking trails in the mountains.

Spectator Diváci

Is there a soccer [football] game [match] this Saturday?	**Bude tuhle sobotu fotbalový zápas?** *boodeh too-hleh sobo-tooh fot-ba-lovee zah-pus*
Which teams are playing?	**Které týmy hrají?** *ktereh tee-mih hra-yee*
Can you get me a ticket?	**Můžete mi obstarat lístek?** *muh-zheteh mih op-sta-rat lees-tek*
What's the admission charge?	**Kolik je vstupné?** *kolik yeh vustoop-neh*
Where's the racetrack [racecourse]?	**Kde je dostihová dráha?** *gdeh yeh dos-tyi-ho-vah drah-ha*
Where can I place a bet?	**Kde mohu podat sázku?** *gdeh mo-hooh podat sahs-kooh*
What are the odds on ...?	**Jaká je šance na výhru ...?** *yukah yeh shan-tseh na-vee-hrooh*
athletics	**atletika** *a-tle-ti-ka*
basketball	**košíková** *ko-shee-kovah*
cycling	**cyklistika** *tsi-klis-tika*
golf	**golf** *golf*
horse racing	**dostihy** *dos-tyi-hih*
soccer [football]	**fotbal** *fot-bal*
swimming	**plavání** *pla-vah-nyee*
tennis	**tenis** *tenis*
volleyball	**volejbal** *vo-leye-bal*

Participating Zapojení do hry

Is there a … nearby?	**Je tady blízko …?** *yeh tadih blees-ko'*
golf course	**golfové hřiště** *gol-fo-veh hurzhish-tyeh*
sports club	**sportovní klub** *spor-tov-nyee kloop*
Are there any tennis courts?	**Jsou tady tenisové kurty?** *yesoh tadih tenisoveh koor-tih*
What's the charge per …?	**Kolik se platí za …?** *kolik seh platyee za*
day / hour	**den/hodinu** *den/ho-dyi-nooh*
game / round (*golf*)	**hru/kolo** *hrooh/kolo'*
Do I need to be a member?	**Musím být členem?** *moo-seem beet chlenem*
Where can I rent …?	**Kde si mohu půjčit …?** *gdeh sih mohooh puhye'-chit*
boots	**boty** *botih*
clubs	**golfové hole** *gol-foveh holeh*
equipment	**vybavení** *vibave-nyee*
a racket	**raketu** *raketooh*
Can I get lessons?	**Mohu si zaplatit hodiny?** *mohooh sih zapla-tyit ho-dyi-nih*
Do you have a fitness room?	**Máte tělocvičnu?** *mah-teh tye-lots-vich-nooh*
Can I join in?	**Mohu se přidat?** *mohooh seh przhi-dat*

Je mi líto, máme obsazeno.	I'm sorry. We're booked up.
Platí se záloha …	There is a deposit of …
Jakou máte velikost?	What size are you?
Budete potřebovat pasovou fotografii.	You need a passport-size photo.

ŠATNY	changing rooms

115

Swimming Plavání

Although landlocked, the Czech Republic has a number of man-made river dams that serve as popular recreational areas. Accommodations in nearby vacation chalets are usually available.

Is there a … here?	**Je tu blízko …?** *yeh tooh blees-ko'*
children's pool	**dětský bazén** *dyets-kee bazehn*
swimming pool	**bazén** *bazehn*
indoor/open-air	**krytý/venkovní** *kri-tee/ven-kov-nyee*
Is it safe to swim/dive here?	**Dá se tady bezpečně plavat/skákat do vody?** *dah seh tadih bes-pech-nyeh plavat/skah-kat do-vodih*
Is it safe for children?	**Je to bezpečné pro děti?** *yeh to' bes-pech-neh pro-dye-tyih*
Is there a lifeguard?	**Je tady plavčík?** *yeh tadih pluf-cheek*
I want to rent a/some …	**Chtěl(a) bych si půjčit …** *khytyel(a) bikh sih puhye'-chit*
deck chair	**skládací lehátko** *sklah-da-tsee le-hah-tko'*
motorboat	**motorový člun** *motorovee chloon*
rowboat	**lodičku** *lo-dyich-kooh*
umbrella [sunshade]	**slunečník** *sloo-nech-nyeek*
water skis	**vodní lyže** *vod-nyee li-zheh*
for … hours	**na … hodin** *na … ho-dyin*

116

Skiing Lyžování

There are many small ski resorts in the mountains that encircle the country as well as in the inland regions. They are particularly good for beginners and cross-country skiers as the slopes are generally not too steep.

Is there much snow?	**Je tam hodně sněhu?** *yeh tum hod-nyeh snye-hooh*
What's the snow like?	**Jaký je sníh?** *yukee yeh snyeekh*
heavy/icy	**těžký/zledovatělý** *tyezh-kee/zledova-tye-lee*
powdery/wet	**prachový/mokrý** *pra-kho-vee/mok-ree*
I'd like to rent some …	**Chtěl(a) bych si půjčit …** *khutyel(a) bikh sih puhye'-chit*
poles	**hole** *holeh*
skates	**brusle** *broos-leh*
ski boots	**lyžařské boty** *li-zharzh-skeh botih*
skis	**lyže** *lizheh*
These are too …	**Tyhle jsou moc …** *ty-hleh yesoh mots*
big/small	**velké/malé** *velkeh/maleh*
They're uncomfortable.	**Nejsou pohodlné.** *ne-yesoh poho-dul-neh*
A lift pass for a day/five days, please.	**Permanentku na vlek na den/na pět dní, prosím.** *per-ma-nent-kooh na-vlek na-den/na-pyet dnyee proseem*
I'd like to join the ski school.	**Chtěl(a) bych se zapsat do lyžařské školy.** *khutyel(a) bikh seh zapsat do-li-zharzh-skeh shko-lih*
I'm a beginner. *(masc./fem.)*	**Jsem začátečník/začátečnice.** *yesem zachah-tech-nyeek/ zachah-tech-nyi-tseh*
I'm experienced. *(masc./fem.)*	**Jsem zkušený lyžař/zkušená lyžařka.** *yesem skoo-she-nee li-zharzh/ skoo-she-nah li-zharzh-ka*

LANOVKA	cable car/gondola
SEDAČKOVÝ VLEK	chair lift
LYŽAŘSKÝ VLEK	drag lift

Making friends Seznamujeme se

Greetings vary according to how well you know someone. It is polite to shake hands when you meet and again on leaving; men shake hands first with women and then with men. When addressing relations and close friends, the intimate form of "you" (**ty**, with the verb in singular) and the person's first name is used; colleagues are usually addressed by their first name and the polite form of "you" (**vy**, and the verb in plural). All other people are addressed as Mr./Mrs. (**pane/paní**), with their surname or academic title and the polite form of "you" (**vy**, and the verb in plural), until you are invited to use a more familiar form.

The use of the academic title is worth noting. People in various professions are awarded special titles upon graduation from university-level establishments, such as **JUDr.** for lawyers, **MUDr.** for doctors, and **Ing** for technical specialists. These titles, or their shorter versions (**doktor** for **JUDr.** or **MUDr.**), are used in day-to-day communication. For example, it is normal to address your doctor or lawyer as "Mr. Doctor" (**pane doktore**).

Hello. We haven't met.	**Dobrý den. My se ještě neznáme.** *dob-ree den. mih seh yesh-tyeh nez-nah-meh*
My name is …	**Jmenuji se …** *yeme-noo-yih seh*
May I introduce …?	**Dovolte, abych vám představil(a) …** *dovolteh abikh vahm przhet-stavil(a)*
Pleased to meet you.	**Těší mě.** *tye-shee myeh*
What's your name?	**Jak se jmenujete?** *yuk seh yeme-noo-yeteh*
How are you?	**Jak se máte?** *yuk seh mah-teh*
Fine, thanks. And you?	**Dobře, děkuji. A vy?** *dob-rzheh dyekoo-yeih. a vih*

– Dobrý den. Jak se máte?
(Hello. How are you?)

– *Dobře, děkuji. A vy?*
(Fine, thanks. And you?)

– Dobře, děkuji.
(Fine, thanks.)

Where are you from? Odkud jste?

Where are you from?	**Odkud jste?** *ot-koot yesteh*
Where were you born?	**Kde jste se narodil(a)?** *gdeh yesteh seh naro-dyil(a)*
I'm from …	**Jsem z(e) …** *yesem z(eh)*
Australia	**Austrálie** *a-oos-trah-li-yeh*
Britain	**Británie** *bri-tah-ni-yeh*
Canada	**Kanady** *kanadih*
England	**Anglie** *an-gli-yeh*
Ireland	**Irska** *irs-ka*
Scotland	**Skotska** *skots-ka*
the U.S.	**Spojených států** *spo-ye-neekh stah-tuh*
Wales	**Walesu** *veyel-sooh*
Where do you live?	**Kde žijete?** *gdeh zhi-ye-teh*
What part of (the) … are you from?	**Z které části … jste?** *sukte-reh chah-styih … yesteh*
Czech Republic	**České republiky** *ches-keh re-poo-blikih*
Poland/Germany	**Polska/Německa** *pols-ka/nye-mets-ka*
Austria/Slovakia	**Rakouska/Slovenska** *ra-koh-ska/slo-vens-ka*
We come here every year.	**Jezdíme sem každý rok.** *yez-dyee-meh sem kuzh-dee rok*
It's my/our first visit.	**Jsem/Jsme tady poprvé.** *yesem/yesmeh tadih po-pr-veh*
Have you ever been to …?	**Byl(a/i) jste někdy v …?** *bil(a/ih) yesteh nyeg-dih v*
the U.K./U.S.	**Británii/Spojených státech** *bri-tah-ni-yih/spo-ye-neekh stah-tekh*
Do you like it here?	**Líbí se vám tady?** *lee-bee seh vahm tadih*
What do you think of the …?	**Co si myslíte o …?** *tso' sih mis-leeteh o'*
I love the food here.	**Moc mi tady chutná jídlo.** *mots mih tadih khoot-nah yeed-lo'*
I love the people here.	**Moc se mi tady líbí lidé.** *mots seh mih tadih lee-bee li-deh*
I don't really like the food here.	**Moc mi tady nechutná jídlo.** *mots mi tadih ne-khoot-nah yeed-lo'*
I don't really like the people here.	**Moc se mi tady nelíbí lidé.** *mots seh mih tadih ne-lee-bee li-deh*

Who are you with? S kým tady jste?

Who are you with?	**S kým tady jste?**	*skeem tadih yesteh*
I'm on my own.	**Jsem tady sám(sama).**	
	yesem tadih sahm(samah)	
I'm with a friend. *(masc./fem.)*	**Jsem tady s přítelem/s přítelkyní.**	*yesem tadih suprzhee-telem/ suprzhee-tel-ki-nyee*
I'm with my …	**Jsem tady s(e) …**	*yesem tadih s(eh)*
husband/wife	**manželem/manželkou**	*man-zhelem/man-zhel-koh*
family	**rodinou**	*ro-dyi-noh*
children/parents	**dětmi/rodiči**	*dyet-mih/ro-dyi-chih*
boyfriend/girlfriend	**přítelem/přítelkyní**	*przhee-telem/przhee-tel-ki-nyee*
father/son	**otcem/synem**	*ot-tsem/sinem*
mother/daughter	**matkou/dcerou**	*mut-koh/tse-roh*
brother/uncle	**bratrem/strýcem**	*brat-rem/stree-tsem*
sister/aunt	**sestrou/tetou**	*ses-troh/tetoh*
What's your son's/ wife's name?	**Jak se jmenuje váš syn/vaše manželka?**	*yuk seh yemenoo-yeh vah-sh sin/va-sheh man-zhel-ka*
Are you married? *(to a man/woman)*	**Jste ženatý/vdaná?**	*yesteh zhena-tee/vda-nah*
I'm married. *(for man/woman)*	**Jsem ženatý/vdaná.**	*yesem zhenatee/vda-nah*
I'm single. *(for man/woman)*	**Jsem svobodný/svobodná.**	*yesem svobod-nee/svobod-nah*
I'm divorced. *(for man/woman)*	**Jsem rozvedený/rozvedená.**	*yesem roz-vedenee/roz-vedenah*
I'm engaged. *(for man/woman)*	**Jsem zasnoubený/zasnoubená.**	*yesem zas-noh-benee/zas-noh-benah*
We live together.	**Žijeme spolu.**	*zhi-yemeh spo-looh*
Do you have any children?	**Máte děti?**	*mah-teh dye-tyih*
We have two boys and a girl.	**Máme dva chlapce a děvče.**	*mah-meh dva khlap-tseh ah dyev-cheh*
How old are they?	**Kolik je jim let?**	*kolik yeh yim let*
They're ten and twelve.	**Je jim deset a dvanáct.**	*yeh yim deset ah dva-nah-tsut*

What do you do? Čím jste?

What do you do?	**Čím jste?** *cheem yesteh*
What are you studying?	**Co studujete?** *tso' stoo-doo-yeteh*
I'm studying …	**Studuji …** *stoo-doo-yih*
I'm in …	**Věnuji se …** *vye-noo-yih seh*
business	**podnikání** *pod-nyi-kah-nyee*
engineering	**strojírenství** *stro-yee-rens-tvee*
sales	**odbytu** *od-bi-tooh*
Who do you work for …?	**Pro koho pracujete …?** *pro' koho' pra-tsoo-yeteh*
I work for …	**Pracuji pro …** *pra-tsoo-yih pro'*
I'm (a/an) …	**Jsem …** *yesem*
accountant	**účetní** *uh-chet-nyee*
housewife	**v domácnosti** *vdo-mahts-nos-tyih*
student	**student(-ka)** *stoo-dent(-kah)*
retired	**v důchodu** *vduh-kho-dooh*
self-employed	**soukromník** *soh-krom-nyeek*
between jobs	**právě bez zaměstnání** *prah-vyeh bez-za-myest-nah-nyee*
What are your interests/ hobbies?	**Jaké máte zájmy/koníčky?** *yukeh mah-teh zahye'-mih/ko-nyeech-kih*
I like …	**Mám rád(a) …** *mahm raht(rah-da)*
music	**hudbu** *hood-booh*
reading	**knihy** *knyi-hih*
sports	**sport** *sport*
I play …	**Hraji …** *hra-yih*
Would you like to play …?	**Chtěl(a) byste si zahrát …?** *khutyel(a) bis-teh sih za-hraht*
cards	**karty** *kartih*
chess	**šachy** *sha-khih*

What weather! To počasí!

What a lovely day!	**Dnes je ale krásně!** *dnes yeh aleh krahs-nyeh*
What terrible weather!	**Dnes je ale hrozné počasí!** *dnes yeh aleh hroz-neh po-cha-see*
It's hot/cold today!	**Dnes je horko/zima!** *dnes yeh horko'/zima*
Is it usually this warm?	**Je normálně tak horko?** *yeh nor-mahl-nyeh tak horko'*
Do you think it's going to … tomorrow?	**Myslíte, že zítra bude …?** *mis-lee-teh zheh zeet-ra boodeh*
be a nice day	**hezky** *hes-kih*
rain	**pršet** *pr-shet*
snow	**sněžit** *snye-zhit*
What's the weather forecast for tomorrow?	**Jaká je na zítra předpověď počasí?** *yukah yeh na-zeet-ra przhet-po-vyetye' pocha-see*
It's …	**Bude …** *boo-deh*
cloudy	**zamračeno** *za-mra-che-no'*
foggy	**mlha** *mul-ha*
frosty/icy	**mráz** *mrahs*
stormy	**bouřka** *boh-rzhuka*
windy	**vítr** *veetr*
It's raining.	**Prší.** *prshee*
It's snowing.	**Sněží.** *snye-zhee*
It's sunny.	**Svítí slunce.** *svee-tyee sloon-tseh*
Has the weather been like this for long?	**Už tohle počasí trvá dlouho?** *oozh to-hleh pocha-see trvah dloh-ho'*
What's the pollen count?	**Jaká je hladina pylu?** *yukah yeh hla-dyi-na pi-looh*
high/medium/low	**vysoká/střední/nízká** *viso-kah/sutrzhed-nyee/nyees-kah*
Will it be good weather for skiing?	**Bude hezky na lyžování?** *boo-deh hes-kih na-li-zho-vah-nyee*

PŘEDPOVĚĎ POČASÍ   weather forecast

122

Enjoying your trip? Líbí se vám tady?

Jste na dovolené?	Are you on vacation?
Jak jste sem přijel(a)?	How did you get here?
Kde jste ubytovaný(á)?	Where are you staying?
Jak už jste tady dlouho?	How long have you been here?
Jak dlouho tady budete?	How long are you staying?
Co jste zde zatím dělal(a)?	What have you done so far?
Kam jedete potom?	Where are you going next?
Líbí se vám tady?	Are you enjoying your vacation?

I'm here on …	**Jsem tady …** *yesem tadih*
business	**služebně** *sloo-zheb-nyeh*
vacation [holiday]	**na dovolené** *na-do-vo-leneh*
We came by …	**Přijeli jsme …** *przhi-ye-lih yesmeh*
train/bus/plane	**vlakem/autobusem/letadlem** *vlakem/ow-to-boo-sem/letad-lem*
car	**autem** *ow-tem*
I have a rental [hire] car.	**Mám auto z půjčovny.** *mahm ow-to' zupuh-ye'-chov-nih*
We're staying in/at …	**Bydlíme …** *bid-leemeh*
a campsite	**v kempu** *fkem-pooh*
a guest house/pension	**v penziónu** *fpen-zi-aunooh*
a hotel	**v hotelu** *vhote-looh*
a youth hostel	**v mládežnické ubytovně** *vmlah-dezh-nyits-keh oobi-tov-nyeh*
with friends	**u přátel** *oo-przhah-tel*
Can you suggest …?	**Můžete mi doporučit …?** *muh-zheteh mih dopo-roo-chit*
things to do	**nějakou činnost** *nye-yukoh chinost*
places to eat	**kde se najíst** *gdeh seh na-yeest*
places to visit	**kam se podívat** *kum se po-dyee-vat*
We're having a great time.	**Máme se skvěle.** *mah-meh seh skvye-leh*
We're having a terrible time.	**Nelíbí se nám tady.** *ne-leebee seh nahm tadih*

Invitations Pozvání

Would you like to have dinner with us on …?	**Přišli byste k nám v … na večeři?** *przhi-shlih bis-teh knahm v … na-ve-che-rzhih*
Are you free for lunch?	**Mohu vás pozvat na oběd?** *mohooh vahs pozvat na-obyet*
Can you come for a drink this evening?	**Můžete dnes večer přijít na skleničku?** *muh-zheteh dnes vecher przhi-yeet na-skle-nyich-kooh*
We're having a party. Can you come?	**Budeme mít večírek. Můžete přijít?** *boo-demeh meet ve-chee-rek. muh-zheteh purzhi-yeet*
May we join you?	**Můžeme se k vám připojit?** *muh-zhemeh seh kvahm przhi-po-yit*
Would you like to join us?	**Chcete se k nám připojit?** *khutseteh seh knahm przhi-po-yit*

Going out Volný čas

What are your plans for …?	**Jaké máte plány na …?** *yukeh mah-teh plah-nih na*
today / tonight	**dnešek/dnes večer** *dne-shek/dnes vecher*
tomorrow	**zítra** *zeet-ra*
Are you free this evening?	**Máte dnes večer volno?** *mah-teh dnes vecher volno'*
Would you like to …?	**Chtěl(a) byste jít …?** *khutyel(a) bis-teh yeet*
go dancing	**tančit** *tun-chit*
go for a drink	**na skleničku** *na-skle-nyich-kooh*
go out for a meal	**na večeři** *na-ve-che-rzhih*
go for a walk	**na procházku** *na-pro-khahs-kooh*
go shopping	**nakupovat** *na-koo-povat*
I'd like to go to …	**Chtěl(a) bych jít do/na …** *khutyel(a) bikh yeet do'/na*
I'd like to see …	**Chtěl(a) bych vidět …** *khutyel(a) bikh vi-dyet*
Do you enjoy …?	**Máte rád(a) …?** *mah-teh raht(rah-da)*

Accepting/Declining Přijetí/Odmítnutí

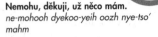

Thank you. I'd love to. **Děkuji. Velice rád(a).**
dyekoo-yeih. veli-tseh raht(rah-da)

Thank you, but I'm busy. **Nemohu, děkuji, už něco mám.**
(*ne-mohooh dyekoo-yeih oozh nye-tso' mahm*

May I bring a friend? **Mohu přijít s přítelem/přítelkyní?**
(*man/woman*) *mohooh przhi-yeet su przhee-telem/ przhee-tel-ki-nyee*

Where shall we meet? **Kde se setkáme?**
gdeh seh set-kah-meh

I'll meet you … **Počkám na vás …**
poch-kahm na-vahs

in front of your hotel **před hotelem** *przhet ho-telem*

I'll pick you up at 8. **Přijdu pro vás v osm.**
przhiye'-dooh pro-vahs vosum

Could we make it a bit **Šlo by to o něco později/dříve?**
later/earlier? *Shlo' bih to' o-nye-tso' poz-dye-yih/ drzhee-veh*

How about another day? **Šlo by to někdy jindy?**
shlo' bih to' nyeg-dih yind-dih

That will be fine. **To mi vyhovuje.**
to' mih vi-hovoo-yeh

Dining out/in Večeře v restauraci/doma

If invited to have drinks and/or dinner in someone's home, it is
customary to bring flowers for the hostess.

Let me buy you a drink. **Mohu vám objednat něco k pití?**
mohooh vahm ob-yed-nut nye-tso' kupi-tyee

Do you like …? **Chcete …?** *khutse-teh*

What are you going to have? **Co si dáte?** *tso' sih dah-teh*

That was a lovely lunch/dinner. **To byl(a) výborný oběd/výborná večeře.**
to' bil(a) vee-bor-nee ob-yet/vee-bor-nah ve-che-rzheh

Encounters Setkání

Do you mind if …?	**Bude vám vadit, když …?** *boo-deh vahm va-dyit gdizh*
I sit here / I smoke	**si tu sednu / si zapálím** *sih tooh sed-nooh / sih za-pah-leem*
Can I get you a drink?	**Mohu vám objednat něco k pití?** *mohooh* *vahm ob-yed-nut nye-tso' kupi-tyee*
I'd love to have some company.	**Budu vděčný(á) za společnost.** *bo-dooh vdyech-nee(ah) za-spo-lech-nost*
What's so funny?	**Co je vám k smíchu?** *tso' yeh vahm kusmee-khooh*
Is my Czech that bad?	**Mluvím česky tak špatně?** *mloo-veem ches-kih tuk shput-nyeh*
Shall we go somewhere quieter?	**Půjdeme někam do tiššího prostředí?** *puhye'-demeh nye-kum do-tyi-shee-ho' pro-sutrzhe-dyee*
Leave me alone, please!	**Nechte mě, prosím!** *nekh-teh myeh proseem*
You look great!	**Vypadáte báječně!** *vi-pa-dah-teh bah-yech-nyeh*
Would you like to come home with me?	**Chcete jít ke mně domů?** *khutse-teh yeet ke-mnyeh do-muh*
I'm not ready for that.	**Na to je ještě moc brzy.** *na-to' yeh yesh-tyeh mots brzih*
I'm afraid we have to leave now.	**Je mi líto, ale už opravdu musíme jít.** *yeh mih lee-to' aleh oozh oprav-dooh moo-see-meh yeet*
Thank you for the evening. *(singular/plural)*	**Děkuji/děkujeme za příjemný večer.** *dyekoo-yeih/dyekoo-yemeh za-przhee-yem-nee ve-cher*
It was great.	**Bylo to skvělé.** *bilo' to' skvye-leh*
Can I see you again tomorrow?	**Mohli bychom se zítra zase setkat?** *mohlih bi-khom seh zeet-ra zaseh set-kut*
See you soon.	**Brzy na shledanou.** *brzih na-sukhle-danoh*
Can I have your address?	**Dáte mi adresu?** *dah-teh mih adre-sooh*

SAFETY ➤ 65

Telephoning Telefonování

Calls can be made from public coin-/card-operated telephones in the street, in subway [metro] stations, and bus and train stations. To phone home from the Czech Republic, dial 00 followed by: 61, Australia; 1, Canada; 353, Ireland; 64, New Zealand; 27, South Africa; 44, the U.K.; 1, the U.S.

Can I have your telephone number?	**Dáte mi vaše telefonní číslo?** *dah-teh mih va-sheh tele-fo-nyee chees-lo'*
Here's my number.	**Tady je moje číslo.** *tadih yeh mo-yeh chees-lo'*
Please call me.	**Zavolejte mi.** *zavo-leye'-teh mih*
I'll give you a call.	**Zavolám vám.** *zavo-lahm vahm*
Where's the nearest telephone booth?	**Kde je nejbližší telefonní budka?** *gdeh yeh neye'bli-shee tele-fo-nyee boot-ka*
May I use your phone?	**Mohu si od vás zatelefonovat?** *mohooh sih ot-vahs zatele-fonovat*
It's an emergency.	**Je to naléhavé.** *yeh to' na-leh-ha-veh*
I'd like to call someone in England.	**Chtěl(a) bych zavolat někomu v Anglii.** *khutyel(a) bikh zavolat nye-komooh van-gli-yih*
What's the area [dialling] code for …?	**Jaké je směrové číslo na …?** *yukeh yeh smye-ro-veh chee-slo' na*
I'd like a phone card, please.	**Chtěl(a) bych telefonní kartu.** *khutyel(a) bikh tele-fo-nyee kar-tooh*
What's the number for Information [Directory Enquiries]?	**Jaké číslo mají telefonní informace?** *yukeh chee-slo' ma-yee tele-fo-nyee in-for-ma-tseh*
I'd like the number for …	**Chtěl(a) bych číslo na …** *khytyel(a) bikh chee-slo' na*
I'd like to call collect [reverse the charges].	**Chtěl(a) bych hovor na účet volaného.** *khytyel(a) bikh hovor na-uh-chet vola-neh-ho'*

Speaking Hovor

Hello. This is …	**Dobrý den. Tady je …** *dob-ree den. tadih yeh*
I'd like to speak to …	**Chtěl(a) bych mluvit s …** *khytyel(a) bikh mloo-vit s*
Extension …	**Linka …** *lin-ka*
Speak louder, please.	**Mluvte hlasitěji, prosím.** *mloof-teh hla-si-tye-yih proseem*
Speak more slowly, please.	**Mluvte pomaleji, prosím.** *mloof-teh poma-le-yih proseem*
Could you repeat that, please?	**Mohl(a) byste to zopakovat?** *mohul(a) bis-teh to' zo-pa-kovat*
I'm afraid he's/she's not in.	**Bohužel tady není.** *bo-hoo-zhel tadih ne-nyee*
You have the wrong number.	**Máte špatné číslo.** *mah-teh shput-neh chees-lo'*
Just a moment, please.	**Okamžik, prosím.** *okam-zhik proseem*
Hold on, please.	**Počkejte chvilku, prosím.** *poch-keye'-teh khuvil-kooh proseem*
When will he/she be back?	**Kdy se vrátí?** *gdih seh vrah-tyee*
Will you tell him/her that I called?	**Řekněte mu/jí prosím, že jsem volal(a).** *rzhek-nye-teh mooh/yee proseem zheh yesem volal(a).*
My name is …	**Jmenuji se …** *yeme-noo-yih seh*
Would you ask him/her to call me?	**Mohl(a) byste mu/jí říci, aby mi zavolal(a)?** *mohul(a) bis-teh mooh/yee rzhee-tsih abih mih zavo-lal(a)*
I must go now.	**Už musím končit.** *oozh moo-seem kon-chit*
Thank you for calling.	**Děkuji za zavolání.** *dyekoo-yeih za-za-volah-nyee*
I'll be in touch.	**Zase se ozvu.** *zaseh seh oz-vooh*
Bye.	**Na shledanou.** *na-sukhle-da-noh*

128

Stores & Services

Supermarkets and small food stores usually accept cash payments only. However, an increasing number of department and other stores take credit cards.

ESSENTIAL

I'd like …	**Chtěl(a) bych …** khutyel(a) bikh
Do you have …?	**Máte …?** mah-teh
How much is that?	**Kolik to stojí?** kolik to' sto-yee
Thank you.	**Děkuji.** dey-koo-yih

OTEVŘENO	open
ZAVŘENO	closed
VÝPRODEJ	sale

Stores and services
Obchody a služby

Where is …? Kde je …?

Where's the nearest …?	**Kde je nejbližší …?** *gdeh yeh neye'-bli-shee*
Is there a good …?	**Je tady dobrý …?** *yeh tadih dob-ree*
Where's the main shopping mall [centre]?	**Kde je hlavní obchodní centrum?** *gdeh yeh hlav-nyee op-khod-nyee tsen-troom*
Is it far from here?	**Je to odtud daleko?** *yeh to' ot-tood daleko'*
How do I get there?	**Jak se tam dostanu?** *yuk seh tum dos-tanooh*

Stores Obchody

bakery	**pekařství** *pekarzh-sutvee*
bank	**banka** *bun-ka*
bookstore	**knihy** *knyi-hih*
butcher	**řezník** *rzhez-nyeek*
camera store	**fotoaparáty** *foto-apa-rah-tih*
cigarette kiosk [tobacconist]	**tabák** *tabahk*
clothing store [clothes shop]	**oděvy** *odye-vih*
convenience store	**potraviny** *potra-vinih*
department store	**obchodní dům** *op-khod-nyee duhm*
drugstore	**drogerie** *drogeri-yeh*
fish and poultry store	**ryby a drůbež** *ribih a druh-bezh*
florist	**květiny** *kvye-tyi-nih*

gift store	**dárky** *dahr-kih*
greengrocer	**ovoce a zelenina** *ovotseh a zelenyina*
health food store	**zdravá výživa** *zdra-vah veezhiva*
jeweler	**klenoty** *klenotih*
liquor store [off-licence]	**víno a lihoviny** *veeno' a li-hovinih*
music store	**gramofonové desky** *gramofonoveh deskih*
newsstand [newsagent]	**noviny** *novinih*
pastry shop	**cukrárna** *tsook-rahrna*
pharmacy [chemist]	**lékárna** *leh-kahrna*
shoe store	**obuv** *oboof*
souvenir store	**suvenýry** *soove-neerih*
sporting goods store	**sportovní potřeby** *spor-tov-nyee pot-rzhebih*
supermarket	**samoobsluha** *samo-op-sloo-ha*
toy store	**hračky** *hruch-kih*

Services Služby

clinic	**zdravotní středisko** *zdra-vot-nyee sutrzhe-dyis-ko'*
dentist	**zubař** *zoo-barzh*
doctor	**lékař** *leh-karzh*
dry cleaner	**čistírna** *chis-tyeer-na*
hairdresser/barber	**kadeřnictví/holičství** *kaderzh-nyits-tvee/holich-sutvee*
hospital	**nemocnice** *nemots-nyitseh*
laundromat	**prádelna** *prah-delna*
optician	**optika** *optika*
police station	**policejní stanice** *poli-tseye'-nyee sta-nyitseh*
post office	**pošta** *posh-ta*
travel agency	**cestovní kancelář** *tses-tov-nyee kan-tselah-rzh*

Opening hours Otvírací doba

Stores are generally open from 8 a.m. to 6 p.m. Monday through Friday, and on Saturdays from 8 a.m. to 12 noon. Tourist stores and currency exchanges [bureaux de change], particularly in Prague, are open late. Some are also open on Sundays.

When does the … open/close?	**Kdy … otvírá/zavírá?** gdih … ot-feerah/zaveerah
Are you open in the evening?	**Máte otevřeno večer?** mah-teh otev-rzheno' vecher
Where's the …?	**Kde je …?** gdeh yeh
cashier [cash desk]	**pokladna** pok-lud-na
escalator	**eskalátor** eska-lah-tor
elevator [lift]	**výtah** veetah
store directory [guide]	**informační tabule** infor-much-nyee tabooleh
It's in the basement.	**Je to v suterénu.** yeh to' vsoo-tereh-nooh
It's on the …	**Je to …** yeh to'
first [ground (Brit.)] floor	**v přízemí** vuprzhee-zemee
second [first (Brit.)] floor	**v prvním poschodí** vupr-vnyeem pos-kho-dyee
Where's the … department?	**Kde je oddělení …?** gdeh yeh od-dyelenyee

OTVÍRACÍ DOBA	business [opening] hours
VCHOD	entrance
ESKALÁTOR	escalator
VÝCHOD	exit
NOUZOVÝ VÝCHOD	emergency/fire exit
VÝTAH	elevator [lift]
SCHODIŠTĚ	stairs
W.C./TOALETY	restroom

Service Obsluha

Can you help me?

Můžete mi pomoci?
muh-zheteh mih pomotsih

I'm looking for ...

Potřebuji ...
potrzhe-boo-yeih

I'm just browsing.

Jen se dívám. *yen seh dyee-vahm*

It's my turn.

Je řada na mně.
yeh rzhada na-mnyeh

Do you have any ...?

Máte ...? *mah-teh*

I'd like to buy ...

Chtěl(a) bych si koupit ...
khutyel(a) bikh sih koh-pit

Could you show me ...?

Můžete mi ukázat ...?
muh-zheteh mih ookah-zat

How much is that?

Kolik to stojí? *kolik to' sto-yee*

That's all, thanks.

To je všechno, děkuji.
to' yeh vshekh-no' dyekoo-yeih

Dobré den/dobré odpoledne.	Good morning/afternoon.
Co byste si přál(a)?/Přejete si?	Can I help you?
Počkejte chvilku, podívám se.	I'll just check that for you.
Bude to všechno?	Is that everything?
Něco dalšího?	Anything else?

– *Přejete si? (Can I help you?)*

– Děkuji. Jen se dívám.
(No thanks. I'm just browsing.)

– *Dobře. (Fine.)*

– Promiňte, prosím. (Excuse me.)

– *Ano, co byste si přál(a)?*
(Yes, can I help you?)

– Kolik to stojí? (How much is that?)

– *Počkejte chvilku, podívám se. ...*
Stojí to pět set padesát korun.
(Um, I'll just check. ... That's 550 korun.)

SAMOOBSLUHA	self-service
VÝPRODEJ	clearance

Preferences Výběr

I want something …	**Chtěl(a) bych něco …** *khutyel(a) bikh nyetso'*
big/small	**velkého/malého** *velkeh-ho/maleh-ho*
cheap/expensive	**levného/drahého** *levneh-ho/draheh-ho*
dark/light (color)	**tmavého/světlého** *tmaveh-ho/svyet-leh-ho*
light/heavy	**lehkého/těžkého** *leh-keh-ho/tyezh-keh-ho*
oval/round/square	**oválného/kulatého/čtvercového** *ovahl-neh-ho/koolateh-ho/* *chutuver-tsoveh-ho*
It must be genuine.	**Musí to být originál.** *moo-see to' beet originahl*
I don't want anything too expensive.	**Nechci nic moc drahého.** *nekh-tsih nyits mots draheh-ho'*
In the region of 400 korun.	**Asi kolem čtyř set korun.** *asih kolem chutirzh set koroon*

Jakou barvu/jaký tvar byste chtěl(a)?	What color/shape would you like?
Jakou kvalitu/jaké množství byste chtěl(a)?	What quality/quantity would you like?
Kolik byste jich chtěl(a)?	How many would you like?
Jaký druh byste chtěl(a)?	What sort would you like?
V jakém cenovém rozmezí?	What price range are you thinking of?

Do you have anything …?	**Máte něco …?** *mah-teh nyetso'*
larger/smaller	**většího/menšího** *vyet-sheeho'/men-sheeho'*
better quality	**kvalitnějšího** *kvalit-nyey'-sheeho'*
cheaper	**levnějšího** *lev-nyey'-sheeho'*
Could you show me …?	**Můžete mi ukázat …?** *muh-zheteh mih ookah-zat*
this one/these	**tenhle/tyhle** *ten-hleh/ti-hleh*
that one/those	**tamten/tamty** *tum-ten/tum-tih*
the one in the window/ display case	**ten ve výloze/ve vitríně** *ten ve-veelozeh/ve-vit-ree-nyeh*
some others	**nějaké jiné** *nye-yukeh yeineh*

Conditions of purchase Nákupní podmínky

Is there a guarantee?
Je na to záruka?
yeh na-to' zah-rooka

Are there any instructions with it?
Je k tomu návod?
yeh kuto-mooh nah-vot

Out of stock Vyprodáno

Je mi líto. Žádné nemáme.	I'm sorry. We don't have any.
Je to vyprodané.	We're out of stock.
Mohu vám ukázat něco jiného/ podobného?	Can I show you something else / a different kind?
Chcete, abychom vám to objednali?	Shall we order it for you?

Can you order it for me?
Můžete mi to objednat?
muh-zheteh mih to' ob-yed-nut

How long will it take?
Jak dlouho to bude trvat?
yuk dloh-ho' to' boodeh tr-vat

Decisions Rozhodnutí

That's not quite what I want.
Není to úplně ono.
nenyee to' uh-pul-nyeh ono'

No, I don't like it.
Ne, to se mi nelíbí.
neh to' seh mih ne-leebee

That's too expensive.
To je moc drahé. *to' yeh mots draheh*

I'd like to think about it.
Ještě si to rozmyslím.
yesh-tyeh sih to' roz-mis-leem

I'll take it.
Vezmu si to. *vez-mooh sih to'*

– Dobrý den. Potřebuji koupit tričko.
(Good morning. I'm looking for a sweatshirt.)

– Jistě. Jakou barvu si přejete?
(Certainly. What color would you like?)

– Oranžovou. A chtěl(a) bych něco velkého.
(Orange. And I want something big.)

– Prosím. Stojí pět set padesát korun.
(Here you are. That's 550 korun.)

– Mmm, to není úplně ono. Děkuji.
(Hmm, that's not quite what I want. Thank you.)

Paying Placení

Sales tax [VAT], generally charged at a rate of 22 percent, is included in the price where appropriate.

Where do I pay?	**Kde zaplatím?** *gdeh zapla-tyeem*
How much is that?	**Kolik to stojí?** *kolik to' sto-yee*
Could you write it down, please?	**Můžete mi to napsat, prosím?** *muh-zheteh mih to' nap-sat proseem*
Do you accept traveler's checks [cheques]?	**Berete cestovní šeky?** *bereteh tses-tov-nyee shekih*
I'll pay by …	**Zaplatím …** *zaplatyeem*
cash	**hotově** *hotovyeh*
credit card	**kreditní kartou** *kredit-nyee kar-toh*
I don't have any smaller change.	**Nemám menší drobné.** *nemahm men-shee drob-neh*
Sorry, I don't have enough money.	**Promiňte, nemám dost peněz.** *prominye'-teh ne-mahm dost pe-nyez*
Could I have a receipt, please?	**Můžete mi dát stvrzenku, prosím?** *muh-zheteh mih daht sutvur-zen-kooh proseem*
I think you've given me the wrong change.	**Myslím, že jste mi nevrátil(a) správně.** *mis-leem zhe yesteh mih ne-vrah-tyil(a) sprah-vnyeh*

Jak budete platit?	How are you paying?
Nedostal(a) jsem autorizaci.	This transaction has not been approved / accepted.
Tahle karta je neplatná.	This card is not valid.
Máte ještě nějaký průkaz totožnosti?	May I have additional identification?
Nemáte menší drobné?	Do you have any smaller change?

POKLADNA   cashier [cash desk]

Complaints Stížnosti

This doesn't work.
Tohle nefunguje.
to-hleh ne-foon-goo-yeh

Can I exchange this?
Můžete mi to vyměnit?
muh-zheteh mih to' vi-mye-nyit

I'd like a refund.
Chtěl(a) bych vrátit peníze.
khutyel(a) bikh vrah-tyit pe-nyee-zeh

Here's the receipt.
Tady je stvrzenka.
tadih yeh sutvur-zen-ka

I don't have the receipt.
Nemám stvrzenku.
ne-mahm sutvur-zen-kooh

I'd like to see the manager.
Chtěl(a) bych mluvit s vedoucím.
khutye(a) bikh mloovit sve-doh-tseem

Repairs/Cleaning Opravy/Čistírna

This is broken. Can you repair it?
Je to rozbité. Můžete to opravit?
yeh to' roz-bi-teh. muh-zheteh to' opravit

Do you have … for this?
Máte k tomu …?
mah-teh kuto-mooh

a battery
baterii *bateri-yeih*

replacement parts
náhradní díly *nah-hrad-nyee dyee-lih*

There's something wrong with …
Něco se stalo s …
nye-tso' seh stalo' s

Can you … this?
Můžete to …? *muh-zheteh to'*

clean
vyčistit *vi-chis-tyit*

press
vyžehlit *vi-zhe-hlit*

patch
spravit *spravit*

Could you alter this?
Můžete to upravit?
muh-zheteh to' oopravit

When will it be ready?
Kdy to bude hotové?
gdih to' boodeh hotoveh

This isn't mine.
To není moje. *to' nenyee mo-yeh*

There's … missing.
Chybí na tom … *khibee na-tom*

TIME ➤ 220; DATES ➤ 218

Bank/Currency exchange
Banka/Směnárna

Banks are open from 8 a.m. to 6 p.m. Monday through Friday. A few major banks have cash machines, where you can get local currency using a major credit card. You will need your passport to exchange foreign currency at a bank; bank rates are usually better than those offered at currency exchange offices [bureaux de change] (**směnárna**) and hotels. Note: currency exchange kiosks on the streets mostly charge horrendous commission, sometimes up to 18 percent.

Where's the nearest …?	**Kde je nejbližší …?** *gdeh yeh neye'bli-shee*
bank	**banka** *bun-ka*
currency exchange office [bureau de change]	**směnárna** *smye-nahr-na*

Changing money Výměna peněz

Can I exchange foreign currency here?	**Mohu si tady vyměnit peníze?** *mohooh sih tadih vy-mye-nyit pe-nyee-zeh*
I'd like to change some dollars/pounds into korun.	**Chtěl(a) bych si vyměnit dolary/libry na koruny.** *khutyel(a) bikh sih vy-mye-nyit dolarih/lib-rih na-ko-roo-nih*
I want to cash some traveler's checks [cheques].	**Chtěl(a) bych si vyměnit cestovní šeky.** *khutyel(a) bikh sih vy-mye-nyit tses-tov-nyee shekih*
What's the exchange rate?	**Jaký je kurz?** *yukee yeh koors*
How much commission do you charge?	**Kolik si účtujete provizi?** *kolik sih uhch-too-yeteh provizih*
Could I have some small change, please?	**Mohu dostat mi dát drobné?** *mohooh dostat mih daht drob-neh*
I've lost my traveler's checks. These are the numbers.	**Ztratil(a) jsem cestovní šeky. Tady jsou jejich čísla.** *stra-tyil(a) yesem tses-tov-nyee shekih. tadih yesoh ye-yikh chees-la*

SMĚNÁRNA	currency exchange
OTEVŘENO/ZAVŘENO	open/closed
POKLADNA	cashiers [cash desk]

Security Bezpečnost

Ukažte mi laskavě ...	Could I see ...?
pas	your passport
průkaz totožnosti	some identification
bankovní kartu	your bank card
Jakou máte adresu?	What's your address?
Kde bydlíte?	Where are you staying?
Vyplňte tento formulář.	Fill out this form, please.
Tady se podepište.	Please sign here.

ATMs [Cash machines] Bankomaty

Can I withdraw money on my credit card here?	**Mohu si tady vybrat peníze na kreditní kartu?** *mohooh sih tadih vibrat pe-nyee-zeh na-kredit-nyee kar-tooh*
Where are the ATMs [cash machines]?	**Kde jsou bankomaty?** *gdeh yesoh bun-komatih*
Can I use my ... card in the cash machine?	**Mohu v bankomatu použít ... kartu?** *mohooh vbun-koma-tooh po-oozheet ... kar-tooh*
The cash machine has eaten my card.	**Bankomat mi nevrátil kartu.** *bun-komat mih ne-vrah-tyil kar-tooh*

BANKOMAT	automated teller (ATM) [cash machine]

The monetary unit is the **česká koruna** (**kč**), the Czech koruna (*plural korun*), which is divided into 100 **haléřů** (**h**), haleru (*singular haler*).

Banknotes: 20, 50, 100, 200, 500, 1,000, 2,000, and 5,000 korun (**Kč**)

Coins: 10, 20, and 50 haleru (**h**); 1, 2, 5, 10, and 20 korun (**Kč**)

Pharmacy Lékárna

Pharmacies (**lékárny**) keep normal business hours ➤ 132, but all large cities have a duty pharmacy with an emergency service. Several pharmacies in Prague are open 24 hours; their addresses and telephone numbers are usually displayed in all pharmacies. If you need help finding a pharmacy, ask at your hotel.

Where's the nearest (all-night) pharmacy?	**Kde je nejbližší (noční) lékárna?** *gdeh yeh neye'bli-shee (noch-nyee) leh-kahr-na*
When does the pharmacy open/close?	**Kdy lékárna otvírá/zavírá?** *gdih leh-kahr-na ot-fee-rah/zavee-rah*
Do you close for lunch?	**Zavíráte přes poledne?** *zaveerah-teh przhes poled-neh*
Can you make up this prescription for me?	**Můžete mi vydat léky na tento předpis?** *muh-zheteh mih vi-dut leh-kih na-ten-to' przhet-pis*
Should I wait?	**Mám si počkat?** *mahm sih poch-kat*
I'll come back for it.	**Přijdu si později.** *przhiye'-dooh poz-dye-yih*

Dosage instructions Dávkování

How much should I take?	**Kolik mám užívat?** *kolik mahm oozhee-vat*
How many times a day should I take it?	**Kolikrát denně to mám užívat?** *kolik-raht denyeh to' mahm oozhee-vat*
Is it suitable for children?	**Je to vhodné pro děti?** *yeh to' vhod-neh pro-dye-tyih*

Užívejte ...	Take ...
... tablety/ ... lžičky	... tablets/... teaspoons
před jídlem/po jídle	before meals/after meals
zapijte vodou	with water
celé	whole
ráno/večer	in the morning/at night
... dní	for ... days

DOCTOR ➤ 161

Asking advice Žádost o radu

I'd like some medicine for …	**Chtěl(a) bych nějaký lék na …** *khutyel(a) bikh nye-yukee lehk na*
a cold	**rýmu** *ree-mooh*
a cough	**kašel** *kashel*
diarrhea	**průjem** *pruh-yem*
a hangover	**kocovinu** *ko-tso-vinooh*
hay fever	**sennou rýmu** *se-noh ree-mooh*
insect bites	**štípance** *shtyee-pun-tseh*
a sore throat	**bolení v krku** *bole-nyee vurk-kooh*
sunburn	**spálení sluncem** *spah-le-nyee sloon-tsem*
motion [travel] sickness	**cestovní nemoc** *tses-tov-nyee nemots*
an upset stomach	**bolení břicha** *bole-nyee brzhi-kha*
Can I get it without a prescription?	**Je to k dostání bez předpisu?** *yeh to' gdos-tah-nyee bes-przhet-pi-sooh*
Can I have some …?	**Mohu dostat …?** *mohooh dos-tat*
antiseptic cream	**antiseptický krém** *un-ti-sep-tits-kee krehm*
aspirin	**aspirin** *us-pirin*
condoms	**kondom** *kon-dom*
cotton [cotton wool]	**vatu** *va-tooh*
gauze [bandages]	**obinadlo** *obi-nud-lo'*
insect repellent	**repelent proti hmyzu** *repelent protyih hmi-zooh*
painkillers	**lék proti bolesti** *lehk protyih bo-les-tyih*
band aid® [plasters]	**náplasti** *nah-plus-tyih*
vitamins	**vitamínové tablety** *vita-meenoveh tub-le-tih*

Toiletries Hygienické potřeby

I'd like some …	**Chtěl(a) bych …** *khutyel(a) bikh*
after-shave	**vodu po holení** *vo-dooh po-ho-le-nyee*
after-sun lotion	**olej po opalování** *oleye' po-opalo-vah-nyee*
deodorant	**deodorant** *de-odo-runt*
razor blades	**žiletky** *zhilet-kih*
sanitary napkins [towels]	**dámské vložky** *dahm-skeh vlosh-kih*
soap	**mýdlo** *meed-lo'*
sunscreen	**krém na opalování** *krehm na-opalovah-nyee*
factor …	**faktor …** *fuk-tor*
tampons	**tampony** *tum-ponih*
tissues	**papírové kapesníky** *papeeroveh ka-pes-nyee-kih*
toilet paper	**toaletní papír** *to-alet-nyee papeer*
toothpaste	**zubní pastu** *zoob-nyee pus-tooh*

Haircare Péče o vlasy

comb	**hřeben** *hurzhe-ben*
conditioner	**kondicionér** *kon-di-tsi-onehr*
hair mousse/gel	**pěna/gel na vlasy** *pyenah/gel na-vla-sih*
hair spray	**lak na vlasy** *luk na-vla-sih*
shampoo	**šampon** *shum-pon*

For the baby Pro kojence

baby food	**kojenecká výživa** *ko-yenets-kah vee-zhiva*
baby wipes	**navlhčené ubrousky** *na-vluh-che-neh oobroh-skih*
diapers [nappies]	**plenky** *plen-kih*
sterilizing solution	**sterilizační roztok** *ste-rili-zuch-nyee rostok*

Clothing Oděvy

Summers are hot and dry, so bring cotton clothing and light sweaters for the evening. Winter temperatures can dip to well below freezing, and snow is likely, so be prepared.

General Všeobecně

I'd like ...	**Chtěl(a) bych ...** *khutyel(a) bikh*
Do you have any ...?	**Máte ...?** *mah-teh*

DÁMSKÉ ODĚVY	ladieswear	
PÁNSKÉ ODĚVY	menswear	
DĚTSKÉ ODĚVY	childrenswear	

Color Barva

beige	**béžový** *beh-zhovee*
black	**černý** *chernee*
blue	**modrý** *modree*
brown	**hnědý** *hnyedee*
gray	**šedý** *shedee*
green	**zelený** *zelenee*
orange	**oranžový** *oran-zhovee*
pink	**růžový** *ruh-zhovee*
purple	**fialový** *fi-alovee*
red	**červený** *cher-venee*
white	**bílý** *beelee*
yellow	**žlutý** *zhloo-tee*
light ...	**světle ...** *svyet-leh*
dark ...	**tmavě ...** *tma-veyh*
I'm looking for something in yellow.	**Chtěl(a) bych něco žlutého.** *khutyel(a) bikh nye-tso' zhloo-teh-ho'*
I want a darker/lighter shade.	**Chtěl(a) bych tmavší/světlejší odstín.** *khutyel(a) bikh tmav-shee/svyet-leye'-shee ot-styeen*
Do you have the same in ...?	**Máte to samé v ...?** *mah-teh to' sameh v*

Clothes and accessories Oděvy a doplňky

belt	**pásek**	*pah-sek*
bikini	**bikiny**	*bikinih*
blouse	**blůza**	*bluh-za*
bra	**podprsenka**	*pot-pr-sen-ka*
briefs	**spodní kalhotky**	*spod-nyee kal-hot-kih*
cap	**čepice**	*chepi-tseh*
coat	**kabát**	*ka-baht*
dress	**šaty**	*shutih*
handbag	**kabelka**	*kabel-ka*
hat	**klobouk**	*klo-bohk*
jacket	**sako**	*sako'*
jeans	**džíny**	*dzhee-nih*
leggings	**kamaše**	*kamasheh*
pants (U.S.)	**kalhoty**	*kul-hotih*
panty hose [tights]	**punčochové kalhoty**	*poon-cho-khoveh kal-hotih*
raincoat	**kabát do deště**	*kabaht do-desh-tyeh*
scarf	**šátek**	*shah-tek*
shirt (men's)	**košile**	*ko-shileh*
shorts	**krátké kalhoty**	*kraht-keh kal-hotih*
skirt	**sukně**	*sook-nyeh*
socks	**ponožky**	*ponozh-kih*
stockings	**punčochy**	*poon-cho-khih*
suit (man's/woman's)	**oblek/kostým**	*ob-lek/kos-teem*
sweater	**svetr**	*svetr*
sweatshirt	**tričko**	*trich-ko'*
swimming trunks/swimsuit	**pánské plavky/dámské plavky**	*pahn-skeh plav-kih/dahm-skeh plav-kih*
T-shirt	**tričko**	*trich-ko'*
tie	**kravata**	*kravata*
trousers	**kalhoty**	*kal-hotih*
underpants	**pánské spodky**	*pahn-skeh spot-kih*
with long/short sleeves	**s krátkým/dlouhým rukávem**	*skraht-keem/dloh-heem rookah-vem*
with a V-/round neck	**s véčkem/s kulatým výstřihem**	*svehch-kem/skoo-lateem vees-trzhi-hem*

Shoes Boty

boots / shoes	**boty** *botih*
flip-flops	**sandály** *sun-dah-lih*
running [training] shoes	**tenisky** *tenis-kih*
sandals	**sandály** *sun-dah-lih*
slippers	**papuče** *papoocheh*

Walking / Hiking gear Vybavení na túry

knapsack	**ruksak** *rook-suck*
walking boots	**pohorky** *po-hor-kih*
waterproof jacket [anorak]	**nepromokavá bunda** *nepromokavah boon-da*
windbreaker [cagoule]	**větrovka** *vyet-rof-ka*

Fabric Látky

I want something …	**Chtěl(a) bych něco …** *khutyel(a) bikh nye-tso'*
in cotton	**z bavlny** *zba-vulnih*
in denim	**z džínsoviny** *zudzheen-sovinih*
in lace	**z krajky** *skraye'-kih*
in leather	**z kůže** *skuh-zheh*
in linen	**ze lnu** *ze-lunooh*
in wool	**z vlny** *zuvul-nih*
Is this …?	**Je to …?** *yeh to'*
pure cotton	**čistá bavlna** *chis-tah ba-vulna*
synthetic	**umělé vlákno** *oomye-leh vlahk-no'*
Is it hand / machine washable?	**Pere se to v ruce/v pračce?** *pereh seh to' vroo-tseh/vuprach-tseh*

ČISTIT POUZE CHEMICKY	dry clean only
PRÁT POUZE V RUCE	handwash only
NEŽEHLIT	do not iron
NEČISTIT CHEMICKY	do not dry clean

Does it fit? Sedí to?

Can I try this on?	**Mohu si to zkusit?**
	mohooh sih to' skoo-sit
Where's the fitting room?	**Kde je zkušební kabina?**
	gdeh yeh skoo-sheb-nyee kabina
It fits well. I'll take it.	**Je mi to dobře. Vezmu si to.**
	yeh mih to' dob-rzheh. vez-mooh sih to'
It doesn't fit.	**Není mi to dobře.**
	ne-nyee mih to' dob-rzheh
It's too …	**Je to moc …** *yeh to' mots*
short/long	**krátké/dlouhé** *kraht-keh/dloh-heh*
tight/loose	**těsné/volné** *tyes-neh/vol-neh*
Do you have this in size …?	**Máte to ve velikosti …?**
	mah-teh to've-velikos-tyih
What size is this?	**Jaká je to velikost?** *yukah yeh to' velikost*
Could you measure me, please?	**Mohl(a) byste mě změřit?**
	mohul(a) bis-teh myeh zumye-rzhit
I don't know Czech sizes.	**Neznám české velikosti.**
	nez-nahm ches-keh velikos-tyih

Size Velikost

	Dresses/Suits						Women's shoes			
American	8	10	12	14	16	18	6	7	8	9
British	10	12	14	16	18	20	$4^{1/2}$	$5^{1/2}$	$6^{1/2}$	$7^{1/2}$
Continental	36	38	40	42	44	46	37	38	40	41

	Shirts				Men's shoes								
American British }	15	16	17	18	5	6	7	8	$8^{1/2}$	9	$9^{1/2}$	10	11
Continental	38	41	43	45	38	39	41	42	43	43	44	44	45

VELMI VELKÉ	extra large (XL)
VELKÉ	large (L)
STŘEDNÍ	medium (M)
MALÉ	small (S)

1 centimeter (cm.) = 0.39 in.	1 inch = 2.54 cm.
1 meter (m.) = 39.37 in.	1 foot = 30.5 cm.
10 meters = 32.81 ft.	1 yard = 0.91 m.

Health and beauty
Kosmetický salon

I'd like a …	**Chtěl(a) bych …** *khutyel(a) bikh*
facial	**masáž obličeje** *ma-sah-zh ob-li-che-yeh*
manicure	**manikýru** *mani-kee-rooh*
massage	**masáž** *ma-sah-zh*
waxing	**voskování** *vos-ko-vah-nyee*

Hairdresser Kadeřnictví

A tip of 10–20 Kč, depending on the service, is appreciated.

I'd like to make an appointment for …	**Chtěl(a) bych se objednat na …** *khutyel(a) bikh seh ob-yed-nut na*
Can you make it a bit earlier / later?	**Máte volno o něco dříve/později?** *mah-teh vol-no' o-nye-tso' drzhee-veh/ poz-dye-yeih*
I'd like a …	**Chtěl(a) bych …** *khutyl(a) bikh*
cut and blow-dry	**ostříhat a vyfoukat** *os-trzhee-hut a vi-foh-kat*
shampoo and set	**umýt a usušit** *oo-meet a oo-soo-shit*
trim	**zastřihnout** *za-strzhih-noht*
I'd like my hair …	**Chtěla bych …** *khutyel(a) bikh*
highlighted	**tónování** *tau-no-vah-nyee*
permed	**trvalou** *trvaloh*
Don't cut it too short.	**Nestříhejte mě moc nakrátko.** *nes-trzhee-heye'-teh meyh mots na-kraht-ko'*
A little more off the …	**Trochu víc …** *tro-khooh veets*
back / front	**vzadu/vpředu** *vza-dooh/vprzhe-dooh*
neck / sides	**na krku/po stranách** *na-kur-kooh/po-stra-nah-kh*
top	**nahoře** *na-ho-rzheh*
That's fine, thanks.	**To stačí, děkuji.** *to' sta-chee dyekoo-yeih*

Household articles
Domácí potřeby

I'd like a(n)/ some …	**Chtěl(a) bych …** *khutyel(a) bikh*
adapter	**adaptér** *adap-tehr*
alumin[i]um foil	**alobal** *alobal*
bottle opener	**otvírač na láhve** *ot-fee-ruch na-lah-hveh*
can [tin] opener	**otvírač na plechovky** *ot-fee-ruch na-ple-khov-kih*
clothes pins [pegs]	**kolíčky** *ko-leech-kih*
corkscrew	**vývrtku** *vee-vrut-kooh*
light bulb	**žárovku** *zhah-rof-kooh*
matches	**zápalky** *zah-pal-kih*
paper napkins	**papírové ubrousky** *papeero-veh oob-rohs-kih*
plastic wrap [cling film]	**potravinovou fólii** *pot-ra-vinovoh fo-li-yeih*
plug	**zástrčku** *zahs-tr-chukooh*
scissors	**nůžky** *nuh-shkih*
screwdriver	**šroubovák** *shroh-bo-vahk*

Cleaning items Čisticí potřeby

bleach	**odbarvovací prostředek** *od-bar-vova-tsee pros-trzhe-dek*
detergent [washing powder]	**prášek na praní** *prah-shek na-pra-nyee*
dishcloth	**hadr na nádobí** *hadr na-nah-dobee*
dishwashing [washing-up] liquid	**prostředek na mytí nádobí** *pros-trzhe-dek na-mi-tyee nah-dobee*
garbage [refuse] bags	**pytle na odpadky** *pit-leh na-ot-pat-kih*
sponge	**houba** *hoh-ba*

Dishes/Utensils [Crockery/Cutlery] Nádobí/Příbory

bowls	**misky** *mis-kih*
cups/glasses	**šálky/sklenice** *shah-lkih/skle-nyi-tseh*
knives/forks	**nože/vidličky** *no-zheh/vidlich-kih*
mugs	**hrnky** *hrun-kih*
plates	**talíře** *ta-lee-rzheh*
spoons/teaspoons	**lžíce/lžičky** *luzhee-tseh/luzhich-kih*

Jeweler Klenoty

Could I see …? — **Mohl(a) bych se podívat na …** *mohul(a) bikh seh po-dyee-vat na*

this/that — **tohle/tamto** *to-hleh/tum-to'*

It's in the window/ display cabinet. — **Je to ve výloze/ve vitríně.** *yeh to' ve-vee-lo-zeh/ve-vit-ree-nyeh*

alarm clock — **budík** *boo-dyeek*

battery — **baterie** *bate-ri-yeh*

bracelet — **náramek** *nah-ramek*

brooch — **brož** *brosh*

chain — **řetízek** *rzhe-tyee-zek*

clock — **hodiny** *ho-dyi-nih*

earrings — **náušnice** *nah-oosh-nyi-tseh*

necklace — **náhrdelník** *nah-hrudel-nyeek*

ring — **prsten** *pr-sten*

watch — **hodinky** *ho-dyin-kih*

Materials Materiály

Is this real silver/gold? — **Je to pravé stříbro/zlato?** *yeh to' pra-veh strzhee-bro'/zlato'*

Is there a certificate for it? — **Máte na to osvědčení?** *mah-teh na-to' os-vyet-che-nyee*

Do you have anything …? — **Máte něco …?** *mah-teh ney-tso'*

in copper — **z mědi** *zumye-dyih*

in crystal (quartz) — **z křemene** *zukurzhe-meneh*

in cut glass — **z broušeného skla** *zubroh-she-neh-ho' skula*

with diamonds — **s diamanty** *sdi-amantih*

in enamel — **s emailem** *se-maye'-lem*

in gold — **ze zlata** *ze-zla-ta*

in gold plate — **pozlaceného** *po-zla-tse-neh-ho'*

in pearl — **s perlami** *sper-lamih*

in pewter — **z cínu** *sutsee-nooh*

in platinum — **z platiny** *zupla-tinih*

in silver — **ze stříbra** *ze-strzhee-bra*

in silver plate — **postříbřeného** *pos-trzhee-brzhe-neh-ho'*

in stainless steel — **z nerezové oceli** *zne-rezoveh o-tse-lih*

149

Newsstand [Newsagent]/ Tobacconist Novinový stánek/ Tabák

Newsstands in major cities have foreign newspapers, although these are usually a day or so old. Cigarettes, cigars, and tobacco can be bought at newsstands, tobacconists (**tabák**), vending machines, and supermarkets. Smoking is prohibited on public transportation (as well as in subway [metro] stations), and in theaters, concert halls (a smoking room is usually provided), and movie theaters [cinemas].

Do you sell English-language books/newspapers?	**Prodáváte anglické knihy/noviny?** *pro-dah-vah-teh anglits-keh knyi-hih/novinih*
I'd like a(n)/some …	**Chtěl(a) bych …** *khutyel(a) bikh*
book	**knihu** *knyi-hooh*
candy [sweets]	**bonbóny** *bon-bo-nih*
chewing gum	**žvýkačku** *zhvee-kuch-kooh*
chocolate bar	**čokoládu** *chokolah-dooh*
cigars	**doutníky** *doht-nyee-kih*
dictionary	**slovník** *slov-nyeek*
English–Czech	**anglicko-český** *anglits-ko' ches-kee*
envelopes	**obálky** *obahl-kih*
guidebook of …	**průvodce …** *pruh-vot-tseh*
lighter	**zapalovač** *zapalo-vach*
magazine	**časopis** *chasopis*
map	**mapu** *mapooh*
map of the town	**plán města** *plahn myes-ta*
matches	**zápalky** *zah-pal-kih*
newspaper	**noviny** *novinih*
American/English	**americké/anglické** *ame-rits-keh/anglits-keh*
pack of cigarettes	**krabičku cigaret** *kra-bich-kooh tsi-garet*
pen	**pero** *pero'*
road map of …	**automapu …** *ow-tomapooh*
stamps	**známky** *znahm-kih*
tobacco	**tabák** *tabahk*
writing paper	**dopisní papír** *dopis-nyee papeer*

Photography Fotografie

I'm looking for a(n) … camera.	**Chtěl(a) bych … fotoaparát.**
	khutyel(a) bikh …
	foto-apa-raht
automatic	**automatický** ow-toma-tits-kee
compact	**kompaktní** kom-pakt-nyee
disposable	**na jedno použití** na-yed-no' po-oozhi-tyee
SLR (single lens reflex)	**s jednoduchou reflexní čočkou**
	s-yed-no-doo-khoh re-flex-nyee choch-koh
I'd like a(n) …	**Chtěl(a) bych …** khutyel(a) bikh
battery	**baterii** bate-ri-yeih
camera case	**pouzdro na fotoaparát**
	pohz-dro' na-foto-apa-raht
electronic flash/filter	**elektrický blesk/filtr**
	elek-trits-kee blesk/fil-tr
lens/lens cap	**čočku/víčko na čočku**
	choch-kooh/veech-ko' na-choch-kooh

Film/Processing Film/Vyvolání

I'd like a … film.	**Chtěl(a) bych … film.**
	khutye(a) bikh … film
black and white	**černobílý** cher-no-beelee
color	**barevný** barev-nee
I'd like a … film.	**Chtěl(a) bych film …**
	khutye(a) bikh film
24-/36-exposure	**s dvaceti čtyřmi/třiceti šesti snímky**
	sudva-tse-tyih chutirzh-mih/trzhi-tse-tyih
	snyeem-kih
I'd like this film developed, please.	**Chtěl(a) bych tento film vyvolat.**
	khutyel(a) bikh ten-to' film vivolat
Would you enlarge this, please?	**Mohli byste to zvětšit?**
	mo-hli bis-teh to' zvyet-shit
How much do … exposures cost?	**Kolik stojí … snímků?**
	kolik sto-yee … snyeem-kuh
When will my photos be ready?	**Kdy budou fotografie hotové?**
	gdih boo-doh foto-gra-fi-yeh hotoveh
I'd like to pick up my photos.	**Chtěl(a) bych si vyzvednout fotografie.**
	khutye(a) bikh sih viz-ved-noht foto-gra-fi-yeh
Here's the receipt.	**Tady je lístek.** tadih yeh lees-tek

Post office Pošta

General queries Všeobecné dotazy

Post offices (**pošta**) provide mail, fax, telegram, telex, and
telephone services. Stamps (**známky**) can also be bought at
newsstands and tobacconists. The main post office in Prague
(Jindřišká 14, just off Wenceslas Square) is open 24 hours. Other post
offices are open from 8 a.m. to 6 p.m. Monday through Friday, and 8 a.m.
to 1 p.m. on Saturday. Mailboxes are painted orange.

Where's the post office?	**Kde je pošta?** *gdeh yeh posh-ta*
What time does the post office open/close?	**V kolik hodin pošta otvírá/zavírá?** *fkolik ho-dyin posh-ta ot-fee-rah/za-vee-rah*
Does it close for lunch?	**Zavírá přes poledne?** *za-vee-rah przhes poled-neh*
Where's the mailbox [postbox]?	**Kde je poštovní schránka?** *dgeh yeh posh-tov-nyee sukhurahn-ka*
Is there any mail for me?	**Mám tady nějakou poštu?** *mahm tadih nye-yukoh posh-tooh*

Buying stamps Nákup známek

I'd like to send these postcards to ...	**Chtěl(a) bych poslat tyto pohlednice do ...** *khutyel(a) bikh pos-lat tito' po-hled-nyi-tseh do'*
A stamp for this postcard/letter, please.	**Známku na pohlednici/dopis, prosím.** *znahm-kooh na-po-hled-nyi-tsih/dopis proseem*
An 8 Kč stamp, please.	**Osmikorunovou známku, prosím.** *os-mi-ko-roo-novoh znahm-kooh proseem*
What's the postage for a letter to ...?	**Kolik je poštovné za dopis do ...?** *kolik yeh posh-tov-neh za-dopis do'*

> – Dobrý den, chtěl(a) bych poslat tyto pohlednice
> do Spojených států.
> (Hello, I'd like to send these postcards to the U.S.)
> – *Kolik jich máte? (How many?)*
> – Devět. (Nine.)
> – *To je devětkrát osm korun: sedmdesát dvě koruny, prosím.*
> *(That's 8 korun times nine: 72 korun please.)*

Sending packages Posílání balíků

I want to send this package [parcel] by …	**Chtěl(a) bych poslat tento balík …** *khutye(a) bikh pos-lat ten-to' baleek*
airmail	**letecky** *letets-kih*
special delivery [express]	**spěšně** *spyesh-nyeh*
registered mail	**doporučeně** *dopo-roo-che-nyeh*
It contains …	**Je v něm …** *yeh vnyem*

Vyplňte laskavě celní prohlášení.	Please fill out the customs declaration form.
Jakou má hodnotu?	What's the value?
Co v něm je?	What's inside?

Telecommunications Telekomunikace

I'd like a phone card, please.	**Chtěl(a) bych telefonní kartu.** *khutyel(a) bikh tele-fo-nyee kar-tooh*
10/20/50 units	**deset/dvacet/padesát jednotek** *deset/dva-tset/pade-saht yed-notek*
Do you have a photocopier?	**Máte kopírku?** *mah-teh ko-peer-kooh*
I'd like to send a message …	**Chtěl(a) bych poslat zprávu …** *khutyel(a) bikh pos-lat zuprah-vooh*
by e-mail/fax	**elektronickou poštou/faxem** *elek-tro-nits-koh posh-toh/fa-ksem*
What's your e-mail address?	**Jakou máte adresu elektronické pošty?** *yukoh mah-teh adresooh elek-tro-nits-keh posh-tih*
Can I access the Internet here?	**Mohu se odtud připojit na Internet?** *mo-hooh seh ot-tood przhi-po-yeit na-in-ter-net*
What are the charges per hour?	**Jaká je hodinová sazba?** *yakah yeh ho-dyi-novah saz-ba*
How do I log on?	**Jak se přihlásím?** *yuk seh przhi-hlah-seem*

Souvenirs Suvenýry

Cut crystal (**broušené sklo**), Czech garnets – usually set in gold-plated silver (**české granáty**) – porcelain, folk crafts – pottery, embroidery, and wooden objects (**výrobky lidových řemesel**) – and CDs of Czech classical music, folk music, and jazz are the most popular souvenirs.

Becher brandy (➤ 49)	**Becherovka®** _be-khe-rof-ka_
cut crystal	**broušené sklo** _broh-she-neh sukulo'_
Czech garnets	**české granáty** _ches-keh gra-nah-tih_
dolls	**panenky** _pa-nen-kih_
embroidery	**výšivky** _vee-shiv-kih_
lace	**krajka** _kraye'-ka_
native art	**lidová tvorba** _lidovah tvor-ba_
painted egg shells	**velikonoční vajíčka** _veliko-noch-nyee va-yeech-ka_
pictures	**obrázky** _ob-rahs-kih_
plates	**talíře** _ta-lee-rzhe_
porcelain	**porcelán** _por-tse-lahn_
pottery	**keramika** _keramika_
puppets	**loutky** _loht-kih_
wooden toys	**dřevěné hračky** _drzhe-vye-neh hrach-kih_

Gifts Dárky

bottle of wine	**láhev vína** _lah-hef vee-na_
box of chocolates	**bonboniéra** _bon-bo-ni-yeh-ra_
calendar	**kalendář** _ka-len-dah-rzh_
key ring	**přívěšek ke klíčům** _purzhee-vye-shek ke-klee-chuhm_
postcards	**pohlednice** _po-hled-nyi-tseh_
scarf	**šátek** _shah-tek_
souvenir guide	**obrázkový průvodce** _ob-rahs-ko-vee pruh-vot-tseh_
tea towel	**utěrka** _oo-tyer-ka_
T-shirt	**tričko** _trich-ko'_

Music Hudba

I'd like a …	**Chtěl(a) bych …** *khutyel(a) bikh*
cassette	**kazetu** *kazetooh*
compact disc	**kompaktní disk** *kom-pakt-nyee disk*
record	**gramofonovou desku** *gramofonovoh des-kooh*
videocassette	**videokazetu** *vide-o-kazetooh*
Who are the popular native singers/bands?	**Kdo jsou místní populární zpěváci/ skupiny?** *gdo' yesoh meest-nyee popoolahr-nyee spye-vah-tsih/skoo-pinih*

Toys and games Hračky a hry

I'd like a toy/game …	**Chtěl(a) bych hračku/hru …** *khutyel(a) bikh hrach-kooh/hrooh*
for a boy	**pro chlapce** *pro-khlap-tseh*
for a 5-year-old girl	**pro pětiletou holčičku** *pro-pye-tyi-letoh hol-chich-kooh*
ball	**míč** *meech*
chess set	**šachy** *sha-khih*
doll	**panenku** *pa-nen-kooh*
electronic game	**elektronickou hru** *elek-tro-nits-koh hrooh*
teddy bear	**medvídka** *med-veet-ka*
pail and shovel [bucket and spade]	**kyblík s lopatkou** *kib-leek slo-pat-koh*

Antiques Starožitnosti

How old is this?	**Jak je to staré?** *yuk yeh to' stareh*
Do you have anything from the … era?	**Máte něco z … období?** *mah-teh nye-tso' z … ob-dobee*
Can you send it to me?	**Můžete mi to poslat?** *muh-zheteh mih to' pos-lat*
Will I have problems with customs?	**Budu mít problémy na celnici?** *boo-dooh meet prob-leh-mih na-tsel-nyi-tsih*
Is there a certificate of authenticity?	**Máte osvědčení pravosti?** *mah-teh os-vyet-che-nyee pra-vos-tyih*

WHO?/WHAT?/WHEN? ➤ 104

Supermarket/Minimart
Samoobsluha/Potraviny

Some Western food chains now have stores in Prague.
You will also find local supermarkets in most towns. However,
fresh fruit and vegetables direct from the farm are best bought at street
markets (**tržnice**).

At the supermarket V samoobsluze

Excuse me. Where can I find …?	**Promiňte, prosím. Kde je/jsou …?** *prominye'-teh proseem. gdeh yeh/yesoh*
Do I pay for this here?	**Platí se tady?** *pla-tyee seh tadih*
Where are the carts [trolleys]/baskets?	**Kde jsou vozíky/košíky?** *gdeh yesoh vozeekih/kosheekih*
Is there a pharmacy here?	**Je tady lékárna?** *yeh tadih leh-kahr-na*
Is there a delicatessen here?	**Jsou tady lahůdky?** *yesoh tadih la-huht-kih*

ČERSTVÉ RYBY	fresh fish
ČERSTVÉ MASO	fresh meat
DOMÁCÍ POTŘEBY	household goods
DRŮBEŽ	poultry
CHLÉB A PEČIVO	bread and cakes
KONZERVY	canned foods
MLÉČNÉ VÝROBKY	dairy products
MRAŽENÉ ZBOŽÍ	frozen foods
OVOCE A ZELENINA	fruit and vegetables
VÍNO A LIHOVINY	wines and spirits

Weights and measures

- **1 kilogram** or **kilo (kg.)** = **1000 grams (g.)**; **100 g.** = 3.5 oz.; **1 kg.** = 2.2 lb
  1 oz. = **28.35 g.**; 1 lb. = **453.60 g.**
- **1 liter (l.)** = 0.88 imp. quart or 1.06 U.S. quart; 1 imp. quart = **1.14 l.**
  1 U.S. quart = **0.951 l.**; 1 imp. gallon = **4.55 l.**; 1 U.S. gallon = **3.8 l.**

Food hygiene Hygiena potravin

⊙ PO OTEVŘENÍ SPOTŘEBUJTE DO … DNÍ	eat within … days of opening
USCHOVEJTE V CHLADU	keep refrigerated
VHODNÉ PRO MIKROVLNNÉ TROUBY	microwaveable
⊙ SPOTŘEBUJTE DO …	use by …

At the minimart V potravinách

I'd like some of that/those.	**Chtěl(a) bych tamto.** *khutyel(a) bikh tum-to'*
this one/that one	**tenhle/tamten** *ten-hleh/tum-ten*
these/those	**tyhle/tamty** *ti-hleh/tum-tih*
to the left/right	**vlevo/vpravo** *vlevo'/fupravo'*
over there/here	**tam/tady** *tum/tadih*
Where is/are the …?	**Kde je/jsou …?** *gdeh yeh/yesoh*
I'd like …	**Chtěl(a) bych …** *khutyel(a) bikh*
a kilo (of)/half a kilo (of)	**kilo/půl kila** *kilo'/puhl kilah*
a liter (of)/half a liter (of)	**litr/půl litru** *litur/puhl lit-rooh*
apples	**jablek** *yab-lek*
tomatoes	**rajčat** *raye'-chut*
milk	**mléka** *mleh-ka*
I'd like two slices of ham.	**Chtěl(a) bych dva plátky šunky.** *khutyel(a) bikh dva plaht-kih shoon-kih*
I'd like some …	**Chtěl(a) bych …** *khutyel(a) bikh*
beer	**pivo** *pivo'*
bread	**chleba** *khleba*
cheese	**sýr** *seer*
coffee	**kávu** *kah-vooh*
cookies [biscuits]	**sušenky** *sooshenkih*
eggs	**vejce** *veye'-tseh*
jam	**marmeládu** *mar-me-lah-dooh*
potato chips [crisps]	**bramborové lupínky** *brum-boroveh loo-peen-kih*
soft drinks	**nealkoholické nápoje** *ne-al-koholits-keh nah-po-yeh*
That's all, thanks.	**To je všechno, děkuji.** *to' yeh vshekh-no' dyekoo-yeih*

Provisions/Picnic Potraviny/Piknik

beer	**pivo** *pivo'*
butter	**máslo** *mahs-lo'*
cakes	**zákusky** *zah-koos-kih*
cheese	**sýr** *seer*
cookies [biscuits]	**sušenky** *soo-shen-kih*
grapes	**hroznové víno** *hroz-noveh vee-no'*
instant coffee	**instantní káva** *ins-tant-nyee kah-va*
lemonade	**limonáda** *limonah-da*
margarine	**margarín** *mar-gareen*
oranges	**pomeranče** *pome-run-cheh*
rolls (bread)	**rohlíky** *ro-hlee-kih*
salami	**salám** *salahm*
sausage	**klobása** *klobah-sa*
sliced meats	**krájené maso** *krah-ye-neh maso'*
tea bags	**sáčkovaný čaj** *sahch-kovanee chaye'*
wine	**víno** *vee-no'*
yogurt	**jogurt** *yeo-goorut*

Czech bakeries and supermarkets sell a rich variety of black and white bread (**chléb**) as loaves and rolls. The most common types include wheat bread (**pšeničný**), rye bread (**žitný chléb**), and French-style baguettes. Russian-style dark bread and bread with sunflower seeds can also be found. Slightly sweet rolls called **loupáčky** are similar to French croissants.

Police Policie

Any crime, theft, accident, or lost property should be
reported at the nearest police station (**policie**). The officers
rarely speak English, so try to find an interpreter. To contact
the police in an emergency, ☎ 158.

Where's the nearest police station?	**Kde je nejbližší policejní stanice?** gdeh yeh neye'bli-shee poli-tseye'-nyee sta-nyi-tseh
Does anyone here speak English?	**Mluví tady někdo anglicky?** mloo-vee tadih nyeg-do' anglits-kih
I want to report a(n) ...	**Chtěl(a) bych ohlásit ...** khutye(a) bikh o-hlah-sit
accident/attack	**nehodu/napadení** ne-ho-dooh/napade-nyee
mugging/rape	**přepadení/znásilnění** przhe-pade-nyee/znah-sil-nye-nyee
My child is lost.	**Ztratilo se mi dítě.** stra-tyi-lo' seh mih dyee-tyeh
Here's a photo of him/her.	**Tady je jeho/její fotografie.** tadih yeh ye-ho'/ye-yee foto-gra-fi-yeh
I need an English-speaking lawyer.	**Potřebuji anglicky mluvícího právníka.** pot-rzhe-boo-yeih anglits-kih mloo-vee-tsee-ho' prahv-nyee-ka
I need to make a phone call.	**Potřebuji si zatelefonovat.** pot-rzhe-boo-yeih sih zatele-fono-vat
I need to contact the ... Consulate.	**Potřebuji se spojit s ... konzulátem.** pot-rzhe-boo-yeih seh spo-yeit s ... kon-zoo-lah-tem
American/British	**americkým/britským** amerits-keem/brits-keem

Můžete ho/ji popsat?	Can you describe him/her?
muž/žena	male/female
světlé vlasy/tmavé vlasy	blond(e)/brunette
zrzavé vlasy/šedé vlasy	red-headed/gray-haired
dlouhé/krátké vlasy/pleš	long/short hair/balding
přibližná výška	approximate height ...
(přibližný) věk	aged (approximately) ...
Měl(a) na sobě ...	He/She was wearing ...

CLOTHES ➤ 144; COLOR ➤ 143

Lost property/Theft Ztráty/Krádež

I want to report a theft.	**Chtěl(a) bych ohlásit krádež.** *khutye(a) bikh o-hlah-sit krah-dezh*
My bag was snatched.	**Vytrhli mi kabelku.** *vi-tr-hlih mih kabel-kooh*
My ... has been stolen from my car.	**Ukradli mi z auta ...** *oo-krad-lih mih zow-ta*
I've been robbed/mugged.	**Okradli/přepadli mě.** *o-krad-lih/przhe-pud-lih myeh*
I've lost my ...	**Ztratil(a) jsem ...** *stratyil(a) yesem*
My ... has been stolen.	**Ukradli mi ...** *oo-krad-lih mih*
bag	**tašku** *tash-kooh*
bicycle	**kolo** *kolo'*
camera	**fotoaparát** *foto-apa-raht*
(rental) car	**auto (z půjčovny)** *ow-to' (zpuhye'-chov-nih)*
credit cards/money	**kreditní karty/peníze** *kredit-nyee kar-tih/pe-nyee-zeh*
handbag	**kabelku** *kabel-kooh*
passport	**pas** *pus*
purse/wallet	**peněženku** *penye-zhen-kooh*
ticket	**jízdenku** *yeez-den-kooh*
watch	**hodinky** *ho-dyi-nkih*
What should I do?	**Co mám dělat?** *tso' mahm dye-lat*
I need a police report for my insurance claim.	**Potřebuji zprávu od policie pro pojišťovnu.** *pot-rzhe-boo-yeih sprah-vooh ot-po-li-tsi-yeh pro-po-yeish-tyov-nooh*

Co chybí?	What's missing?
Co bylo zcizeno?	What's been taken?
Kdy vám to ukradli?	When was it stolen?
Kdy se to stalo?	When did it happen?
Kde bydlíte?	Where are you staying?
Odkud to bylo zcizeno?	Where was it taken from?
Kde jste v té době byl(a)?	Where were you at the time?
Objednali jsme vám tlumočníka.	We're getting an interpreter for you.
Vyšetříme to.	We'll look into the matter.
Vyplňte laskavě tento formulář.	Please fill out this form.

Health

Doctor (general) Lékař (všeobecně)

Before you leave, make sure your health insurance policy covers any illnesses or accidents while you are away.

An increasing number of medical/dental practices are private; you will be asked for a fee, which your insurer should reimburse, but ask the doctor for a receipt. The U.K. and the Czech Republic have a reciprocal arrangement for emergency medical treatment, but you may still be asked to produce insurance documents. Your hotel or the nearest pharmacy (**lékárna**) can recommend a doctor. In an emergency, ☏ 155 for an ambulance.

Where can I find a hospital/dental office [surgery]?	**Kde najdu nemocnici/zubní středisko?** *geh naye-dooh nemots-nyi-tsih/ zoob-nyee strzhe-dyis-ko*
Where's there a doctor/dentist who speaks English?	**Mluví tam některý lékař/zubař anglicky?** *mloovee tum nyek-teree leh-karzh/ zoo-barzh an-glits-kih*
What are the office [surgery] hours?	**Kdy mají na středisku otevřeno?** *gdih ma-yee na-sturzhe-dyis-kooh otev-rzhe-no'*
Could the doctor come to see me here?	**Mohl by mě lékař navštívit tady?** *mohul bih myeh leh-karzh nav-shtyee-vit tadih*
Can I make an appointment for …?	**Mohu se objednat na …?** *mo-hooh seh ob-yed-nat na*
today/tomorrow	**dnešek/zítra** *dne-shek/zeetrah*
as soon as possible	**co nejdříve** *tso' neye-drzhee-veh*
It's urgent.	**Je to naléhavé.** *yeh to' naleh-haveh*
I have an appointment with Doctor …	**Jsem objednaný(á) u doktora …** *yesem ob-yed-nanee(ah) oodok-torah*

TIME ➤ 220; DATES ➤ 218

161

Accident and injury Nehoda a úraz

My ... is hurt/injured.	**Můj ... je zraněný.**
	muh-ye' ... yeh zra-nye-nee
husband/son/friend *(male)*	**manžel/syn/přítel**
	man-zhel/sin/przhee-tel
My ... is hurt/injured.	**Moje ... je zraněná.**
	mo-yeh ... yeh zra-nye-nah
wife/daughter/friend *(female)*	**žena/dcera/přítelkyně**
	zhenah/tse-rah/przhee-tel-kinye
My child is hurt/injured.	**Moje dítě je zraněné.**
	mo-yeh dyee-tyeh yeh zra-nye-neh
He/She is ...	**Je ...** *yeh*
unconscious	**v bezvědomí** *vbez-vye-domee*
(seriously) injured	**(vážně) zraněný(á)**
	(vah-zhnyeh) zra-nye-nee(ah)
He/She is bleeding (heavily).	**(Silně) krvácí.** *(sil-nyeh) kur-vah-tsee*
I have a(n) ...	**Mám ...** *mahm*
blister/boil	**puchýř/vřídek** *poo-khee-rzh/vrzhee-dek*
bruise/burn	**modřinu/popáleninu**
	mod-rzhi-nooh/popah-le-nyi-nooh
lump/swelling	**bouli/oteklinu** *boh-lih/otek-linooh*
rash/sting	**vyrážku/žihadlo** *virah-zh-kooh/zhi-had-lo'*
strained muscle	**natažený sval** *natazhenee sval*
I have a cut.	**Pořezal(a) jsem se.**
	po-rzhe-zal(a) yesem seh
I have a scrape [graze].	**Odřel(a) jsem se.** *od-rzhel(a) yesem seh*
I have an insect bite.	**Jsem poštípaný(á).**
	yesem posh-tyee-panee(ah)
My ... hurts.	**Bolí mě ...** *bolee mye*

Symptoms Příznaky

I've been feeling ill for … days.	**Necítím se dobře už … dní.** *ne-tsee-tyeem seh dob-rzhe oozh … dnyee*
I feel faint.	**Je mi mdlo.** *yeh mih mudulo'*
I have a fever.	**Mám horečku.** *mahm horech-kooh*
I've been vomiting.	**Zvracel(a) jsem.** *zuvra-tsel(a) yesem*
I have diarrhea.	**Mám průjem.** *mahm pruh-yem*
It hurts here.	**Tady to bolí.** *tadih to' bolee*
I have a backache.	**Bolí mě v zádech.** *bolee myeh vzah-dekh*
I have a cold.	**Jsem nachlazený(á).** *yesem na-khla-zenee(ah)*
I have cramps.	**Mám křeče.** *mahm krzhe-cheh*
I have an earache.	**Bolí mě ucho.** *bolee myeh oo-kho'*
I have a headache.	**Bolí mě hlava.** *bolee meyh hlavah*
I have a sore throat.	**Bolí mě v krku.** *bolee myeh fkur-kooh*
I have a stomachache.	**Bolí mě břicho.** *bolee myeh brzhi-kho'*
I have sunstroke.	**Mám úžeh.** *mahm uh-zhekh*

Conditions Choroby

I have arthritis.	**Mám artritidu.** *mahm ar-tri-ti-dooh*
I have asthma.	**Mám astma.** *mahm ast-mah*
I'm …	**Jsem …** *yesem*
deaf	**hluchý(á)** *hloo-khee(ah)*
diabetic	**diabetik** *di-a-be-tik*
epileptic	**epileptik** *epilep-tik*
handicapped	**tělesně postižený(á)** *tyeles-nyeh pos-tyi-zhenee(ah)*
(… months) pregnant	**(… měsíců) těhotná** *(… mye-see-tsuh) tye-hot-nah*
I have a heart condition.	**Mám srdeční chorobu.** *mahm sur-dech-nyee khorobooh*
I have high/low blood pressure.	**Mám vysoký/nízký krevní tlak.** *mahm visokee/nyees-kee krev-nyee tlak*
I had a heart attack … years ago.	**Před … lety jsem měl(a) infarkt.** *przhet … letih yesem myel(a) in-farukut*

Doctor's inquiries Dotazy lékaře

Jak dlouho už se tak cítíte?	How long have you been feeling like this?
Je to poprvé?	Is this the first time you've had this?
Užíváte nějaké jiné léky?	Are you taking any other medication?
Jste na něco alergický(á)?	Are you allergic to anything?
Máte očkování proti tetanu?	Have you been vaccinated against tetanus?
Máte chuť k jídlu?	Is your appetite OK?

Examination Vyšetření

Změřím vám teplotu/krevní tlak.	I'll take your temperature/ blood pressure.
Vyhrňte si rukáv.	Roll up your sleeve, please.
Svlékněte se do pasu.	Please undress to the waist.
Položte se.	Please lie down.
Otevřete ústa.	Open your mouth.
Dýchejte zhluboka.	Breathe deeply.
Zakašlete.	Cough, please.
Kde to bolí?	Where does it hurt?
Bolí to tady?	Does it hurt here?

Diagnosis Diagnóza

Chci vás poslat na rentgen.	I want you to have an X-ray.
Potřebuji vzorek krve/stolice/moči.	I want a specimen of your blood/stool/urine.
Chci aby vás prohlédl specialista.	I want you to see a specialist.
Chci vás poslat do nemocnice.	I want you to go to a hospital.
Je to zlomené/vyvrtnuté.	It's broken/sprained.
Je to vykloubené/natržené.	It's dislocated/torn.

Máte ...	You have (a/an) ...
zánět slepého střeva	appendicitis
infekci močových cest	cystitis
chřipku	flu
otravu potravinami	food poisoning
zlomeninu	fracture
gastritidu	gastritis
hemoroidy	hemorrhoids
kýlu	hernia
zánět ...	inflammation of ...
neštovice	measles
zápal plic	pneumonia
ischias	sciatica
angínu	tonsilitis
nádor	tumor
pohlavní nemoc	venereal disease
Je to zanícené.	It's infected.
Je to nakažlivé.	It's contagious.

Treatment Léčba

Dám vám ...	I'll give you some ...
antiseptikum	antiseptic
lék proti bolesti	painkillers
Předepíšu vám ...	I'm going to prescribe ...
dávku antibiotik	a course of antibiotics
čípky	some suppositories
Jste alergický(á) na nějaké léky?	Are you allergic to any medication?
Vezměte si jednu tabletu ...	Take one pill ...
každé dvě/tři/čtyři hodiny	every 2/3/4 hours
každých pět/šest/sedm hodin	every 5/6/7 hours
... krát denně	... times a day
před jídlem/po jídle	before each meal/after each meal
v případě bolesti	in case of pain
dva/tři/čtyři dny	for 2/3/4 days
pět/šest/sedm dní	for 5/6/7 days
Až přijedete domů, běžte k lékaři.	Consult a doctor when you get home.

Parts of the body Části těla

appendix	**slepé střevo**	*slepeh strzhe-vo'*
arm	**paže**	*pazheh*
back	**záda**	*zah-dah*
bladder	**měchýř**	*mye-kheerzh*
bone	**kost**	*kost*
breast	**prso**	*pr-so'*
chest	**prsa**	*pr-sah*
ear	**ucho**	*oo-kho'*
eye	**oko**	*oko'*
face	**obličej**	*ob-li-cheye'*
finger/thumb	**prst/palec**	*purusut/pa-lets*
foot/toe	**chodidlo/prst na noze**	*kho-dyi-dlo'/purusut nanozeh*
gland	**žláza**	*zhlah-zah*
hand	**ruka**	*rooka*
head	**hlava**	*hlava*
heart	**srdce**	*sur-tseh*
jaw	**čelist**	*che-list*
joint	**kloub**	*klohp*
kidney	**ledvina**	*led-vinah*
knee	**koleno**	*koleno'*
leg	**noha**	*noha*
lip	**ret**	*ret*
liver	**játra**	*yah-tra*
mouth	**ústa**	*uh-sta*
muscle	**sval**	*sval*
neck	**krk**	*kuruk*
nose	**nos**	*nos*
rib	**žebro**	*zheb-ro'*
shoulder	**rameno**	*rameno'*
skin	**pokožka**	*pokozh-ka*
stomach	**žaludek**	*zhaloodek*
thigh	**stehno**	*ste-hno'*
throat	**krk**	*kuruk*
tongue	**jazyk**	*ya-zik*
tonsils	**mandle**	*man-dleh*
vein	**žíla**	*zheela*

Gynecologist Gynekolog

I have …	**Mám …** *mahm*
abdominal pains	**bolesti v břiše** *boles-tyih vubrzhi-sheh*
period pains	**bolestivé měsíčky** *boles-tyi-veh mye-seech-kih*
a vaginal infection	**vaginální infekci** *vagi-nahl-nyee in-fek-tsih*
I haven't had my period for … months.	**Už … měsíců jsem neměla měsíčky.** *oozh … mye-see-tsuh yesem ne-mye-la mye-seech-kih*
I'm on the Pill.	**Beru antikoncepční pilulky.** *berooh unti-kon-tsep-chnyee pilool-kih*

Hospital Nemocnice

Please notify my family.	**Uvědomte laskavě mou rodinu.** *oovye-domteh laska-vyeh moh ro-dyi-nooh*
I'm in pain.	**Mám bolesti.** *mahm boles-tyih*
I can't eat/sleep.	**Nemohu jíst/spát.** *nemo-hooh yeest/spaht*
When will the doctor come?	**Kdy přijde lékař?** *gdih przhiye-deh leh-karzh*
Which ward is … in?	**Na kterém oddělení je …?** *nakte-rehm od-dye-lenyee yeh*
I'm visiting …	**Jdu navštívit …** *yedooh nav-shtyee vit*

Optician Optik

I'm near- [short-] sighted/ far- [long-] sighted.	**Jsem krátkozraký(á)/dalekozraký(á).** *yesem kraht-ko-zra-kee(ah)/daleko-zra-kee(ah)*
I've lost …	**Ztratila(a) jsem …** *stra-tyil(a) yesem …*
one of my contact lenses	**jednu kontaktní čočku** *yed-nooh kon-takt-nyee choch-kooh*
my glasses/a lens	**brýle/čočky** *bree-leh/choch-kih*
Could you give me a replacement?	**Mohli byste mi dát náhradní?** *mo-hlih bis-teh mih daht nah-hrad-nyee*

Dentist Zubař

I have a toothache.	**Bolí mě zub.**
	bolee myeh zoop
This tooth hurts.	**Bolí mě tento zub.**
	bolee myeh ten-to' zoop
I've lost a tooth / filling.	**Vypadl(a) mi zub/plomba.**
	vipadul(vipadlah) mih zoop/plom-bah
Can you repair this denture?	**Můžete mi opravit protézu?**
	muh-zheteh mih opravit pro-teh-zooh
I don't want it extracted.	**Nechci ho vytrhnout.**
	nekh-tsih ho' vi-tr-hnoh-t

Dám vám injekci/anestetikum.	I'm going to give you an injection / an anesthetic.
Potřebujete plombu/korunku.	You need a filling / cap (crown).
Budu to muset vytrhnout.	I'll have to take it out.
Mohu to spravit jen dočasně.	I can only fix it temporarily.
… hodin nic nejezte.	Don't eat anything for … hours.

Payment and insurance Placení a pojištění

How much do I owe you?	**Kolik vám dlužím?**
	kolik vahm dloo-zheem
I have insurance.	**Mám pojištění.**
	mahm po-yish-tye-nyee
Can I have a receipt for my insurance?	**Mohu dostat stvrzenku pro pojišťovnu?**
	mo-hooh dos-tat sutvur-zenkooh pro-po-yish-tyov-nooh
Would you fill out this insurance form, please?	**Vypište laskavě tento formulář pro pojišťovnu.** *vi-pish-teh laska-vyeh tento' for-moolah-rzh pro-po-yish-tyov-nooh*

Dictionary

English – Czech

Most terms in this dictionary are either followed by an example or cross-referenced to pages where the word appears in a phrase. Only the masculine ending (**-ý/-í**) of adjectives is given in the dictionary. The feminine and neuter endings are **-á** and **-é**, respectively. The notes below provide some basic grammar guidelines.

Nouns

There are three genders in Czech: masculine (m.), feminine (f.), and neuter (n.) ▶ 15. The endings of nouns vary according to their "role" in the sentence. There are seven different cases in both the singular and plural. The following notes give an overview of how the cases are used.

Nominative: refers to the subject of the sentence – the person or thing performing the action.

Genitive: used to designate a person/object to whom/which somebody or something belongs (it can often be translated by *of* or *'s* in English).

Dative: designates the person/object to whom/which something is given or done.

Accusative: usually denotes the direct object of an action.

Vocative: used to address a person.

Locative: always used with a preposition. The most common prepositions are **na**, **v** (*on, in*), and **o** (*about*).

Instrumental: answers the questions "By whom?", "By what means?", and "How?".

Adjectives

Adjectives agree in number, gender, and case with the noun they modify. Here are three singular nouns, each with an adjective, showing the different endings for three cases: nominative, genitive, and accusative.

Case	Masculine (old suit)	Feminine (nice woman)	Neuter (small car)
Nom.	**starý oblek**	**milá žena**	**malé auto**
Gen.	**starého obleku**	**milé ženy**	**malého auta**
Acc.	**starý oblek**	**milé ženě**	**malé auto**

Verbs

The infinitive of most verbs ends in **-t**. Czech verbs conjugate (change their endings) according to the subject of the verb – I (**já**), you (**ty**), he/she/it (**on/ona/ono**), we (**my**), you plural/formal (**vy**), they (**oni/ony**).

	dělat (to do)	**vidět** (to see)	**kupovat** (to buy)
já	**dělám**	**vidím**	**kupuji**
ty	**děláš**	**vidíš**	**kupuješ**
on/ona/ono	**dělá**	**vidí**	**kupuje**
my	**děláme**	**vidíme**	**kupujeme**
vy	**děláte**	**vidíte**	**kupujete**
oni/ony	**dělají**	**vidí**	**kupují**

The negative is formed by adding the prefix **ne-** to the verb.

I understand	**rozumím**	I don't understand	**nerozumím**

a.m. dopoledne

about *(approx.)* asi 15

abroad v cizině/ v zahraničí

accept: to ~ *(authorize)* autorizovat 136; **do you ~ …?** berete …? 42, 136

accident *(road)* nehoda f 92, 159

accidentally neúmyslně 28

accompany: to ~ doprovodit 65

accountant účetní m 121

acne akné

across přes 12

acrylic akrylik m

actor/actress herec/herečka m/f

adapter adaptér m 26, 148

address adresa f 23, 84, 93, 126

adjoining room sousední pokoj m 22

admission charge vstupné n 114

adult *(noun)* dospělý m 100

afraid: I'm ~ *(I'm sorry)* je mi líto 126

after *(time)* po 13, 165; *(place)* za 95

after-shave voda po holení f 142

after-sun lotion olej po opalování m 142

afternoon: in the ~ odpoledne 221

age věk n 159

ago před 221; **… years ~** před … lety 163

agree: I don't agree nesouhlasím

air: ~ conditioning klimatizace f 22, 25; **~ mattress** nafukovací matrace f 31; **~ pump** stlačený vzduch m 87; **~ sickness bag** sáček na zvracení m 70; **~mail** letecky 153; **~port** letiště m 84, 96

aisle seat sedadlo do chodbičky/ uličky 69, 74

alarm clock budík m 149

alcoholic *(drink)* alkoholický

all všichni

allergy alergie f

allergic: to be ~ být alergický 164, 165

allowance povolené zboží n 67

almost skoro

alone sám; **leave me ~!** nechte mě! 126

already už 28

also také 19

alter: to ~ upravit 137

alumin[i]um foil alobal m 148

always vždy 13

am: I am já jsem

amazing obdivuhodný 101

ambassador velvyslanec m

ambulance sanitka f 92

American *(adj.)* americký 150, 159

American Plan [A.P.] *(full board)* plná penze f 24

amount *(money)* částka f 42

amusement arcade prostor s hracími automaty m 113

and a 19

anesthetic anestetikum n 168

animal zvíře n 106

anorak nepromokavá bunda f 145

another jiný 21, 25; *(time)* někdy jindy 125

antibiotics antibiotika npl 165

antifreeze nemrznoucí směs f

antique *(noun)* starožitnost f 155

antiseptic antiseptikum n 165; **~ cream** antiseptický krém m 141

any jakýkoliv

anyone někdo 67; **does ~ speak English?** mluví někdo anglicky?

anything else? něco dalšího?

apartment byt m 28

apologize: I ~ omlouvám se

appendicitis zánět slepého střeva m 165

appendix slepé střevo n 166

appetite chuť k jídlu f 164

apples jablka npl 157

appointment: to make an ~ objednat se 147

approximately přibližně 159

April duben m 218

architect architekt m 104

are: are there …? jsou tam …? 17

area code směrové číslo n 127

arm paže f 166

around *(place)* po 12; *(time)* kolem 13

arrive: to ~ přijet 13, 71, 76

art gallery galerie f 99

arthritis: to have ~ mít artritidu 163

artificial sweetener umělé sladidlo n 38

ashtray popelník m 39

ask: I asked for … objednal jsem si … 41

aspirin aspirin m 141

asthma: to have ~ mít astma 163

at: *(place)* u 12; *(time)* v 13, 84, 221; **at last!** konečně! 19; **at least** nejméně 23

athletics atletika f 114

attack napadení m 159

attractive přitažlivý

audio-guide audio průvodce m 100

August srpen m 218

aunt teta f 120

Australia Austrálie f 119

Austria Rakousko n 119

authentic: is it ~? je to pravé?

authenticity pravost f 155

automated teller (ATM) bankomat m 139

automatic: *(car)* s automatickou převodovkou 86; **~ camera** automatický fotoaparát m 151

automobile automobil m

autumn podzim m 219

available *(free)* volný 77

avalanche lavina f

B **baby** dítě m 39, 113; **~ food** kojenecká výživa f 142; **~-sitter** paní k dětem f 113; **~ wipes** navlhčené ubrousky mpl 142

back: *(head)* vzadu 147; *(body)* záda 166; **I have ~ache** bolí mě v zádech 163

back: to be ~ *(return)* vrátit se 98

bad špatný 14

bag kabelka f 160

baggage: zavazadlo n 32, 71; **~ check** úschovna zavazadel f 71, 73; **~ reclaim** výdej zavazadel m 71

bakery pekařství n 130

balcony balkón m 29

ball míč m 155

ballet balet m 108, 111

band *(musical group)* skupina f 111, 155

bandage obinadlo n 141

bank banka f 96, 130, 138

bar bar m 26, 112

barber holičství n 131

basement suterén m

basket košík m 156

basketball košíková f 114

bath: vana f 21; **~room** koupelna f 29; **~ towel** ručník m 27

bathroom *(toilet)* záchod m 26, 98, 113

battery baterie f 88, 137, 149, 151

battle site bitevní pole n 99

be: to ~ být 17, 121
beach pláž f 107
beam (headlights) světla m 86
beard vousy
beautiful krásný 14, 101
because: protože 15; **~ of** kvůli 15
bed postel f 21; **~room** ložnice f 29;
~ **and breakfast** nocleh se snídaní
m 24
bedding přikrývky a povlečení 29
beer pivo n 40, 157, 158
before (time) před/do 13, 165, 221
begin: to ~ začít
beginner začátečník m/
začátečnice f 117
behind za 95
beige béžový 143
belong: this belongs to me
to je moje
belt pásek m 144
berth lůžko n 74, 77
best nejlepší
better lepší 14
between: (time) mezi 221;
~ **jobs** (unemployed) právě bez
zaměstnání 121
bib bryndáček m
bicycle jízdní kolo n 75, 83, 160
bidet bidet m
big velký 14, 117, 134; **bigger**
větší 24
bikini bikiny 144
bill (restaurant, etc.) účet m 32, 42
bin liner sáček do odpadkového
koše m
binoculars dalekohled m
bird pták m 106
birthday narozeniny 219
biscuits sušenky fpl 157, 158

bite (insect) štípnutí n
bitten: I've been ~ by a dog pokousal
mě pes
bitter hořký 41
bizarre prapodivný 101
black: černý 143; **~ coffee** černá
káva f 40; **~ and white film** (camera)
černobílý film m 151
bladder měchýř m 166
blanket přikrývka f 27
bleach odbarvovací prostředek m 148
bleeding: he's ~ krvácí 162
blind roleta f 25
blister puchýř m 162
blocked: to be ~ být ucpaný 25
blood: krev f 164; **~ group** krevní
skupina; **~ pressure** krevní tlak m
163, 164
blouse blůza f 144
blow-dry vyfoukat 147
blue modrý 143
board: on ~ (bus) v autobuse 78
boarding card palubní vstupenka
f 70
boat trip výlet lodí m 97
boil (ailment) vřídek m 162
boiled (cooking) vařený
boiler kotel m 29
bone kost f 166
book kniha f 150; **~store** knihy 130
booted: to be ~ (car) dostat
botičku 87
boots boty fpl 115, 145
boring nudný 101
born: to be ~ narodit se 119; **I was ~
in ...** narodil jsem se v ...
borrow: may I borrow your ...?
mohu si půjčit váš ...?
botanical garden botanická zahrada
f 99

bottle láhev f 37, 40; **~ of wine** láhev vína f 154; **~-opener** otvírač na láhve m 148

bowel střevo n

bowls misky fpl 148

box krabička f 110; **~ of chocolates** bonboniéra f 154

boy chlapec m 120, 155; **~friend** přítel m 120

bra podprsenka f 144

bracelet náramek m 149

brakes *(bicycle)* brzdy fpl 83

bread chléb m 38, 157

break: to ~ rozbít 28

breakdown porucha f 88; **~ truck** havarijní služba f 88

breakfast snídaně f 27

breast prso n 166

breathe: to ~ dýchat 92, 164

bridge most m 95, 107

briefs *(clothing)* spodní kalhotky 144

bring: to ~ přivést 113, 125

Britain Británie f 119

British britský 159

brochure brožura f

broken: to be ~ být rozbitý 25, 137; *(bone)* být zlomený 164

bronchitis bronchitida f

brooch brož f 149

brother bratr m 120

brown hnědý 143

browse: to ~ *(look around)* dívat se 133

bruise modřina f 162

bucket kyblík m 155

building budova f

built: to be ~ postavit 104

bulletin board nástěnka f 26

bureau de change směnárna f 138

burger karbanátek m 40; **~ stand** stánek s párky m 35

burn popálenina f 162

bus autobus m 70, 71, 79, 123; **~ route** autobusová trasa f 96; **~ station** autobusové nádraží n 78; **~ stop** autobusová zastávka f 65, 78, 96

business: ~ class obchodní třída f 68; **to be in ~** věnovat se podnikání n 121; **on ~** služebně 66, 123

busy: to be ~ *(occupied)* něco mít 125; *(full)* obsazeno 36

but ale 19

butane gas plyn m 30, 31

butcher řezník m 130

butter máslo n 38, 158

button knoflík m

buy: to ~ koupit 79, 80, 98, 133; *(order)* objednat 125

by *(near)* u 36; *(time)* před/do 13, 221; **~ bus** autobusem 17; **~ car** autem 17, 94; **~ cash** hotově 17; **~ credit card** kreditní kartou 17; **~ train** vlakem 17

bye! nashledanou!

C **cabaret** kabaret m 112
café kavárna f 35

cagoule větrovka f 145

cake *(large)* dort m; **cakes** zákusky mpl 158

calendar kalendář m 154

call: to ~ collect hovor na účet volaného 127; **to ~ for someone** přijít pro někoho 125; *(telephone)* zavolat 87, 92, 127, 128; **call the police!** zavolejte policii! 92

called: to be ~ jmenovat se 94

camera fotoaparát m 151, 160; **~ case** pouzdro na fotoaparát m 151; **~ store** fotoaparáty mpl 130

camp: ~site kempink m 30, 123; **~bed** stanové lůžko n 31

camp: to ~ tábořit

can: I can/I can't mohu/nemohu 18; **~ I have ...?** mohu dostat ...? 18

Canada Kanada f 119

canal kanál m 107

cancel: to ~ zrušit 68

cancer (disease) rakovina f

candy bonbóny mpl 150

can opener otvírač na plechovky m 148

cap (clothing) čepice f 144; (dental) korunka f 168

car auto n 30, 73, 86, 88, 93, 123, 160; **by ~** autem 95; **~ park** parkoviště n 26, 96; **~ rental** půjčovna aut 70; (train compartment) vagón m 75

carafe džbánek m 37, 40

caravan obytný přívěs m 30

cards karty fpl 121

careful: be ~! buďte opatrný!

carpet (rug) koberec m

carrier bag sáček m

carry-cot přenosná taška na dítě f

cart vozík m 156

case (suitcase) zavazadlo n 69

cash (money) hotovost f 42, 136; **~ desk** pokladna f 132; **~ machine** bankomat m 139

cash: to ~ (exchange) vyměnit 138

cashier pokladna f 132

casino kasino n 112

cassette kazeta f 155

castle hrad m 99

cathedral chrám m 99

Catholic katolický 105

cave jeskyně f 107

CD kompaktní disk m; **~-player** přehrávač kompaktních disků m

cemetery hřbitov m 99

center of town centrum m 21

central heating ústřední topení n

ceramics keramika f

certificate osvědčení n 149, 155

chain (necklace) řetízek m 149

change (coins) drobné 84, 87, 136

change: (transportation) přestoupit 75, 79, 80; (money) vyměnit 138; (reservation) změnit 68; **to ~ a baby** přebalit dítě 39;

changing facilities prostor na přebalování n

charcoal dřevěné uhlí n 31

charges sazba f 153

charter flight speciál m

cheap levný 14, 134; **cheaper** levnější 21, 24, 109, 134

check [cheque] book šeková knížka f

check: to ~ in (hotel) ubytovat se 68; **to ~ out** (hotel) uvolnit pokoj 32; **~-in desk** přepážka k odbavení f 69

cheers! na zdraví!

cheese sýr m 157, 158

chemist lékárna f 131

chess šachy 121, 155

chest (body) prsa npl 166

chewing gum žvýkačka f 150

child dítě n 159, 162; **~'s cot** dětská postýlka f 22; **~minder** hlídání n; **~'s seat** dětská sedačka f 39; **children** děti npl 22, 24, 39, 66, 74, 100, 113, 116, 120, 140

Chinese (cuisine) čínský 35

chocolate: ~ bar čokoláda f 150; (flavor) čokoládový 40; **~ ice cream** čokoládová zmrzlina f 110

Christmas Vánoce 219

church kostel m 96, 99, 105

cigarette kiosk tabák m 130

cigarettes cigarety fpl 150

cigars doutníky mpl 150

cinema kino n 110

claim check *(baggage)* zavazadlový lístek m 71

clamped: to be ~ dostat botičku 87

clean čistý 14, 39

clean: to ~ vyčistit 137

cliff útes m 107

cling film potravinová fólie f 148

clinic zdravotní středisko n 131

cloakroom šatna f 109

clock hodiny 149

close *(near)* blízko 93, 95

close: to ~ *(store)* zavírat 100, 140, 152

clothes pins [pegs] kolíčky mpl 148

clothing store oděvy mpl 130

cloudy: to be ~ být zamračeno 122

clubs *(golf)* golfové hole fpl 115

coach autobus m 78; *(train compartment)* vagón m 75; **~ station** autobusové nádraží n 78

coast pobřeží n

coat kabát m 144; **~check** šatna f 109; **~hanger** ramínko n

cockroach šváb m

code *(area [dialing])* kód m

coffee káva f 40, 157

coin mince f

cold studený 14, 41; **cold** *('flu)* rýma f 141; *(weather)* zima 122

cold: to have a ~ být nachlazený 163

collapse: he's collapsed zhroutil se

collect: to ~ vyzvednout 113, 151

color barva f 143; **~ film** barevný film m 151

comb hřeben m 142

come: to ~ přijít 36, 124, 126; **to ~ back** *(return)* přijít znovu 36

comfortable pohodlný 117

commission provize f 138

compact: ~ camera kompaktní fotoaparát m 151; **~ disc** kompaktní disk m 155

company *(business)* firma f; *(companionship)* společnost f 126

composer skladatel m 111

computer počítač m

concert koncert m 108, 111; **~ hall** koncertní síň f 111

concession sleva f

concussion: he has a ~ má otřes mozku

conditioner *(hair)* kondicionér m 142

condom kondom m 141

conductor dirigent m 111

confirm: to ~ *(reservation)* potvrdit 22, 68

congratulations! *(from me/from us)* blahopřeji!/blahopřejeme!

connection *(train)* spojení n 76

conscious: he's ~ je při vědomí

constant nepřetržitý 113

constipation zácpa f

consulate konzulát m 159

consult: to ~ jít k 165

contact lens kontaktní čočka f 167

contact: to ~ spojit se 28

contagious: to be ~ být nakažlivý 165

contain: to ~ obsahovat 153

contemporary dance moderní tanec m 111

contraceptive antikoncepce f

cook: to ~ vařit; *(chef)* kuchař/kuchařka m/f

cooker *(appliance)* vařič m 28, 29

cookies sušenky fpl 157, 158

cooking *(cuisine)* kuchyně f; **~ facilities** kuchyňské vybavení n 30

coolbox lednice f

copper měď f 149

copy kopie f

corkscrew vývrtka f 148

correct správný
cosmetics kosmetika f
cost: to ~ stát 84, 89
cottage chata f 28
cotton bavlna f 145; **~ wool**
vata f 141
cough kašel m 141
cough: to ~ zakašlat 164
could: ~ I have …?
mohu dostat …? 18
country (nation) země f
country music country hudba f 111
courier (guide; masc./fem.) průvodce/
průvodkyně m/f
course (meal) chod m; (track, path)
cesta f 106; (medication) dávka
f 165
cousin bratranec m/sestřenice f
cover charge kuvert m 112
craft store obchod s uměleckými
řemesly m
cramps křeče fpl 163
crèche jesle
credit card kreditní karta f
42, 109, 136, 139, 160; **~ number** číslo
kreditní karty n 109
crib kolébka f 22
crisps bramborové lupínky mpl 157
crockery nádobí ns 29
cross (crucifix) kříž m
cross: to ~ přejít přes 95
crowded přeplněný 31
crown (dental) korunka f 168
cruise (noun) zábavní plavba f
crutches berle fpl
crystal (quartz) křemen m 149
cup šálek m 39, 148
cupboard skříň f
currency měna f 67, 138; **~ exchange**
směnárna f 70, 73, 138
curtains záclony fpl

customs celní prohlídka f 67, 155
cut (hair) ostříhat 147
cut glass broušené sklo n 149
cutlery příbory mpl 29
cycle route cyklistická stezka 106
cycling cyklistika f 114
cystitis zánět močových cest m 165
Czech český 35, 110, 126

D **daily** denně
damage: to ~ poškodit 71;
to be damaged být poškozený 28
damp (noun) vlhkost f; (adj.) vlhký
dance: tanec m 111; **to ~** tančit 111;
to go dancing jít tančit 124
dangerous nebezpečný
dark (color) tmavě 143
dark tmavý 14, 24, 134, 143; **darker**
tmavší 143
daughter dcera f 120, 162
dawn úsvit m 221
day: den m 23, 97, 122, 221; **~ ticket**
denní jízdenka f; **~ trip** jednodenní
výlet m
dead (battery) vybitý 88
deaf: to be ~ být hluchý 163
December prosinec m 218
deck chair skládací lehátko n 116
declare: to ~ přihlásit 67
deduct: to ~ (money) odečíst
deep hluboký
defrost: to ~ rozmrazit
degrees (temperature) stupně mpl
delay zpoždění n 70
delicatessen lahůdky 156
delicious chutný 14
deliver: to ~ doručit
denim džínsovina m 145
dental floss vlákno na čištění
mezizubních prostorů n
dentist zubař m 131, 168

denture protéza f 168

deodorant deodorant m 142

depart: to ~ *(train, bus)* odjíždět

department store obchodní dům m 96, 130

departure lounge odjezdová hala f

deposit záloha f 24, 83

describe: to ~ popsat 159

details podrobnosti fpl

detergent prášek na praní m 148

develop: to ~ *(photos)* vyvolat 151

diabetic: *(noun)* diabetik m 39; **to be ~** být diabetik 163

dialling code směrové číslo n 127

diamond diamant m 149

diapers plenky fpl 142

diarrhea průjem n 141; **to have ~** mít průjem 163/mám průjem

dice kostky fpl

dictionary slovník m 150

diesel: *(fuel)* nafta f 87; *(vehicle)* dieselový motor m

diet: I'm on a ~ jsem na dietě

difficult těžký 14

dining: ~ car jídelní vůz m 75, 77; **~ room** jídelna f 26, 29

dinner večeře 125; **~ jacket** smoking m; **to have ~** jít na večeři 124

direct *(train, flight)* přímý 75

direction: in the ~ of ... směrem na ... 95

director *(company)* ředitel m

directory *(telephone)* telefonní seznam m

dirty špinavý 14, 28

disabled *(noun)* tělesně postižený 22/ invalida m 100

discotheque diskotéka f 112

discount sleva f 24

dish *(meal)* jídlo n 37, 39

dishcloth hadr na nádobí m 148

dishes nádobí ns 29

dishwashing liquid prostředek na mytí nádobí m 148

dislocated: to be ~ být vykloubený 164

display cabinet/case vitrína f 134, 149

disposable camera fotoaparát na jedno použití m 151

distilled water destilovaná voda f

disturb: don't ~ nerušit

dive: to ~ skákat do vody 116

divorced: to be ~ být rozvedený 120

dizzy: I feel ~ točí se mi hlava

do: to ~ dělat 123; **what do you do?** čím jste 121

doctor doktor m 92, 131, 167

doll panenka f 155

dollar dolar m 67, 138

door dveře 25

double: ~ bed manželská postel f 21; **~ room** dvoulůžkový pokoj m 21

downtown centrum města m 83, 99

dozen tucet m 217

draft [draught] točené 40

dress šaty 144

drink: *(noun)* pití n 37, 70, 125, 126; **drinking water** pitná voda f 30

drip: the faucet [tap] drips kohoutek kape

driver řidič m; **driver's license** řidičský průkaz m 93

drive: to ~ jet 93

drop: to ~ someone off vysadit někoho 83

drowning: someone is ~ někdo se topí

drugstore drogerie f 130

drunk opilý

dry cleaner čistírna f 131**

A-Z

dry-clean: to ~ chemicky vyčistit

dubbed: to be ~ být dabovaný 110

dummy *(pacifier)* dudlík m

during během 221

dustbins popelnice fpl 30

duvet peřina f

E e-mail elektronická pošta f 153; ~ address adresa elektronické pošty f 153

ear: ucho n 166; ~ drops kapky do uší fpl; I have ~ache bolí mě ucho 163; ~rings náušnice fpl 149

earlier dříve 125, 147

early brzo 14, 221

east východ m 95

Easter Velikonoce 219

easy snadný 14

eat: to ~ jíst 167; *(dine)* najíst se 123; *(damaged by machine)* nevrátit 139

economy class ekonomická třída f 68

eggs vejce npl 157

elastic *(adj.)* elastický

electric: ~ meter elektrické hodiny 28; ~ razor [shaver] elektrický holicí strojek m; electrical outlets elektrické zásuvky fpl 30

electronic: elektronický 69; ~ flash *(camera)* elektrický blesk m 151; ~ game elektronická hra f 155

elevator výtah m 26, 132

else: something ~ něco jiného

embassy velvyslanectví n

emerald smaragd m

emergency *(adj.)* naléhavý 127; ~ exit nouzový východ m 132

empty prázdný 14

enamel email m 149

end: to ~ končit 108; at the ~ na konci m 95

engaged: to be ~ být zasnoubený 120

engine motor m

engineering strojírenství n 121

England Anglie f 119

English: anglický f 11, 67, 150, 159; in ~ v angličtině f 100, 110; ~-speaking anglicky mluvící 98, 159

enjoy: to ~ líbit se 110/mít rád 124

enlarge: to ~ *(photos)* zvětšit 151

enough dost 15, 42, 136

ensuite bathroom pokoj s koupelnou m

entertainment guide kulturní přehled m

entrance fee vstupné n 100

entry visa vstupní vízum n

envelope obálka f 150

epileptic: to be ~ být epileptik 163

equipment *(sports)* vybavení n 115

era období n 147

error chyba f

escalator eskalátor m 132

essential nezbytný 89

Eurocheque Eurocheque m

evening večer m 109, 124, 132, 221

every: každý 119; ~ day každý den; ~ hour každou hodinu 76; ~ week každý týden m 13

examination *(medical)* vyšetření n

example: for ~ například

except kromě

excess baggage nadváha f 69

exchange rate kurz m 138

exchange: to ~ vyměnit 137, 138

excursion výlet m 97

excuse me *(apology)* promiňte 10

excuse me: *(getting attention)* promiňte 10, 94; *(may I get past?)* dovolte prosím 10; excuse me! promiňte! 94; *(please repeat)* prosím? 11

exhausted: I'm ~ jsem vyčerpaný 106

exit (*noun*) východ m 70, 132; (*highway*) sjezd m 83

expensive drahý 14, 134

experienced zkušený 117

expire: when does the card ~? kdy karta přestane platit? 109

exposure (*photos*) snímek m 151

express spěšně 153

extension linka f 128

extra (*additional*) ještě jeden 23; (*another*) navíc 27

extract: to ~ (*tooth*) vytrhnout 168

eye oko n 166

F **fabric** látka f 145

face obličej m 166

facial masáž obličeje f 147

facilities vybavení n 22, 30

factor ... (*sunscreen*) faktor ... m 142

faint: to feel ~ cítit se mdle 163

fairground lunapark m 113

fall podzim 219

family rodina f 66, 74, 120, 167

famous známý

fan (*ventilation*) větrák m 25

far: daleko 12, 95, 130; **~-sighted** dalekozraký 167; **how ~ is it?** jak je to daleko? 73, 94, 106

farm statek m 107

fast: rychlý 17, 93; (*clock*) napřed 221; **~-food restaurant** rychlé občerstvení n 35

father otec m 120

faucet kohoutek m 25

faulty: this is ~ je to vadné

favorite oblíbený

fax: fax m 22, 153; **~ machine** fax m 153

February únor m 218

feed: to ~ nakojit 39

feeding bottle dětská láhev f

feel: to ~ ill necítit se dobře 163

female žena f 159

fever horečka f 163

few: málo 15; **a few of ...** několik ... 15

fiancé(e) snoubenec/snoubenka m/f

field pole n 107

fifth pátý 217

fight (*brawl*) rvačka f

fill: to ~ out (*form*) vyplnit 168; **to ~ up** (*with fuel*) plná nádrž 87

filling (*dental*) plomba f 168

film: (*movie*) film m 108, 110; (*camera*) film m 151

filter filtr m 151

find: to ~ najít 18

fine (*well*) dobře 118/fajn 19; (*penalty*) pokuta f 93

finger prst m 166

fire: ~ alarm požární hlásič m; **~ department [brigade]** hasiči mpl 92; **~ escape** požární schodiště n; **~ exit** nouzový východ m 132; **~ extinguisher** hasicí přístroj m; **there's a ~!** hoří!; **~wood** palivové dříví n

first první 68, 75, 132, 217; **~ floor** (*U.K.*) přvn patro m 132; **~ class** první třída f 68, 74

fish and poultry store ryby a drůbež 130

fish restaurant rybí restaurace f 35

fit: to ~ (*clothes*) být dobře 146

fitting room zkušební kabina f 146

fix: to ~ spravit 168

flashlight ruční svítilna f 31

flat (*puncture*) píchlý 83, 88

flavor: what flavors do you have? jaké máte příchutě?

flea blecha f

flight: letadlo n 68, 70; **~ number** let číslo 68

flip-flops sandály mpl 145

floor (level) poschodí n 132

florist květiny fpl 130

flower květina f 106

flu (influenza) chřipka f 165

flush: the toilet won't ~ záchod nesplachuje

fly (insect) moucha f

foggy: it is ~ je mlha f 122

folk: ~ art lidové umění n; **~ music** lidová hudba f 111

follow: to ~ (pursue) chodit 159

food jídlo n 39, 119; **~ poisoning** otrava potravinami f 165

foot chodidlo n 166

football fotbal m 114

footpath pěšina f 107

for (time) na 116; **~ a day** na den 86; **~ a week** na týden 86; (towards) do 94

foreign currency peníze 138

forest les m 107

forget: to ~ zapomenout 42

fork vidlička f 39, 41, 148

form formulář m 23, 168

formal dress formální oblečení n 111

fortnight čtrnáct dní

fortunately naštěstí 19

fountain kašna f 99

four: ~-door car čtyřdveřové auto n 86; **~-wheel drive** (car) se čtyřkolovým pohonem 86

fourth čtvrtý 217

foyer (hotel, theater) foyer m

fracture zlomenina f 165

frame (glasses) obroučky

free (available) volný 36; (no charge) zadarmo 69

freezer mraznička m 29

French dressing francouzská zálivka f 38

frequent: how ~? jak často? 76; **frequently** často

fresh čerstvý 41

Friday pátek m 218

fried smažený

friend (masc./fem.) přítel / přítelkyně m / f 123, 125, 162

friendly přátelský

fries hranolky mpl 38, 40

frightened: to be ~ mít strach

from z 12, 70, 73; (time) od 13, 221; **where are you ~?** odkud jste? 119

front (adj.) přední 83; (head) vpředu 147

frost mráz f 122

frying pan pánev f 29

fuel (gasoline [petrol]) palivo m/ benzín m 86

full (adj.) plný 14; **~ board** plná penze f 24; **to be ~** být obsazeno 21, 36

fun: to have ~ bavit se

furniture nábytek m

fuse pojistka f 28; **~ box** pojistky fpl 28

G **game** (sport) zápas m 114; (toy) hra f 155

garage (parking) garáž f 26; (repair) servis m 88

garbage bags pytle na odpadky mpl 148

garden zahrada f 35

gas (gasoline) benzín m 88; **~ bottle** plynová bomba f 28; **~ station** benzínová pumpa f 87; **I smell ~!** cítím plyn!

gastritis gastritida f 165

gate *(airport)* východ m 70

gauze gáza f 141

gay club klub pro homosexuály m 112

genuine originál m 134

Germany Německo n 119

get: to ~ to přijet 77; **to ~ back** *(return)* vrátit se 98; **to ~ off** *(bus, etc.)* vystoupit 79; **how do I get to …?** jak se dostanu …? 70, 73, 94; *(buy)* opatřit si 30

gift dárek m 67, 154; **~ store** dárky mpl 130

girl děvče n 120; *(little girl)* holčička f 155; **~friend** přítelkyně f 120

give: to ~ dát 70

gland žláza f 166

glass sklenice f 37, 39, 40, 148

glasses *(optical)* brýle 167

glossy finish *(photos)* na lesklý papír

glove rukavice f

go: to ~ *(on foot)* jít 18, 124; **~ for a walk** jít na procházku 124; **~ out for a meal** jít na večeři 124; *(by vehicle)* jet 66, 93; **~ shopping** jít nakupovat 124; **where does this bus ~?** kam jede tento autobus?; **let's ~!** jdeme!; **~ away!** běžte pryč!; **~ on!** ale jděte! 19

goggles potápěčské brýle

gold zlato n 149; **~ plate** pozlacený 149

golf golf m 114; **~ course** golfové hřiště n 115

good: dobrý 14, 35; **~ afternoon** dobré odpoledne n 10; **~-bye** nashledanou 10; **~ evening** dobrý večer m 10; **~ morning** *(for early morning)* dobré ráno n; *(for late morning)* dobrý den m 10; **~ night** dobrou noc f 10; *(delicious)* výborný 42

grandparents prarodiče mpl

grapes hroznové víno n 158

grass tráva f

gray šedý 143

great moc dobře 19

green zelený 143

greengrocer ovoce a zelenina 130

grilled grilovaný

grocer *(grocery store)* potraviny

ground *(earth)* zem f 31; **~ floor** přízemí n

groundcloth [groundsheet] podlážka f 31

group skupina f 66, 100

guarantee záruka f 135

guest house penzión m 123

guide *(masc./fem.)* průvodce m/průvodkyně f 98; **~book** průvodce m 100, 150; **guided tour** prohlídka s průvodcem f 100; **guided walk** vycházka s průvodcem f 106

guitar kytara f

gum žvýkačka f

guy rope kotevní lano n 31

gynecologist gynekolog m 167

H **hair** vlasy mpl 147; **~dresser** kadeřnictví n 131, 147; **~ mousse** pěna na vlasy f 142; **~ spray** lak na vlasy 142 **to have a ~cut** nechat se ostříhat

half *(noun)* půl f 217; **~ past** půl 220; **~ board** polopenze f 24

ham šunka f 157

hammer kladivo n 31

hand baggage příruční zavazadlo n 69

hand *(body)* ruka f 166; **~bag** kabelka f 144, 160; **~ washable** prát v ruce 145

handicap (*golf*) handicap m

handicapped: to be ~ být tělesně postižený 163

handicrafts řemesla npl

handkerchief kapesník m

hanger ramínko n 27

hangover (*noun*) kocovina f 141

happen: to ~ stát se 93

harbor přístav m

hard (*firm*) tvrdý 31; (*difficult*) obtížný 106

hat klobouk m 144

have: to ~ mít 18, 42, 120, 133; **could I ~ …?** mohu dostat …? 38; **does the hotel ~ …?** je v hotelu …? 22; **I'll ~ …** vezmu si 37

hay fever senná rýma f 141

head hlava f 166; **I have a ~ache** bolí mě hlava 163

head waiter vrchní m 41

health: ~ food store zdravá vyživa 130; **~ insurance** zdravotní pojištění n 168

hear: to ~ slyšet

hearing aid sluchadlo n

heart srdce n 166; **~ attack** infarkt m 163; (*cards*) srdce npl

heat [heating] topení n 25

heavy těžký 14, 69, 117, 134

height výška f 159

hello nazdar 10

help: can you ~ me? můžete mi pomoci? 18, 92, 133

hemorrhoids hemoroidy mpl 165

her(s) její 16; **it's hers** je to její

here (*motion*) sem 12; (*place*) tady 17, 31, 106, 119/tu 35, 77

hernia kýla f 165

hi ahoj 10

high vysoký 122, 163

highlight: to ~ hair tónování m 147

highway dálnice f 88, 92, 94

hiking: (*noun*) pěší turistika f; **~ gear** vybavení na turistiku n

hill kopec m 107

hire půjčit 83

his jeho 16; **it's his** je to jeho

historic site památková oblast f 99

HIV-positive HIV pozitivní

hobby (*pastime*) koníček m 121

hold: to ~ on (*wait*) počkat 128

hole (*in clothes*) díra f

holiday dovolená f 123; **on ~** na dovolené f 66; **~ resort** rekreační středisko v

home domů 126; **we're going ~** jedeme domů

homosexual (*adj.*) homosexuální

honeymoon: we're on our ~ jsme na svatební cestě

hopefully snad 19

horse kůň m; **~ racing** dostihy mpl 114

hospital nemocnice f 96, 131, 164, 167

hot horký 14; (*weather*) horko n 122; **~ dog** párek v rohlíku 110; **~ spring** horký pramen m; **~ water** horká voda f 25

hotel hotel m 21, 123

hour hodina f 97, 116; **in an ~** za hodinu f 84

house dům m

housewife být v domácnosti 121

how jak? 17; **~ long …?** jak dlouho …? 23, 68, 75, 76, 78, 88, 94, 98, 106, 135; **~ many times …?** kolikrát …? 140; **~ many …?** kolik …? 15, 79, 80; **~ much …?** kolik …? 21, 65, 68, 79, 89, 100, 109, 136, 140; **~ old …?** jak starý …? 120, 147; **~ are you?** jak se máte? 118; **~ are things?** jak se máte? 19

hundred sto n 217

hungry: I'm ~ mám hlad

hurry: I'm in a ~ spěchám

hurt: to ~ bolet 164; **to be ~** být zraněný 162; **my ... hurts** bolí mě ... 162

husband manžel m 120, 162

I ice led m 38; **~ cream** zmrzlina f 40; **~-cream parlor** cukrárna se zmrzlinou f 35

icy zledovatělý 117

identification identifikace f

ill: I'm ~ jsem nemocný

illegal: is it ~? je to nezákonné?

imitation napodobenina f 134

in *(place)* v 12, 88; *(within period of time)* za 13; **~ front of** před 125

include zahrnovat 24

included: to be ~ být zahrnutý 42; **is ... included?** je v tom zahrnuté ...? 86; **is ... included in the price?** je ... zahrnutý do ceny? 98

incredible neuvěřitelný 101

indicate: to ~ ukázat

indigestion porucha trávení f

indoor pool krytý bazén m 116

inexpensive levný 35

infected: to be ~ být zanícený 165

infection infekce f 167

inflammation zánět m 165

informal *(dress)* neformální

information informace f 97; **~ desk** informace fpl 73; **~ office** informační kancelář f 96

injection injekce f 168

injured: to be ~ být zraněný 92, 162

innocent nevinný

insect hmyz m 25; **~ bite** štípanec m 141; **to have an ~ bite** být poštípaný 162; **~ repellent** repelent proti hmyzu m 141

inside uvnitř 12

insomnia nespavost f

instant coffee instantní káva f 158

instead of místo 38

instructions návod m 135

instructor instruktor m

insulin inzulín m

insurance *(car)* pojištění n 86; *(company)* pojišťovna f 89, 160, 168; **~ card [certificate]** pojistka f 93; **~ claim** pojistná škoda f

interest *(hobby)* zájem m 121

interested: to be ~ in ... mít zájem o ... 111

interesting zajímavý 101

International Student Card mezinárodní studentský průkaz m 29

Internet Internet m 153

interpreter tlumočník m 160

intersection křižovatka f 95

into do 70

introduce oneself: to ~ představit se 118

invite: to ~ pozvat 124

iodine jód m

Ireland Irsko n 119

is: is it ...? je to ...? 17; **is there ...?** je tam ...? 17; **it is ...** to je ... 17

Italian *(cuisine)* italský 35

itch: it itches svědí to

item předmět m 69

itemized bill rozepsaný účet m 32

J jacket sako n 144

jam marmeláda f 157

jammed: to be ~ nejít otevřít 25

January leden m 218

jaw čelist f 166

jazz džez m 111

jeans džíny 144

jellyfish medúza f

jet lag: I'm jet lagged nevyrovnal jsem se s časovým posunem

jeweler klenoty mpl 130, 149

job: what's your ~? kde pracujete?

join: to ~ zapsat si 117; **to ~ in** přidat se 115; **can we ~ you?** můžeme se k vám připojit? 124

joint kloub m 166; **~ passport** společný pas m 66

joke vtip m

journalist novinář m

journey cesta f 76, 78

jug (water) džbánek m

July červenec m 218

jump leads spojovací kabel m

jumper svetr m

junction křižovatka f 95

June červen m 218

keep: to ~ nechat si 84; **~ the change!** nechejte si drobné!

kerosene petrolej m; **~ stove** primus m 31

ketchup kečup m

kettle konvice f 29

key klíč m 27, 28, 88; **~ ring** přívěšek ke klíčům 154

kiddie pool dětský bazén m 113

kidney ledvina f 166

kilometer kilometr m 88

kind (pleasant) hodný

kind: what ~ of ... jaký ...

kiss: to ~ políbit

kitchen kuchyň f 29

knapsack ruksak m 31, 145

knee koleno n 166

knickers spodní kalhotky 144

knife nůž m 39, 41; **knives** nože mpl 148

know: to ~ znát 146

kosher košer

label etiketa f

lace krajka f 145

ladder žebřík m

lake jezero n 107

lamp lampa f 25, 29

land: to ~ (airplane) přistát 70

language course jazykový kurz m

large velký 40, 69; **larger** větší 134

last (in a row/sequence) poslední 14, 68, 75, 80; (year) minulý 218

last: to ~ vydržet

late pozdě 14, 221; **later** později 125, 147

laundromat prádelna f 131

laundry: ~ facilities prádelna f 30; **~ service** prádelní služba f 22

lavatory záchod m

lawyer právník m 159

laxative projímadlo n

lead: to ~ (in a direction) vést 94

lead-free (unleaded) bezolovnatý 87

leader (group) vedoucí m

leak: to ~ (roof, pipe) téct

learn: to ~ (language) učit se

leather kůže f 145

leave: to ~ (aircraft) odlétat 68, 70; (by vehicle) odjíždět 76, 98; (on foot) odejít 41, 126; (deposit) nechat 32, 73; **I've left my bag ...** zapomněla jsem si kabelku ...

left: on the ~ vlevo 76, 95

left-luggage office úschovna zavazadel f 71, 73

leg noha f 166

legal: is it ~? je to legální?

leggings kamaše 144

lemon citrón m 38

lemonade limonáda f 158

lend: could you ~ me ...? můžete mi půjčit ...?

length délka f

lens (camera) čočka f 151; **~ cap** víčko na čočku n 151; (optical) čočky fpl 167

less méně 15

lesson hodina f 115

let me know! dejte mi vědět!

letter dopis m 152; **~box** (street/house) poštovní schránka/schránka na dopisy

level (adj.) rovný 31

library knihovna f

lie down: to ~ položit se 164

life: ~belt záchranný pás m; **~boat** záchranný člun m; **~guard** plavčík m 116; **~jacket** záchranná vesta f

lift výtah m 26, 132

lift (hitchhiking) svezení n 83

lift pass permanentka na vlek m 117

light (color) světlý 14, 134, 143; (weight) lehký 14, 134; **lighter** světlejší 143

light (electric, bicycle) světlo f 25, 83; **~ bulb** žárovka f 148

lighter (cigarette) zapalovač m 150

like: to ~ (people) líbit se 101, 119, 135; (want) chtít 125; (activities, books, etc.) mít rád 121; (food) chutnat 119; **I ~ it** líbí se mi; **I don't ~ it** nelíbí se mi; **I'd ~** chtěl bych 18, 37, 40, 141, 157

like this (similar to) jako tento

limousine limuzína f

line (subway) trasa f 80

linen len m 145

lip ret m 166

lipstick rtěnka f

liqueur likér m

liquor store víno a lihoviny 131

liter litr m 87

little (small) malý; **a ~** trochu 15

live: to ~ žít 119; **to ~ together** žít spolu 120

liver játra 166

living room obývací pokoj m 29

lobby (theater, hotel) vestibul m

local místní 37

lock oneself out: to ~ zabouchnout si pokoj 27

lock zámek m 25

lock: to ~ zamknout 88

log on: to ~ přihlásit se 153

long dlouhý 144, 146; **~-distance bus** dálkový autobus m 78; **~-sighted** dalekozraký 167

look: to ~ for hledat 18/potřebovat 133; **I'm looking for ...** chtěl bych ... 143; **to ~ like** vypadat 71; **I'm just looking** jenom se dívám

loose volný 146

lorry nákladní auto n

lose: to ~ ztratit 28, 138, 160

lost: I've ~ ... ztratily se mi ... 71/ztratil jsem ... 100, 160; **to be ~** ztratit se 159; **I'm ~** ztratil jsem se 106

lost-and-found [lost property] office ztráty a nálezy 73

A-Z

lot: a ~ hodně 15; **lots of fun** zábavný 101
louder hlasitěji 128
love: to ~ (food) moc chutnat 119; (people) moc se líbit 119; **I ~ you** miluji tě
lovely krásně 122/výborný 125
low nízký 122, 163; **lower** (berth) dole 74
low-fat nízkotučný
luck: good ~ hodně štěstí 219
luggage zavazadla npl 32, 69, 71; **~ carts [trolleys]** vozíky mpl 71
lump boule f 162
lunch oběd m 98, 125; **~time** poledne n 152
lung plíce f

M **machine washable** prát v pračce 145
madam paní f
magazine časopis m 150
magnificent velkolepý 101
maid (hotel) pokojská f 27, 28; (home) služebná f
mail (noun) pošta f 27, 152; **by ~** poštou f 22; **~box [postbox]** poštovní schránka f 152
mail: to ~ poslat 27
main hlavní 130; **~ street** hlavní ulice f 95
make a phone call zatelefonovat 159
make up: to ~ vydat léky 140
make-up make-up m
male muž m 159
mallet palice f 31
man pán m 93
manager vedoucí m/f 25, 41, 137
manicure manikýra f 147
manual (car) manuální
many mnoho 15
map mapa f 94, 106, 150

March březen m 218
margarine margarín m 158
market tržnice f 99
married: to be ~ ženatý/vdaná 120
mascara řasenka f
mask (diving) potápěčská maska
mass mše f 105
massage masáž f 147
mat finish (photos) na matový papír
match zápas m 114
matches zápalky fpl 31, 148, 150
matter: it doesn't ~ to nevadí; **what's the ~?** co se děje?
mattress matrace f
May květen m 218
may I mohu 18
maybe možná
meal jídlo n 38, 42, 70, 165
mean: what does this ~? co to znamená? 11
measles neštovice fpl 165
measure: to ~ změřit 146
measurement míra f
meat maso n 41
mechanic mechanik m 88
medication lék m 164, 165
medicine lék m 141
medium (position) obyčejný 40; (size) střední 122
meet: to ~ setkat se 125; **pleased to ~ you** těší mě 118
member člen m 88, 112, 115
men (toilets) muži mpl
mention: don't ~ it to je v pořádku 10
menu jídelní lístek m
message vzkaz m 27
metal kov m
metro station stanice metra f 80, 96
microwave (oven) mikrovlnná trouba f
midday poledne n

midnight půlnoc f 13, 220

migraine migréna f

milk mléko n 157; **with ~** *(coffee)* bílá (káva) f 40

million milión m 217

mind: do you ~? bude vám vadit? 126; vadilo by vám? 77

mine můj 16; **it's ~!** to je moje!

mineral water minerálka f

mini-bar minibar m 32

minimart potraviny 156

minute minuta f

mirror zrcadlo n

missing: to be ~ chybět 137

mistake *(error)* chyba f 32, 42; *(misunderstanding)* omyl m 41

misunderstanding: there's been a ~ došlo k nedorozumění

Modified American Plan [M.A.P.] polopenze 24

moisturizer (cream) zvlhčující krém m

monastery klášter m 99

Monday pondělí m 218

money peníze 139, 160; **~ order** poštovní poukázka f

month měsíc m 218

moped moped m 83

more více 15; **~ slowly** pomaleji 94; **I'd like some ~ ...** chtěl(a) bych ještě ... 39

morning: in the ~ *(early morning/before noon)* ráno/dopoledne 221

mosque mešita f 105

mosquito bite štípnutí komárem n

mother matka f 120

motion sickness cestovní nemoc f 141

motor: ~bike motocykl m 83; **~boat** motorový člun m 116; **~way** dálnice f 92, 94

mountain hora f 107; **~ bike** horské kolo n; **~ pass** horský průsmyk m 107; **~ range** horské pásmo n 107

moustache knír m

mouth ústa 164, 166; **~ ulcer** aft m

move: to ~ *(motion)* hýbat se 92; *(relocate)* přestěhovat se 25; **don't ~ him!** nehýbejte s ním! 92

movie film m 108; **~ theater** kino n 110

Mr. p.

Mrs. pí.

much hodně 15

mugged; I was ~ přepadli mě 160

mugging přepadení n 159

mugs hrnky mpl 148

mumps příušnice

muscle sval m 166

museum muzeum n 99

music hudba f 112, 121

musician hudebník m

must: I ~ musím

mustard hořčice f 38

my můj 16

myself: I'll do it ~ udělám to sám

N **name** jméno n 22, 36, 93, 118, 120; **my ~ is** jmenuji se 118; **what's your ~?** jak se jmenujete? 118

napkin ubrousek m 39

nappies plenky fpl 142

narrow úzký 14

national národní

nationality státní příslušnost f 23

native místní 155

nature: ~ reserve přírodní rezervace f 107; **~ trail** přírodní stezka f 107

nausea žaludeční nevolnost f

near blízko 12/poblíž 35; **nearest** nejbližší 80, 88, 92, 127, 130, 140; **~by** blízko 115/poblíž 21, 87; **~-sighted** krátkozraký 167;

necessary nutný 112

neck *(head)* na krku 147/krk m 166

necklace náhrdelník m 149

need: I ~ to ... potřebuji 18

nephew synovec m

nerve nerv n; **nervous system** nervový systém m

never nikdy 13; **~ mind** nic se nestalo 10

new nový 14

New Year Nový rok m 219

New Zealand Nový Zéland m 119

news: ~agent noviny 131; **~paper** noviny 150; **~stand** novinový stánek m 131

next *(in a row)* další 14, 68, 75, 78, 100; *(in a row)* nejbližší 94; *(in time)* příští 80, 218; **~ stop!** další stanici! 79; **~ to** vedle 12, 95

nice hezký 14

niece neteř f

night: at ~ v noci 221

night: for two nights *(in hotel)* na dvě noci 22; **~club** noční klub m 112

no ne 10; **~ way!** rozhodně ne! 19

no one nikdo 16, 92

noisy hlučný 14, 24

non-alcoholic nealkoholický

non-smoking nekuřáci 36, 69

none žádný 15

nonsense! nesmysl! 19

noon poledne n 220

normal běžný 67

north sever m 95

nose nos m 166

not bad jde to 19

not yet ještě ne 13

nothing nic 16; **~ else** už nic 15

notify: to ~ uvědomit 167

November listopad m 218

now nyní 84/teď 13

number číslo n 138; **~ plate** státní poznávací značka f; **sorry, wrong ~** promiňte, špatné číslo

nurse zdravotní sestra f

nylon nylon m

O **o'clock: it's ...** je ... 220

occasionally občas

occupied obsazený 14

October říjen m 218

odds *(betting)* šance na výhru f 114

of course samozřejmě 19

off-licence víno a lihoviny 131

off-peak mimo špičku

office kancelář f

often často 13

oil olej m 38

okay dobře 10, 19

old starý 14; **~ town** staré město n 99

olive oil olivový olej m

omelet omeleta f 40

on: *(day)* v 13; **~ foot** pěšky 17, 95; **~ the left** vlevo 12; **~ the right** vpravo 12

on/off switch vypínač m

once jednou 217; **~ a day** jednou denně 76

one like that jako tento 16

one-way jedním směrem 65, 79; **~ ticket** *(train)* jízdenka jedním směrem f 74; *(plane)* letenka jedním směrem f 68

open otevřený 14; **~-air pool** venkovní bazén 116

open: to ~ otvírat 77, 100, 132, 140, 152, 164;

opening hours otevírací doba f 100

opera opera f 108, 111; **~ house** operní divadlo n 99

operation (*medical*) operace f

opposite naproti 12, 95

optician optik m 167; optika f 131

or nebo 19

orange (*color*) oranžový 143

oranges pomeranče mpl 158

orchestra orchestr m 111

order: to ~ objednat 32, 37, 41, 135

organized hike/walk organizovaná túra/vycházka f

our(s) náš 16

outdoor venkovní

outrageous nestydatý 89

outside venku 12, 36

oval oválný 134

oven trouba f

over: ~ here tady 157; **~ there** tam 157; tamhle 36

overcharge: I've been overcharged naúčtovali jste mi víc

overdone převařený 41

overheat přehřátí n

overnight přes noc 23

owe: to ~ dlužit 168; **how much do I ~?** kolik jsem dlužen?

own: on my own sám 65, 120; **I'm on my ~** jsem sám 66

owner majitel m

P **p.m.** odpoledne
pacifier dudlík m

pack: to ~ balit 69

package balík m 153

packed lunch studený oběd m

paddling pool dětský bazén m 113

padlock visací zámek m

pail kyblík m 155

pain: to be in ~ mít bolesti 167; **~killer** lék proti bolesti m 141, 165

paint: to ~ malovat

painter malíř m

painting obraz m

pair: a ~ of ... pár ... m 217

palace palác m 99

palpitations bušení srdce n

panorama panoráma n 107

pants (*U.S.*) kalhoty 144

panty hose punčochové kalhoty 144

paper napkins papírové ubrousky mpl 148

paraffin parafín m 31

paralysis ochrnutí n

parcel balík m 153

parents rodiče mpl 120

park park m 96, 99, 107

parking: ~ lot parkoviště n 26, 87, 96; **~ meter** parkovací hodiny 87

parliament building budova parlamentu f 99

partner (*boyfriend/girlfriend*) partner/partnerka m/f

party (*social*) společnost f 124

pass: to ~ (*a place*) projet 77

passport pas m 23, 66, 69, 160; **~ number** číslo pasu 23

pasta těstoviny fpl 38

pastry shop cukrárna f 131

patch: to ~ spravit 137

patient (*noun*) pacient m

pavement: on the ~ na chodníku

pay: to ~ zaplatit 42, 136; **can I ~ in ...** mohu zaplatit v ... 67; **~ phone** telefonní budka f

payment platba f

peak vrchol m 107

pearl perla f 149

pedestrian: ~ **crossing**
přechod pro chodce m
96; ~ **zone** [**precinct**]
pěší zóna f 96

pen pero n 150

people lidé 92, 119

pepper pepř m 38

per: ~ **day** na/za den 30, 83,
86, 87, 115; ~ **hour** hodinový 153,
na/za hodinu 87, 115; ~ **night** jedna
noc f 24, za noc n 21; ~ **week**
na/za týden 24, 30, 83, 86; ~ **round**
(golf) za kolo 115

perhaps možná 19

period (menstrual) měsíčky 167;
~ **pains** bolestivé měsíčky 167

perm trvalá f 147

petrol benzín m 88; ~ **station**
benzínová pumpa f 87

pewter cín m 149

pharmacy lékárna f 131, 140, 156

phone: to ~ telefonovat; ~ **card**
telefonní karta f 127, 153

photo: to take a ~ vyfotografovat;
~**copier** kopírka f 153; ~**graph**
fotografie f 98; ~**grapher** fotograf m

phrase věta f 11; ~ **book**
konverzační příručka f 11

pick up: to ~ vyzvednout si 28

picnic piknik m; ~ **area** místo na
piknik n 107

piece: a ~ of ... kousek ... m 40

pill tableta f 165; (contraceptive)
antikoncepční pilulka f 167

pillow polštář m 27; ~ **case** povlak
na polštář m

pilot light plamínek m

pink růžový 143

pipe (smoking) dýmka f

pitch (for camping) stanoviště n

place: to ~ a bet podat sázku 114

plane letadlo n 68

plans plány mpl 124

plant (noun) rostlina f

plaster náplast f 141

plastic: ~ **bag** igelitová taška f;
~ **wrap** potravinová fólie f 148

plate talíř m 39; **plates** talíře mpl 148

platform nástupiště n 73, 76, 77

platinum platina f 149

play (noun) představení n 108;
~ **group** školka f 113; ~**ground**
dětské hřiště n 113; ~**ing field**
hřiště n 96

play: to ~ hrát 110, 111, 114, 121;
it is ~**ing** (movie, etc.) hraje se 110

pleasant příjemný 14

please prosím 10

plug zástrčka f 148

pneumonia zápal plic m 165

point: ~ **to** ukázat 11

poison jed m

Poland Polsko n 119

police policie f 92, 159; ~ **report**
zpráva od policie f 160; ~ **station**
policejní stanice f 96, 131, 159

pollen count hladina pylu f 122

polyester polyester m

pond rybník m 107

pop (music) pop m 111

popcorn pražená kukuřice f 110

popular populární 111, 155

port (harbor) přístav m

porter nosič m 71

portion porce f 39, 40

possible: as soon as ~ co nejdříve

post (noun) pošta f; ~ **office** pošta f
96, 131, 152; ~**age** poštovné n
152; ~**box** poštovní schránka f
152; ~**card** pohlednice f 152, 154

post: to ~ (in mailbox/at post office)
vhodit do schránky/podat na poště

potato chips bramborové lupínky
mpl 157

potatoes brambory fpl 38

pottery keramika f

pound (sterling) libra (šterlinků) f 67, 138

powdery prachový 117

power: ~ cut výpadek elektrického proudu m; **~ points** elektrické zásuvky fpl 30

pregnant: to be ~ být těhotná 163, 167

premium *(gas)* prémiový 87

prescribe: to ~ předepsat 165

prescription předpis m 140, 141

present *(gift)* dárek m

press: to ~ vyžehlit 137

pretty hezký

price cena f 24

priest kněz m

prison vězení n

profession povolání n 23

program program m 108, 109

pronounce: to ~ vyslovit

Protestant protestantský 105

pub hospoda f

public *(noun)* veřejnost f 100

pump *(gas station)* pumpa f 87

puncture píchlý 83, 88; **have a ~** mit píchlé kolo 83

puppet show představení loutkového divadla n

pure čistý 145

purple fialový 143

purse peněženka f 160

push-chair kočárek m

put: to ~ *(to place)* dát 22; **can you ~ me up for the night?** můžete mě na dnešní noc ubytovat?; **where can I ~ ...?** kam mohu dát ...?

Q **quality** *(adj)* kvalitní 134

quarter: a ~ čtvrt f 217; **a ~ past** *(after)* čtvrt na 220; **a ~ to** *(before)* tři čtvrtě na 220

queue: to ~ stát ve frontě 112

quick rychlý 14; **quickly** rychle 17

quickest: what's the ~ way? jak se tam nejrychleji dostanu?

quiet tichý 14; **quieter** tišší 24, 126

R **rabbi** rabín m

race course dostihová dráha f 114

racetrack dostihová dráha f 114

racket *(tennis, squash)* raketa f 115

railway železnice f

rain: to ~ pršet 122; **~coat** kabát do deště m 144

rape znásilnění n 159

rapids peřeje fpl 107

rare *(steak)* krvavý; *(unusual)* vzácný

rash vyrážka f 162

razor holicí strojek m; **~ blades** žiletky fpl 142

ready: to be ~ být hotový 89, 137, 151

real *(genuine)* pravý 149

rear zadní 83

receipt *(collection ticket)* lístek m 151; *(when paying)* paragon m 89; stvrzenka f 32, 42, 136, 137, 168

reception (desk) recepce f

receptionist recepční m/f

reclaim tag zavazadlový lístek m 71

recommend: to ~ doporučit 21, 37; **can you ~ ...?** můžete mi doporučit ...? 35, 97, 108, 112

record *(L.P.)* gramofonová deska f 155; **~ store** gramofonové desky

S safe *(lock-up)* sejf m 27; *(not dangerous)* bezpečný 116;
to feel ~ cítit se bezpečně 65

safety bezpečí n; ~ pins zavírací špendlíky mpl

salad čerstvý salát m 38

sales *(as job)* odbyt m 121; ~ tax DPH f 24; ~clerk prodavač m

salt sůl f 38, 39; salty slaný

same stejný 75

sand písek m

sandals sandály mpl 145

sandwich sendvič m 40

sandy beach písečná pláž f

sanitary napkin [towel] dámská vložka f 142

satellite TV satelitní televize f 22

satin satén m

satisfied: I'm not ~ with this nejsem s tím spokojený

Saturday sobota f 218

sauce omáčka f 38

sauna sauna f 22

sausage salám m 158

say: how do you ~ ...? jak se řekne ...?

scarf šátek m 144, 154

scheduled flight plánovaný let m

sciatica ischias f 165

scissors nůžky 148

Scotland Skotsko n 119

screwdriver šroubovák m 148

sea moře n 107

seasick: I feel ~ mám mořskou nemoc

season ticket sezónní lístek m

seat *(on train, etc.)* místo n 77 / sedadlo n 74, 75, 77; *(theater)* místo k sezení n 109

second druhý 132, 217; ~ class druhá třída f 74; ~ floor *(U.S.)* první patro n; ~-hand second-hand

secretary sekretářka f

sedative sedativum n

see: to ~ vidět 18, 37, 93, 124; *(inspect)* podívat se 24; ~ you soon! brzo na shledanou! 126

self-employed: to be ~ být soukromník m 121

self-service *(gas [petrol] station)* samoobsluha f 87

sell: to ~ prodávat 133

send: to ~ poslat 153

senior citizen starší občan m 74, 100

separately samostatně 42

September září n 218

serious závažný

service *(in restaurant)* obsluha f 42; *(religious)* bohoslužba f 105

serviette ubrousek m 39

set menu hotové menu n 37

sex pohlavní styk m

shade odstín m 143; shady ve stínu 31

shallow mělký

shampoo šampon m 142; ~ and set umýt a usušit 147

share: to ~ *(room)* mít dohromady

sharp ostrý 69

shaving: ~ brush štětka na holení f; ~ cream krém na holení m

she ona

sheath *(contraceptive)* kondom m

sheet *(bed)* povlečení n 28

shirt *(men's)* košile f 144

shock *(electric)* šok m

shoe: shoes boty fpl 145; ~ repair *(store)* opravna bot f; ~ store obchod s obuví m/obuv f 131

A-Z

shopping: ~ **area** oblast
s obchody f 99; ~ **basket**
nákupní košík m;
~ **mall [centre]** obchodní
centrum n 130; ~ **trolley**
nákupní vozík m;
to go ~ jít nakupovat

short *(opp. long)* krátký 144, 146, 147/
(opp. tall) nízký 14; *(height)* malý;
~**-sighted** krátkozraký 167

shorts krátké kalhoty 144

shoulder rameno n 166

shovel lopatka f 155

show: to ~ ukázat 18, 94, 134;
can you ~ **me?** můžete mi to
ukázat? 106

shower sprcha f 21; **showers** sprchy
fpl 30; ~ **room** sprcha f 26

shut zavřený 14

shut: to ~ zavírat 132; **when do
you** ~? v kolik hodin zavíráte?

shutter okenice f 25

sick: I'm going to be ~ budu zvracet

side: ~ **order** příloha 38; ~ **street**
postranní ulice f 95

sides *(head)* po stranách 147

sights pamětihodnosti fpl

sightseeing: to go ~ jít na prohlídku
památek; ~ **tour** prohlídka f 97

sign *(road sign)* značka f 93, 95

signpost ukazatel m

silk hedvábí n

silver stříbro n 149; ~ **plate**
postříbřený 149

singer zpěvák m 155

single: ~ **room** jednolůžkový pokoj m
21; ~ **ticket** *(train)* jízdenka jedním
směrem f 65, 74; ~ **ticket** *(plane)*
letenka jedním směrem f 65, 68;
to be ~ svobodný 120

sink umyvadlo n 25

sister sestra f 120

sit: to ~ *(be seated)* sedět 77;
(get seated) sednout si 36, 126:
~ **down, please** sedněte si

size velikost f 146

skates brusle fpl 117

ski: ~ **boots** lyžařské boty fpl 117;
~ **poles** lyžařské hole fpl 117; **skis**
lyže fpl 117

skin pokožka f 166

skirt sukně f 144

sleep: to ~ spát 167

sleeping: ~ **bag** spací pytel m 31;
~ **car** lůžkový vůz m 74, 77; ~ **pill**
prášek na spaní m

sleeve rukáv m 144

slice: a ~ **of ...** plátek m 40

sliced meats krájené maso n 158

slippers papuče fpl 145

Slovakia Slovensko n 119

slow pomalý 14; *(clock)*
pozadu 221; ~ **down!** zpomalte!;
to be ~ být pomalý

slowly *(speak)* pomalu 11, 17, 128

SLR camera fotoaparát s
jednoduchou reflexní čočkou m 151

small malý 14, 24, 40, 117, 134;
~ **change** drobné 138; **smaller**
menší 134

smell: there's a bad ~ něco smrdí

smoke: to ~ zapálit si 126

smoking kuřáci 36, 69

snack něco malého k jídlu n; ~ **bar**
občerstvení n 73

sneakers tenisky fpl

snorkel šnorchl m

snow sníh m 117; **to** ~ sněžit 122

soap mýdlo n 27, 142

soccer fotbal m 114

socket zástrčka f

socks ponožky fpl 144

soft drinks nealkoholické nápoje
mpl 157

sole *(shoes)* podrážka f

soloist sólista m 111

soluble aspirin šumivý aspirin m

something něco 16; **~ to eat** něco k jídlu 70

sometimes někdy 13

son syn m 120, 162

soon brzo 13

sore: it's ~ bolí to; **~ throat** bolení v krku 141; **I have a ~ throat** bolí mě v krku 163

sorry! pardon! 10

soul music hudba amerických černochů f 111

sour kyselý 41

south jih m 95

South Africa Jižní Afrika f

South African *(noun)* Jihoafričan m

souvenir suvenýr m 98, 154; **~ guide** obrázkový průvodce m 154; **~ store** suvenýry 131

space místo n 30

spade lopatka f 155

spare *(replacement)* náhradní 28; *(extra)* navíc

speak: to ~ mluvit 11, 18, 41, 67, 128; **do you ~ English?** mluvíte anglicky? 11; **~ to someone** mluvit s někým 128

special zvláštní 86; **~ delivery** spěšně 153

specialist specialista m 164

specimen vzorek m 164

spectacles brýle

spell: to ~ hláskovat 11

spend: to ~ *(time/money)* strávit/utratit

spicy kořeněný

sponge houba f 148

spoon lžíce f 39, 41; **spoons** lžíce fpl 148

sport sport m 121

sporting goods store sportovní potřeby 131

sports: ~ club sportovní klub m 115; **~ ground** hřiště n 96

spot *(place, site)* místo n 31

sprained: to be ~ být vyvrtnutý 164

spring jaro n 219

square náměstí n 95/čtvercový 134

stadium stadion m 96

staff personál m 113

stain skvrna f; **~less steel** nerezová ocel f 149

stairs schodiště n 132

stamp známka f 152; **stamps** známky fpl 150

stand: ~ in line stát ve frontě 112

standby ticket lístek na čekací listině m

start: to ~ *(car, etc.)* nastartovat 88/začínat 108, 112

statement *(police)* prohlášení n 93

stationer's papírnictví n

statue socha f 99

stay: to ~ *(remain)* zůstat 23, 65; *(live)* bydlet 123

steal: to ~ ukrást 71

sterilizing solution sterilizační roztok m 142

stiff neck přeležený krk m

still: I'm ~ waiting stále ještě čekám

stockings punčochy fpl 144

stolen *(adj.)* ukradený 160

stomach žaludek m 166; **I have a ~ache** bolí mě břicho 163

stool *(faeces)* stolice f 164

stop *(bus/tram/etc.)* stanice f 79, 80

stop: to ~ *(train)* stavět 77; *(make a stop)* zastavit 98; **to ~ at** *(train)* stavět v 76

stopcock uzavírací kohout m 28

store guide informační tabule f 132

stormy bouřka f 122

stove vařič m 28, 29

straight ahead přímo před vámi 95

strained muscle natažený svall m 162

strange divný 101

straw brčko n

strawberry jahoda f 40

stream potok m 107

streetcar tramvaj f 79

strong silný

student student m 74, 100, 121

study: to ~ studovat 121

style styl m 104

subtitled: to be ~ být s titulky 110

subway: ~ map plán metra m 80; **~ station** stanice metra f 80, 96

sugar cukr m 38, 39

suggest: to ~ doporučit 123

suit (man's) oblek; (woman's) kostým m 144

suitable vhodný 140; **~ for** vhodný pro

summer léto n 219

sun: ~ block krém na opalování m 142; **to ~bathe** opalovat se; **~burn** spálení sluncem n 141; **~glasses** sluneční brýle; **~shade** slunečník m 116; **~stroke** úžeh m 163; **~tan lotion** krém na opalování m 142; **sunny** na slunci 31

Sunday neděle f 218

super (gas) super m 87

superb skvělý 101

supermarket samoobsluha f 156

supervision dozor m 113

supplement přirážka f 68, 69

suppositories čípky mpl 165

sure: are you ~? určitě?

surname příjmení n

sweater svetr m 144

sweatshirt tričko n 144

sweet (taste) sladký

sweets bonbóny mpl 150

swelling oteklina f 162

swim: to ~ plavat 116; **~suit** dámské plavky 144

swimming plavání n 114; **~ pool** bazén m 22, 26, 116; **~ trunks** pánské plavky 144

swollen: to be ~ být oteklý

symptom (illness) příznak m 163

synagogue synagoga f 105

synthetic umělé vlákno n 145

T

T-shirt tričko n 144, 154

table stůl m 36, 112

take: to ~ (medicine) užívat 140, 165; (time) trvat 78; (carry) vzít 71/vzít si 24; **to ~ away** vzít si s sebou 40; **to ~ out** (extract tooth) vytrhnout 168; **to ~ photographs** fotografovat 100; **I'll ~ it** (room) vezmu si ho 24, 135; **is this seat taken?** je tohle místo obsazené? 77; **~ me to ...** dovezte mě na ... 84

talk: to ~ mluvit

tall vysoký 14

tampons tampony mpl 142

tan (skin color) opálení n

tap kohoutek m 25

taxi taxi m 32, 70, 71, 84; **~ stand [rank]** stanoviště taxi m 96

tea čaj m 40; **~ bags** sáčkovaný čaj mpl 158; **~ towel** utěrka f 154; **~spoons** lžičky fpl 148

teacher učitel m

team tým m 114

teddy bear medvídek m 155

telephone telefon m 22, 92; **to ~** zatelefonovat 127; **~ bill** účet za telefon m 32; **~ booth** telefonní budka f 127; **~ call** telefonický hovor m 32; **~ number** telefonní číslo n 127

tell: to ~ říci 18; **can you ~ me …?** můžete mi … ? 79

temperature *(body)* teplota f 164

temple chrám m 105

temporarily dočasně 168

tennis tenis m 114; **~ court** tenisový kurt m 115

tent stan m 30, 31; **~ pegs** stanové kolíčky mpl 31; **~ pole** stanová tyč f 31

terminus *(bus, etc.)* konečná f 78

terrace terasa f 35

terrible hrozně 19; hrozný 101, 122

terrific báječně 19

tetanus tetanus m 164

thank you děkuji 10, 118

that to 94; **~ one** tamten 16, 134, 157; **~'s true!** to je pravda! 19; **~'s all** to je všechno 133

theater divadlo n 96, 99, 110, 111

theft krádež f 160

their(s) jejich 16

then *(time)* potom 13

there tam 12, 17; **~ are …** jsou tam … 17; **~ is …** je tam … 17; **over ~** tamhle 76

thermometer teploměr m

thermos flask termoska f

these tyto 134, 157

they oni

thick silný 14

thief zloděj m

thigh stehno n 166

thin *(opp. thick)* slabý 14; *(narrow)* tenký; *(opp. fat)* hubený

think: I ~ … myslím … 42; **to ~ about something** rozmyslit si to 135

third třetí 217; **a ~** třetina f 217; **~ party insurance** pojištění odpovědnosti vůči třetí osobě

thirsty: I am ~ mám žízeň

this tenhle 84/tento 218; **~ one** tenhle 16, 134, 157; **~ evening** dnes večer 36

those tamty 134, 157

thousand tisíc m 217

throat krk m 166

thrombosis trombóza f

through přes

thumb palec m 166

Thursday čtvrtek m 218

ticket *(train)* jízdenka f 65, 74, 75, 79, 80, 160; *(plane)* letenka f 68, 69; *(theater, etc.)* vstupenka f 100/lístek m 108, 109, 114; **~ office** pokladna f 73

tie kravata f 144

tight těsný 146

tights punčochové kalhoty 144

till receipt účtenka f

time: is it on ~? *(train, etc.)* jede na čas? 76; **free ~** volný čas m 98; **what's the ~?** kolik je hodin? 220; **~table** jízdní řád m 75

tin opener otvírač na plechovky m 148

tire pneumatika f 83

tired: I'm ~ jsem unavený

tissue papírový kapesník m 142

to *(place)* k 12

tobacco tabák m 150

tobacconist tabák m 130

today dnes 89, 124, 218

toe prst na noze m 166

A-Z

toilet záchod m 25, 26, 29, 78, 98, 113; **~ paper** toaletní papír m 25, 142

tomatoes rajčata npl 157

tomorrow zítra 36, 84, 122, 124, 218

tongue jazyk m 166

tonight dnes večer 108, 110, 124

tonsilitis angína 165

tonsils mandle fpl 166

too (extreme) moc 41, 117, 135, 146 / příliš 17, 93; **~ much** příliš mnoho 15

tooth zub m 168; **~brush** kartáček na zuby m; **~paste** zubní pasta f 142; **I have a ~ache** bolí mě zub

top (head) nahoře 147

torch ruční svítilna f 31

torn: to be ~ (muscle) být natržený 164; **torn: this is ~** je to roztržené

tough (food) tuhý 41

tour zájezd m 98; **~ guide** průvodce m / průvodkyně f 27; **~ operator** cestovní kancelář f 26

tourist turista m; **~ office** turistická kancelář f 97

tow truck havarijní služba f 88

towel ručník m

tower věž f 99

town město n 70, 94; **~ hall** radnice f 99

toy hračka f 155

traditional tradiční 35

traffic doprava f; **~ jam** dopravní zácpa f; **~ light** semafory mpl 95; **~ violation** [offence] dopravní přestupek m

trailer obytný přívěs m 30

train vlak m 13, 73, 75, 77, 123; **~ station** nádraží n 73, 84, 96

trained vyškolený 113

tram tramvaj f 79

transit: to be in ~ projíždět

translate: to ~ přeložit 11

translation překlad m

translator překladatel m

trashcans popelnice fpl 30

travel: ~ agency cestovní kancelář f 131; **~ sickness** cestovní nemoc f 141

traveler's check [cheque] cestovní šek m 136, 138

tray podnos m

tree strom m 106

trim zastřihnout 147

trip cesta f 76, 78

trolley vozík m 156

trousers kalhoty 144; **trouser press** žehlič kalhot m

truck nákladní automobil m

true: that's not ~ to není pravda

try: ~ on (clothes) zkusit si 146

Tuesday úterý n 218

tumor nádor m 165

tunnel tunel m

turn: to ~ down (volume, heat) stáhnout; **to ~ off** vypnout 25; **to ~ on** zapnout 25; **to ~ up** (volume) zesílit

TV televize f 22

tweezers pinzeta f

twice dvakrát 217; **~ a day** dvakrát denně 76

twin beds dvě lůžka npl 21

twist: I've twisted my ankle vyvrtl jsem si kotník

two-door car dvoudveřové auto n 86

type typ m 109; **what ~ of ...?** jaký druh ...? 112

typical typický 37

tyre pneumatika f 83

U **U.K.** Británie f 119

U.S. Spojené státy mpl 119

ugly ošklivý 14, 101

ulcer vřed m

umbrella slunečník m 116

uncle strýc m 120

unconscious: to be ~
být v bezvědomí 92;
he's ~ je v bezvědomí 162

under pod

underdone *(not cooked/rare meat)*
nedovařený 41/nepropečený

underpants pánské spodky 144

understand: to ~ rozumět 11;
do you ~? rozumíte? 11;
I don't ~ nerozumím 11, 67

undress: to ~ svléknout se 164

uneven *(ground)* hrbolatý 31

unfortunately bohužel 19

uniform uniforma f

unit *(for a phone card)* jednotka f 153

unleaded petrol bezolovnatý
benzín m

unlimited mileage počet kilometrů
není omezen

unlock: to ~ odemknout

unpleasant nepříjemný 14

unscrew: to ~ odšroubovat

until do 221

up to až k 12

upper *(berth)* nahoře 74

upset stomach bolení břicha
n 141

urine moč f 164

use: to ~ použít 139; **for my
personal ~** pro mou osobní
potřebu 67

utensils *(knives, etc.)* příbory mpl 29

V **V-neck** véčko 144

vacant volný 14

vacation dovolená f
123; **on ~** na
dovolené 66

**vaccinated against: to
be ~** mít očkování 164

vaginal infection vaginální infekce
f 167

valet service parkovací služby

valid platný 75

validate: to ~ *(tickets)* potvrdit

valley údolí n 107

valuable cenný

valve uzavírací kohout m 28

vanilla *(flavor)* vanilkový 40

VAT DPH f 24; **~ receipt** daňový
doklad m

vegetables zelenina f 38

vegetarian vegetariánský 35, 39

vein žíla f 166

venereal disease pohlavní nemoc
f 165

ventilator větrák m

very velmi 17; **~ good** skvěle 19

video: ~ game video hra f;
~ recorder videorekordér m;
~cassette videokazeta f 155

viewpoint vyhlídka f 99, 107

village vesnice f 107

vinaigrette francouzská zálivka m 38

vinegar ocet m 38

vineyard vinice f 107

visa vízum n

visit: to ~ navštívit 167;
(see sights, etc.) podívat se 123;
(hospital) **visiting hours** návštěvní
hodiny fpl;

vitamin tablet vitamínová tableta
f 141

volleyball volejbal m 114

voltage napětí n

vomit: to ~ zvracet 163

W wait: to ~ čekat 41/ počkat si 140; to ~ for čekat na 76/počkat si na 89; wait! počkejte! 98

waiter/waitress vrchní m 37

waiting room čekárna f 73

wake vzbudit 70; to ~ someone vzbudit někoho 27; ~-up call buzení telefonem n

Wales Wales m 119

walk home: to ~ jít domů 65

walking: ~ boots pohorky 145; ~ gear vybavení na turistiku n; ~ route turistická cesta f 106

wallet peněženka f 42, 160

war memorial památník obětem války m 99

ward (hospital) oddělení n 167

warm teplý 14; (weather) teplo n 122; **warmer** teplejší 24

washbasin umyvadlo n

washing: ~ machine pračka f 29; ~ powder prášek na praní m 148; ~-up liquid prostředek na mytí nádobí m 148

wasp vosa f

watch hodinky 149, 160

water voda f 87; ~ bottle láhev na vodu f; ~ heater ohřívač vody m 28; ~ skis vodní lyže fpl 116; ~fall vodopád m 107; ~proof vodotěsný; ~proof jacket nepromokavá bunda f 145

wave vlna f

waxing voskování n 147

way: I've lost my ~ ztratil(a) jsem se 94; **it's on the ~ to ...** je to směrem na … 83

we my; **we'd like ...** chtěli bychom … 18

wear: to ~ mít na sobě 159

weather počasí n 122; ~ forecast předpověď počasí f 122

wedding svatba f; ~ ring snubní prstýnek m

Wednesday středa f 218

week týden m 23, 97, 218

weekend víkend m 24, 218; ~ rate víkendová sazba f 86

weight: my ~ is... vážím …

welcome to ... vítáme vás v …

well-done (steak) propečený

west západ m 95

wet mokrý 117

wetsuit neoprenový oblek m

what? (asking for a description) jak? 94; (asking for identification) co? 104; ~ kind of ... is it? co je to za …? 106; ~ time? v kolik hodin? 68, 76, 78

wheelchair kolečková židle f

when? kdy 13, 68, 78, 104

where? kde 12, 73, 76, 78, 84, 88, 98; ~ is? kde je? 80, 94, 99; ~ were you born? kde jste se narodil? 119

which? který? 16

whipped cream: with ~ (coffee) Vídeňská (káva)

white bílý 143; ~ wine bílé víno n 40

who? kdo? 16, 104

whose? čí? 16

why proč 15; ~ not proč ne 15

wide široký 14

wife manželka f 120/žena f 162

wildlife divoká příroda f

wind; ~breaker větrovka f 145; ~screen přední sklo n

window okno n 25, 77; (store) výloha f 134, 149; ~ seat sedadlo u okna n 69, 74

windy: to be ~ vítr m 122

wine víno n 40, 158; **~ cellar** vinárna f 35; **~ list** nápojový lístek m 37; **winery** vinný sklep m 107

winter zima f 219

wishes: best ~ všechno nejlepší 219

with s 17, 39

withdraw: to ~ vyzvednout 139

within *(time)* do 13

without bez 17, 38, 141

witness svědek m 93

wood les m 107

wool vlna f 145

work: to ~ *(function)* fungovat 28, 83

work: it doesn't work nefunguje to 25, 137

worse horší 14; **worst** nejhorší

write down: to ~ napsat 136

writing paper dopisní papír m 150

wrong chybný 14; **~ number** špatné číslo n 128; **there's something ~ with ...** něco není v pořádku s ...

X Y Z

x-ray rentgen m 164

yacht jachta f

year rok m 119, 218

yellow žlutý 143

yes ano 10

yesterday včera 218

yogurt jogurt m 158

you *(formal)* vy; *(informal)* ty

young mladý 14

your(s) *(formal)* váš; *(informal)* tvůj

youth hostel mládežnická ubytovna f 29, 123

zebra crossing přechod pro chodce m

zero nula f

zip(per) zip m

zoo zoo n 113

Dictionary
Czech – English

This Czech-English dictionary covers all the areas where you may need to decode written Czech: hotels, public buildings, restaurants, stores, ticket offices, and on transportation. It will also help with understanding forms, maps, product labels, road signs, and operating instructions (for telephones, parking meters, etc.).
If you can't locate the exact sign, you may find key words or terms listed separately.

A   **a.s.** joint-stock company (*in company names*)

administrativní čtvrť administrative district

akce event

aktualizovaný updated

alternativní trasa alternate route

ambasáda embassy

ambulance outpatients (*hospital department*)

angličtina English

autobus bus

autobusová zastávka bus stop

autobusový pruh bus lane

automapa road map

automatické dveře automatic doors

automobilová opravna car mechanic/body shop

Autoturist Czech Automobile Association

B   **balík** package [parcel]

banka bank

bankomat ATM (*automated teller*) [cash machine]

bankovní poplatek bank charges

bar bar

bažina swamp/marsh

běh na lyžích cross-country skiing

benzínová pumpa gas [petrol] station

bez cukru sugar-free

bezlepkový gluten-free

bezolovnatý unleaded (*gasoline*)

bez přestávky no intervals

biskup bishop

bitevní pole battle site

bleší trh flea market

Boží hod velikonoční Easter Sunday

brožovaný výtisk paperback (*book*)

brusle skates

bruslení ice-skating

březen March

burza stock exchange

C   **celní kontrola** customs control

celnice customs
cena za litr price per liter
cena za pokoj room rate
centrum města downtown area
cesta road
cesta uzavřena road closed
cestovní kancelář travel agent
cizí foreign
cizí jazyky foreign languages
cizí měna foreign currency
cukr sugar
cukrárna confectioner
cyklistická stezka cycle lane/path

Č časopisy magazines, periodicals
čekárna waiting room
čekejte na lístek wait for your ticket
čekejte na tón wait for the tone
čekejte prosím please wait
čekejte za přepážkou please wait behind barrier
čerstvě natřeno wet paint
čerstvý fresh
červen June
červenec July
činžovní dům apartment building
číslo letu flight number
číslo pro případ nouze emergency number
číslo sedadla seat number
čistá váha net weight
čistírna dry-cleaner
čtvrtek Thursday

D dabovaný dubbed

A-Z

dálnice highway
dálniční křižovatka highway interchange [motorway junction]
dámské oděvy ladieswear
dámy women (*toilets*)
dárek zdarma free gift
dárky gifts
datum narození date of birth
dávkování dosage
dejte přednost v jízdě yield [give way]
den pracovního klidu national holiday
dětem do … let vstup zákázán no children under …
děti children
dětský bazén kiddie [children's] pool
dieta diet
dlouhé vozidlo extra long vehicle
dnes today
dnes dopoledne this morning (*from about 11 a.m.*)
dnes odpoledne this afternoon
dnes ráno this morning (*before 11 a.m.*)
dnes večer this evening
do until
do … before …
dole downstairs
domácí homemade
domácí adresa home address
dopoledne a.m.

A-Z

doporučená příprava cooking instructions

doporučeno recommended

doporučený dopis registered letter

dopravní policie traffic police

dopravní zácpy traffic jams

dostihová dráha racetrack [racecourse]

dotazy ... for inquiries, see ...

dráha pro středně pokročilé ski trail/slope [piste] for intermediates

dráha pro začátečníky ski trail/slope [piste] for beginners

druhé patro third floor [second floor *(U.K.)*]

dřevo wood

duben April

dům k pronajmutí house for rent

dvakrát denně twice a day

dveře se zavírají ... minut po začátku představení doors close ... minutes after performance begins

dvůr yard

E elektrospotřebiče electrical goods

expresní balík special delivery [express]

expresní poštovní zásilka express mail

externí linka ... dial ... for an outside line

F farma farm

farnost parish

film v původní verzi film in original version

formální oděv/oblečení formal wear

G galerie gallery

guma rubber

H hala hall

hasicí přístroj fire extinguisher

havarijní služby breakdown services *(automobile)*

hedvábí silk

herna game room

hlavní silnice main road

hloubka deep end *(swimming pool)*

hodina hour

hodinář watchmaker

hodiny electric meter

holičství barber

hon hunt

hora mountain

horký hot *(water, tap)*

horolezectví mountaineering/rock climbing

hotovost cash

hovor na účet volaného collect call [reverse-charge call]

hračky toy store / toys

hrad castle

hřbitov cemetery

CH chléb bread

chodci pedestrians

chodci choďte vlevo keep to the left

chodci choďte vpravo keep to the right

chodník sidewalk [pavement]

chráněná historická budova listed historic building

chráněná památka listed historic site

chraňte před dětmi keep out of the reach children

chůze walking, hiking

I identifikační průkaz ID card

informace information desk

informace o letu flight information

informace pro zákazníky customer information

instruktor instructor

intenzivní péče intensive care

J jaro spring

jednosměrka one-way street

jeďte opatrně drive carefully

jenom only

jeskyně cave

jezero lake

jídelna dining room

jih south

jízda na koni horseback riding

jízdenka platí na metro ticket valid for subway [metro]

jízdní řád ve svátky holiday timetable

jižní southern

jméno manžela/manželky name of spouse

jméno za svobodna maiden name

JUDr. lawyer (*title*)

K kadeřnictví hairdresser

kamenitý stoney (*campsite*)

kapky drops (*medication*)

každý týden weekly

klenoty jeweler

klimatizace air-conditioned

knihovna library

knihy bookstore

k pronájmu for rent

kojenecké oblečení babieswear

konferenční místnost conference room

kontejner na láhve bottle bank

kopec hill

koruna koruna (*Czech currency*) / crown (*royal*)

kostel church

kouření smoking

krásná literatura fiction (*section in bookstore*)

A-Z

krém na opalování sun-block cream

krém po opalování after-sun lotion

kreslené příběhy comic books

krevní skupina blood type [group]

kromě ... except on ...

kruhový objezd roundabout (*circulatory traffic system*)

krytý bazén indoor swimming pool

krytý trh covered market

křesla stalls (*area of theater*)

křižovatka intersection [junction]

k sobě pull (*instruction*)

kuchyň kitchen

kůže leather

květen May

květiny florist

Květná neděle Palm Sunday

L lahůdky delicatessen

lanovka cable car

lázně baths

leden January

lehátko deck chair

lékárna pharmacy

len linen

lepší improved

les forest

letadlo plane

letiště airport

letní jízdní řád summer timetable

léto summer

letuška flight attendant (*female*)

libra šterlinku pound sterling

lístek ticket

lístky na dnes večer tickets for tonight

literatura faktu non-fiction (*section in bookstore*)

loď ship

loterie lottery

lov hunt

lunapark amusement park

lyžařská dráha ski trail

lyžování (downhill) skiing

M malý small

matka mother

maximální zatížení load limit

menu za ... Kč set menu for ... Kč (*koruna*)

měřítko: ... scale: ...

měsíčně monthly

městské hradby city wall

mešita mosque

metro subway

mimo provoz out of order

minimální minimum (requirement)

minimální poplatek minimum charge

místa nahoře seats upstairs

místo narození place of birth

místo v uličce aisle seat

mládež young adults/youths

mládežnická ubytovna youth hostel

mléčné výrobky dairy products

mlékárna dairy
mlha fog
mluvíme anglicky English spoken
močál swamp/marsh
modlitebna prayer room
mokrý (sníh) wet (snow)
moře sea
mražený frozen
mražené výrobky frozen foods
muži gentlemen (*toilets*)
muzeum museum

N **nabídka dne** menu of the
day
nábřeží riverbank
nábytek furniture
na den per day
na ... dny for ... days
nadmořská výška height above
sea level
nádraží train station
nádrž reservoir
nafta diesel
nahoře upstairs
nákladní vůz truck
nákup ... currency bought at ...
nákupní košík shopping basket
nákupní středisko shopping mall
[centre]
náměstí square
naplnit nádrž no vacancy
(*hotel/motel*)
nápoje drinks
na prodej on sale
např. e.g.
nástup boarding (*airport*)

nástupiště
platform
na týden per week
návod k použití
instructions for use
návštěvní hodiny visiting hours
(*hospital*)
**návštěvníci jsou povinni nosit
koupací čepice** bathing caps
must be worn
nebezpečí smrti danger (of death)
neblokujte vchod do not block
entrance
neděle Sunday
nedotýkejte se do not touch
nechejte si stvrzenku/lístek keep
your receipt/ticket
nejvyšší povolená rychlost
speed limit
nemluvte za jízdy s řidičem
do not talk to driver
nemocnice hospital
**nenechávejte ve vozidle cenné
předměty** do not leave valuables
in your car
**nenechávejte zavazadla bez
dozoru** do not leave baggage
unattended
neobsahuje ... contains no ...
neodhazujte odpadky don't dump
trash
neoznačená jízdenka je neplatná
no unvalidated tickets
nepřetržitý provoz continuous
performance
nerovný povrch vozovky poor
road surface
nerušit do not disturb

A-Z

neužívat vnitřně not to be taken internally / orally

nevratný non-returnable

nevyklánějte se z oken do not lean out of windows

nevystavuje slunci do not expose to sunlight

nezahrnuto not included (*in the price*)

nezapomeňte ... don't forget to ...

nic k proclení nothing to declare

noc night

noční lékárna all-night pharmacy

noční vrátný night porter

normální normal (*hair, skin*)

nouzová brzda emergency brake

nouzový východ emergency exit / fire exit

nové tituly new titles / new releases (*books/films*)

novinový stánek newsstand

Nový rok New Year

O občanský průkaz ID card

občerstvení refreshments

obchod se smíšeným zbožím general store

obchodní čtvrť business district

obchodní dům department store

objížďka detour [diversion]

obsah tuku fat content

obsazeno occupied

obuv shoes

obyčejný regular (*gasoline*)

obytný přívěs trailer

ocel steel

očistěte si obuv please wipe your feet

od ... commencing ...

od ... do ... between ... and ... (*time*)

oddělení department

odesilatel sender

odevzdejte klíče na recepci leave keys at reception

odpadky trash [rubbish]

odpojeno disconnected

odpoledne p.m.

od sebe push

ochranná přilba [crash] helmet

ochutnávka vín wine tasting

ohňostroj fireworks

okružní silnice outer roadway [ring road]

olej oil (*at gas station*)

olovnatý leaded (*fuel*)

operátor operator (*telephone*)

opožděný delayed

opravy repairs (*car, etc.*)

optik optician

ordinace doctor's office [surgery]

osobní vlak local [stopping] service (*train*)

ošetřovna infirmary / treatment room

otevřeno open

otevřeno do/v ... open until/on ...

otvírací doba business [opening] hours

ovoce a zelenina greengrocer

ovocné šťávy fruit juices

označte si jízdenku validate/punch your ticket

P **padací most** drawbridge
palivo fuel
palubní vstupenka boarding pass [card] (*airport*)
památník obětem války war memorial
pan Mr.
panelový dům apartment building [block of flats]
paní Mrs.
páni gentlemen (*toilets*)
pánské oděvy menswear
papírnictví stationer
parkovací hodiny parking meter
parkovací lístek parking ticket
parkování povoleno parking permitted
parkoviště pro zákazníky customer parking lot
pátek Friday
pavilon pavilion
péče o pleť beauty care
pekařství bakery/pastry shop
peněžní poukázky money orders
pěší zóna traffic-free zone
písečný sandy (*campsite*)
pitná voda drinking water
pivo beer
placené parkoviště pay parking lot
platí do expiration [expiry] date
plátno linen
plavání swimming

plavčík lifeguard
plná penze full board (*American Plan [A.P.]*)
počítače computers
podávání jídel na pokoji room service
podávejte chlazené best served chilled
podchod/podjezd underpass
podlaží poschodí floor (*level in building*)
podle sezóny according to season
podzemní garáže underground garage
podzim fall [autumn]
pohotovost emergency medical service
po jídle (take) after meals (*medication*)
pokladna box office/ticket office; cashier [cash desk]
pokoje k pronajmutí rooms for rent
pole field
poledne noon
policejní stanice police station
poliklinika clinic/health center
poloostrov peninsula
polopenze half board (*Modified American Plan [M.A.P.]*)
poloviční cena half price
pondělí Monday
Pondělí velikonoční Easter Monday
poschodí floor (*level in building*)

A-Z

poslední čerpací stanice před dálnicí last gas station before highway [motorway]

poslední hovor last call

poslední prohlídka v ... last tour at ... p.m.

pošta post office

poštovní přihrádka post office box

potok stream

potraviny grocery store

pouze only

pouze noviny newspapers only

pouze pro holicí strojky razors [shavers] only

pouze s povolením permit-holders only

pouze víkendy weekdays only

použité lístky used tickets

povlečení household linen

povolený limit zavazadel luggage allowance

pozítří the day after tomorrow

pozor warning/caution

pozor na psa beware of dog

pozor schod watch the step

požární stanice fire station

požárníci firefighters

pracovní dny weekdays

prádelna laundry

prachový (sníh) powdery (snow)

prázdninový provoz holiday timetable

prodej ... currency sold at ...

pro dva for two

pro začátečníky for beginners (skiers)

pro zkušené lyžaře for advanced (skiers)

průjezd zakázán access only; no through road

průkaz zdravotního pojištění national insurance card

průsmyk pass (mountain)

první balkón dress circle

první patro second floor [first floor (U.K.)]

první pomoc first aid

první třída first class

před jídlem before meals

předložte registrační dokumenty show your car registration documents

předměstí suburbs

přednost v jízdě right of way

před odchodem předložte zavazadla show your bags before leaving

předpis prescription

před použitím se poraďte s lékařem consult your doctor before use

předpověď počasí weather forecast

předprodej vstupenek ticket agency

představení performance

přechod pro chodce pedestrian crossing [zebra crossing]

přesné drobné exact fare/change

přestoupit v ... change at ...

při bohoslužbě during services

příchuť flavoring

příjezdy arrivals (train station)

příjmení last name

přílety arrivals (airport)

případ nouze emergency

připoutejte se prosím fasten your seat belt

přístav port

přístaviště harbor

přízemí first floor [ground floor (U.K.)]

půjčovna aut car rental

půlnoc midnight

R **radnice** town hall

rampy ramps

ranní mše morning mass

realitní kancelář real estate agent

recepce ... dial ... for reception

registrace check-in counter (*airport*)

revizor subway ticket inspector

rezervace advance bookings (*theater*); conservation area; reserved (*seat, etc.*)

rozpusťte ve vodě dissolve in water

ruční práce handmade

rybářský prut fishing rod

rybník pond

rybolov povolen fishing permitted

Ř **řada** row

řeka river

řezník butcher

říční parníky river boats

řidičský průkaz driver's license

 S **s koupelnou** with bathroom

s titulky subtitled

salónek lounge

samoobsluha self-service restaurant

sanitka ambulance

sauna sauna

se sprchou with shower

sedadlo u okna window seat

sem pull

servis car mechanic/body shop (*car repairs*)

servisní poplatek service charge

sestry nurses

sever(ní) north(ern)

sezónní lístek season ticket

schránky na zavazadla luggage lockers

sídliště housing estate

silnice road

silnice 2. třídy secondary road

silnice uzavřena road closed

Silvestr New Year's Eve

síť network

sjezd na dálnici highway [motorway] entrance

sjezd z dálnice highway [motorway] exit

skokanské prkno diving board

slečna Miss

slepá ulice dead end

sleva reduction/discount

slunečníky umbrellas [sunshades]

služba service

A-Z

služby zákazníkům customer service
směnárna currency exchange (office)
směnný kurz exchange rate
smíšené zboží general store
snídaně breakfast
snížené ceny reduced prices
sobota Saturday
soudní dvůr courthouse
soukromý private
soukromý pozemek private property
soutěž contest
specialita dne dish of the day
spodní prádlo lingerie/underwear
Spojené státy United States
spol. s r.o./s.r.o. Inc. [Ltd.] *(company)*
spořitelna savings bank
spotřebujte do ... best before ... *(date)*
sprchy showers
spropitné tip
srpen August
stadion stadium
stálobarevný colorfast
standardní poplatek standard charge
stanoviště taxi taxi stand [rank]
starožitnosti antique store
statek farm
státní poznávací značka license plate [registration] number
státní svátek national holiday

stěna wall
stevard flight attendant *(male)*
stezka path/footpath
stlačený vzduch air *(gas station)*
stoupání incline [gradient] *(road sign)*
středa Wednesday
středně pokročilá úroveň intermediate level
střední škola high school [secondary school]
studený cold
student student
studio studio
suchá kůže dry skin
suché vlasy dry hair
sůl salt
super premium [super] *(gasoline)*
surf surfboard
sýr cheese

Š **škola** school

T **tablety** pills, tablets
tady here
tam push
tekoucí voda running water
telefonní karta phone card
telefonní seznam phone book/directory
tento autobus jede do ... this bus is going to ...
tento vlak staví v ... this train stops at ...

těstoviny pasta

těžké vozidlo truck [heavy goods vehicle (HGV)]

těžký (sníh) heavy (snow)

toalety bathroom [toilet]

trasa autobusu bus route

travnatý grassy (*campsite*)

trh/tržnice market

třikrát denně three times a day

turistická atrakce tourist attraction

turistická kancelář tourist office

U **ubytování** accommodations

udržujte volný průchod keep clear

ulice street

ulička lane, alley

umyvadlo sink [wash basin]

únor February

upozornění warning/caution

uschovejte v chladu keep in a cool place

úterý Tuesday

útes cliff

uvolněte místo starším osobám please give up this seat to the elderly/disabled

uvolněte pokoj do ... vacate your room by ...

V **v případě havárie, poruchy volejte ...** in case of breakdown, phone ...

v případě nouze rozbijte sklo break glass in case of emergency

v případě požáru ... in the event of fire ...

Vánoce Christmas

večerní provoz evening service

vedlejší účinky side effects

vedoucí manager

Velikonoce Easter

Velká Británie United Kingdom

velvyslanectví embassy

venkovní bazén outdoor swimming pool

veřejné zahrady public gardens

veřejné záchodky public toilet

veřejný park public park

vhodné pro vegetariány suitable for vegetarians

vchod entrance/way in

vchod zadem use back entrance

vítáme vás welcome

vklady a výběry deposits and withdrawals

vlaky InterCity intercity trains

vlna wool

vložte kreditní kartu insert credit card

vložte lístek insert ticket

vložte minci insert coins

vnější okruh bypass *(road)*

vodní lyžování waterskiing

vodovodní kohoutek faucet [tap]

volný vacant

volná místa vacancies

vozíky carts

A-Z

vratná láhev returnable bottle
vrátný caretaker
vstup pouze pro zaměstnance
staff only
vstup zakázán keep out/ no access/no entry
vstup zdarma free admission
všeobecný lékař general practitioner (*doctor*)
výběr withdrawals
vyberte si zónu
select zone (*ticket machine*)
výdej zavazadel
baggage claim [reclaim]
východ exit/way out; gate (*airport*)
východ(ní) east(ern)
východ zakázán no exit
vyjížďkový parník pleasure steamers
výkup a prodej ...
we buy and sell ...
výměna exchange
vypněte motor
turn off your engine
vypnout turn [switch] off
vyprodáno sold out
výprodej clearance [sale]
výroba klíčů na počkání
keys cut while you wait
vyhlídka viewpoint
vyrobeno na míru
made to measure
vyrobeno na zakázku
made to order

vysoké napětí high voltage
vysoušeč vlasů hair dryer
výtah elevator [lift]
vytočte ... dial ...
(*telephone number*)
významný historický objekt
important historical feature
vznášedlo hovercraft

Z
z ... do ... from ... to ...
z provozních důvodů zavřeno
closed for maintenance
(*store sign*)
začíná v ... begins at ...
zadejte PIN enter your PIN
zahradnické středisko garden center
zahrnuto included (*in the price*)
záchranné čluny lifeboats
záchranné vesty life jackets
záchranný pás life preserver [belt]
zakázáno forbidden
zákaz fotografování no photography
zákaz kouření no smoking
zákaz odhazování odpadků no littering
zákaz parkování no parking
zákaz rybolovu no fishing
zákaz skákání do bazénu no diving
zákaz stání no standing
zákaz vjezdu motorových vozidel
no motor vehicles

zákaz vjezdu pro cyklisty a motocyklisty cyclists and motorcyclists not allowed *(road sign)*

zákaz vstupu na trávník keep off the grass

zákaz zastavení no stopping

zakoupené zboží nevyměňujeme sale goods cannot be exchanged

západ(ní) west(ern)

zaplaťte u pultu pay at counter

zapnout dálková světla turn on headlights

zastávka na znamení request stop

zavazadla nad povolenou hmotnost excess baggage

zavazadlový lístek baggage check

zavírejte dveře close the door

zavírejte vrata keep gate shut

závod contest

zavřeno closed

zavřeno: dovolená closed for vacation [holiday]

zazvoňte please ring the bell

zdarma free

zde here

zde odtrhněte tear here

zdravá výživa health food store

zdravotní středisko doctor's office [surgery]/health center

zeď wall

zelenina vegetables

zeptat se na recepci ask at reception

zima winter

zimní jízdní řád winter timetable

zítra tomorrow

zkušební kabina fitting room

zlaté stránky yellow pages *(phone book)*

zlato gold

zledovatělá silnice icy road

známky stamps

zpevněná krajnice hard shoulder

zpomalit slow down

zpoždění … minut/ hodin … minutes/ hours delay

zprávy news

zrušeno canceled

ztráty a nálezy lost and found [lost property]

zubní středisko dentist's office [surgery]

zvedněte sluchátko lift receiver *(telephone)*

zvhlčovač moisturizer

Ž **železářství** hardware store
železniční přejezd railroad [level] crossing

ženský časopis women's magazine

ženy women *(toilets)*

Reference

Numbers

GRAMMAR

Numbers in their basic nominative form
The number "one" and numbers ending in "one" are followed by the nominative singular and "one" agrees with the gender of the noun.

| one book | **jedna kniha** (*fem.*) |
| twenty-one books | **dvacet jedna kniha** (*fem.*) |

The numbers "two," "three," and "four," and numbers ending in them are followed by the nominative plural. The number "two" agrees with the gender of the noun – **dva** (*masc.*), **dvě** (*fem./neuter.*).

| two magazines | **dva časopisy** (*masc.*) |
| fifty-two magazines | **padesát dva časopisy** (*masc.*) |

Other numbers are followed by the genitive plural.

| seven books | **sedm knih** (*fem.*) |
| fifty hotels | **padesát hotelů** (*masc.*) |

For additional information ➤ 169.

0	**nula** *noola*	13	**třináct** *trzhi-nah-tsut*
1	**jedna** *yed-na*	14	**čtrnáct** *chutr-nah-tsut*
2	**dva** *dva*	15	**patnáct** *pat-nah-tsut*
3	**tři** *trzhih*	16	**šestnáct** *shes-nah-tsut*
4	**čtyři** *chuti-rzhih*	17	**sedmnáct** *sedum-nah-tsut*
5	**pět** *pyet*	18	**osmnáct** *osum-nah-tsut*
6	**šest** *shest*	19	**devatenáct** *devate-nah-tsut*
7	**sedm** *sedum*	20	**dvacet** *dva-tset*
8	**osm** *osum*	21	**dvacet jedna** *dva-tset yed-na*
9	**devět** *de-vyet*	22	**dvacet dva** *dva-tset dva*
10	**deset** *deset*	23	**dvacet tři** *dva-tset trzhih*
11	**jedenáct** *ye-de-nah-tsut*	24	**dvacet čtyři** *dva-tset chuti-rzih*
12	**dvanáct** *dva-nah-tsut*	25	**dvacet pět** *dva-tset pyet*

26	**dvacet šest** *dva-tset shest*	first	**první**
27	**dvacet sedm** *dva-tset sedum*		*pr-vnyeeh*
28	**dvacet osm** *dva-tset osum*	second	**druhý** *droo-hee*
29	**dvacet devět** *dva-tset de-vyet*	third	**třetí** *trzhe-tyee*
30	**třicet** *trzhi-tset*	fourth	**čtvrtý** *chutvur-tee*
31	**třicet jedna** *trzhi-tset yed-na*	fifth	**pátý** *pah-tee*
32	**třicet dva** *trzhi-tset dva*	once	**jednou** *yed-noh*
40	**čtyřicet** *chuti-rzhi-tset*	twice	**dvakrát** *dvak-raht*
50	**padesát** *pade-saht*	three times	**třikrát** *trzhik-raht*
60	**šedesát** *shede-saht*	a half	**půl** *puhl*
70	**sedmdesát** *sedum-de-saht*	half an hour	**půl hodiny** *puh-l do-dyi-nih*
80	**osmdesát** *osum-de-saht*	half a tank	**půl nádrže** *puh-l nah-dr-zheh*
90	**devadesát** *devade-saht*	half eaten	**napůl snědený** *napuhl snye-denee*
100	**sto** *sto'*	a quarter	**čtvrt** *chutvurut*
101	**sto jedna** *sto' yed-na*	a third	**třetina** *trzhe-tyi-nah*
102	**sto dva** *sto' dva*	a pair of ...	**pár ...** *pahr ...*
200	**dvě stě** *dvyeh styeh*	a dozen ...	**tucet ...** *too-tset ...*
300	**tři sta** *trzhih sta*	1999	**devatenáct set devadesát devět** *deva-tenah-tsut set devade-saht de-vyet*
400	**čtyři sta** *chuti-rzhih sta*		
500	**pět set** *pyet set*		
1,000	**tisíc** *tyi-seets*	2001	**dva tisíce jedna** *dva tyi-see-tseh yed-na*
10,000	**deset tisíc** *deset tyi-seets*	the 1990s	**devadesátá léta** *devade-sah-tah leh-ta*
35,750	**třicet pět tisíc sedm set padesát** *trzhi-tset pyet tyi-seets sedum set pade-saht*	in the year 2000	**v roce dva tisíce** *vro-tseh dva tyi-see-tseh*
1,000,000	**milión** *mi-li-awn*	the millennium	**tisícileh** *tyi-see-tsi-le-tyee*

217

Days Dny

Monday	**pondělí**	*pon-dye-lee*
Tuesday	**úterý**	*uh-teree*
Wednesday	**středa**	*sturzhe-da*
Thursday	**čtvrtek**	*chutvur-tek*
Friday	**pátek**	*pah-tek*
Saturday	**sobota**	*sobota*
Sunday	**neděle**	*ne-dyeleh*

Months Měsíce

January	**leden**	*leden*
February	**únor**	*uh-nor*
March	**březen**	*brzhe-zen*
April	**duben**	*dooben*
May	**květen**	*kvye-ten*
June	**červen**	*cher-ven*
July	**červenec**	*cher-venets*
August	**srpen**	*sr-pen*
September	**září**	*zah-rzhee*
October	**říjen**	*rzhee-yen*
November	**listopad**	*listopat*
December	**prosinec**	*prosi-nets*

Dates Datum

It's …	**Je …**	*yeh*
July 10	**desátého července**	
	desah-teh-ho' cher-ven-tseh	
Tuesday, March 1	**útery prvního března**	
	uh-teree pr-vnyee-ho' brzhez-nah	
yesterday	**včera**	*fche-rah*
today	**dnes**	*dnes*
tomorrow	**zítra**	*zeet-rah*
this/last	**tento/minulý**	*ten-to'/mi-noolee*
next week	**příští týden**	*przheesh-tyee tee-den*
every month/year	**každý měsíc/rok**	
	kazh-dee mye-seets/rok	
on [at] the weekend	**o víkendu**	*o-vee-ken-dooh*

Seasons Roční doby

spring	**jaro** *yaro'*
summer	**léto** *leh-to'*
fall [autumn]	**podzim** *pod-zim*
winter	**zima** *zima*
in spring	**na jaře** *na-ya-rzheh*
during the summer	**v létě** *vleh-tyeh*
in the fall [autumn]	**na podzim** *na-pod-zim*
in winter	**v zimě** *vzi-myeh*

Greetings Pozdravy

Happy birthday!	**Všechno nejlepší k narozeninám!** *vshekh-no' neye'-lep-shee kna-ro-ze-nyi-nahm*
Merry Christmas!	**Veselé Vánoce!** *veseleh vah-no-tseh*
Happy New Year!	**Šťastný Nový rok!** *shtya-sutnee novee rok*
Happy Easter!	**Veselé Velikonoce!** *veseleh velikono-tseh*
Best wishes!	**Všechno nejlepší!** *vshekh-no' neye'-lep-shee*
Congratulations! *(from me/from us)*	**Blahopřeji/Blahopřejeme!** *bla-ho-przhe-yih/bla-ho-przhe-yemeh*
Good luck! / All the best!	**Hodně štěstí!** *hod-nye shutyes-tyee*
Have a good trip!	**Mějte se hezky!** *myeye'-teh seh hes-kih*
Give my regards to ...	**Pozdravujte ode mě ...** *poz-dra-vooye'-teh odeh myeh*

Public holidays Státní svátky

January 1	**Nový rok**	New Year's Day
May 1	**Svátek práce**	May Day
May 8	**Den osvobození od fašismu**	Victory over Fascism (Liberation Day)
July 5	**Den slovanských zvěrozvěstů Cyrila a Metoděje**	St. Cyril and St. Methodius Day
July 6	**Mistr Jan Hus**	Anniversary of Jan Hus' death
October 28	**Den vzniku samostatného československého státu**	Independence Day (founding of first Czechoslovak Republic)
December 24	**Štědrý den**	Christmas Eve
December 25/26	**Sváty vánoční**	Christmas Day / Boxing Day
moveable date	**Velikonoční pondělí**	Easter Monday

Time Čas

za pět minut ...
hodin(a)
hodina (a)
pět minut
deset
čtvrt na ...
za deset minut půl ...
za pět minut půl ...
půl ...
za deset minut čtvrtě na ...
za pět minut tři čtvrtě na ...
tři čtvrtě na ...
za deset minut ...

Excuse me. Can you tell me the time?	**Prominte. Můžete mi říci, kolik je hodin?** *prominye'-teh muh-zheteh mih rzhee-tsih kolik yeh ho-dyin*
It's ...	**Je ...** *yeh*
five past one	**jedna hodina a pět minut** *yed-na do-dyi-na a pyet mi-noot*
ten past two	**za pět minut čtvrt na tři** *za-pyet mi-noot chutvurut na-trzhih*
a quarter past three	**čtvrt na čtyři** *chutvurut na-chuti-rzhih*
twenty past four	**za deset minut půl páté** *za-deset mi-noot puhl pah-teh*
twenty-five past five	**za pět minut půl páté** *za-pyet mi-noot puhl pah-teh*
half past six	**půl sedmé** *puhl sed-meh*
twenty-five to seven	**za deset minut tři čtvrtě na sedm** *za-deset mi-noot trzhih chutvur-tyeh nasedum*
twenty to eight	**za pět minut tři čtvrtě na osm** *za-pyet mi-noot trzhih chutvur-tyeh na-osum*
a quarter to nine	**tři čtvrtě na devět** *trzhih chutvur-tyeh na-de-vyet*
ten to ten	**za deset minut deset** *za-deset mi-noot deset*
five to eleven	**za pět minut jedenáct** *za-pyet mi-noot ye-de-nah-tsut*
twelve o'clock	**dvanáct hodin** *dva-nah-tsut ho-dyin*

noon/midnight	**poledne/půlnoc** *poled-neh/puhl-nots*
at dawn	**na úsvitu** *na-uh-svi-tooh*
in the morning *(early morning/late morning)*	**ráno/dopoledne** *rah-no'/dopoled-neh*
during the day	**přes den** *przhes den*
before lunch	**před obědem** *przed-o-bye-dem*
after lunch	**po obědě** *po-o-byedyeh*
in the afternoon	**odpoledne** *ot-poled-neh*
in the evening	**večer** *vecher*
at night	**v noci** *vno-tsih*
I'll be ready in five minutes.	**Budu hotový(á) za pět minut.** *boodooh hotovee(ah) za-pyet mi-noot*
He'll be back in a quarter of an hour.	**Vrátí se za čtvrt hodiny.** *vrah-tyee seh za-chutvurut ho-dyi-nih*
She arrived half an hour ago.	**Přišla před půl hodinou.** *przhi-shla przhet-puhl ho-dyi-noh*
The train leaves at …	**Vlak odjíždí …** *vlak od-yeezd-dyee*
13:04	**v třináct nula čtyři** *futrzhi-nah-tsut noola chuti-rzhih*
00:40	**čtyřicet minut po půlnoci** *chuti-rzhi-tset mi-noot po-puhl-no-tsih*
The train is 10 minutes late/early.	**Vlak přijede o deset minut později/dříve.** *vlak purzhi-yedeh o-deset mi-noot poz-dye-yih/drzhee-veh*
It's 5 minutes fast/slow.	**Jde o pět minut napřed/pozadu.** *yedeh o-pyet mi-noot nap-rzhet/ pozadooh*
from 9:00 to 5:00	**od devíti do pěti** *od-devee-tyih do-pye-tyih*
between 8:00 and 2:00	**mezi osmou a druhou** *mezih os-moh a droo-hoh*
I'll be leaving by …	**Odejdu před …** *odeye-dooh przhet*
Will you be back before …?	**Vrátíte se do …?** *vrah-tyee-teh seh do'*
We'll be here until …	**Budeme tady do …** *boo-demeh tadih do'*

Quick reference Krátký glosář

Good morning. *(early/late morning)* — **Dobré ráno./Dobrý den.** *dobreh rah-no'/dobree den*

Good afternoon. — **Dobré odpoledne./Dobrý den.** *dobreh otpoledneh/dobree den*

Good evening. — **Dobrý večer.** *dobree vecher*

Hello. *(familiar use only)* — **Ahoj.** *ahoy*

Good-bye. — **Na shledanou.** *nas-khledanoh*

Excuse me. *(getting attention)* — **Promiňte.** *prominye'-teh*

Excuse me!/Sorry! — **Promiňte!/Pardon!** *prominye'-teh/pardon*

Please. — **Prosím.** *proseem*

Thank you. — **Děkuji.** *dyekoo-yeih*

Do you speak English? — **Mluvíte anglicky?** *mlooveeteh anglitskih*

I don't understand. — **Nerozumím.** *nerozoomeem*

Where is …? — **Kde je …?** *gdeh yeh*

Where are the bathrooms [toilets]? — **Kde jsou záchody?** *gdeh yesoh zah-kho-dih*

Emergency Případy nouze

Help! — **Pomoc!** *pomots*

Go away! — **Jděte pryč!** *yedye-teh prich*

Leave me alone! — **Nechte mě!** *nekh-teh myeh*

Call the police! — **Zavolejte policii!** *zavoleye'-teh poli-tsi-yih*

Stop thief! — **Zastavte zloděje!** *zas-tav-teh zlo-dye-yeh*

Get a doctor! — **Zavolejte lékaře!** *zavoleye'-teh leh-ka-rzheh*

Fire! — **Hoří!** *ho-rzhee*

I'm ill. — **Jsem nemocný(á).** *yesem nemots-nee(ah)*

I'm lost. — **Ztratil(a) jsem se.** *stratyil(a) yesem seh*

Can you help me? — **Můžete mi pomoci?** *muh-zheteh mih pomo-tsih*

Emergency ☎

Fire **150**   Ambulance **155**   Police **158**

Embassies Prague (Praha) ☎

Australia	Canada	Ireland [Eire]
420 2 24 31 07 43	**420 2 24 31 11 08**	**420 2 57 53 00 61**
South Africa	U.K.	U.S.
420 2 67 31 11 14	**420 2 24 53 67 37**	**420 2 24 51 08 47**